October 14th, 1992

To my friend Larry STERNS
I hope this book will give you
a general idea about my small
country Tunisia.
See you in SFAX in few months
from now. Johames SGHAMi

*Created and Directed by Hans Höfer*

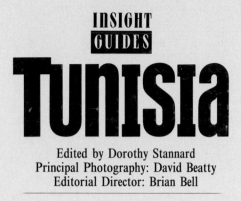

**Edited by Dorothy Stannard**
**Principal Photography: David Beatty**
**Editorial Director: Brian Bell**

APA PUBLICATIONS

# Tunisia

*First Edition*
© **1991 APA PUBLICATIONS (HK) LTD**
*All Rights Reserved*
Printed in Singapore by Höfer Press Pte. Ltd

# ABOUT THIS BOOK

It was on a press trip on a Nile cruise from Aswan to Cairo in the early 1980s that this book's project editor **Dorothy Stannard** first felt the lure of Arab culture. Within three months she was back in Egypt. This time, travelling independently and delving into all the places that press trips prefer to by-pass, she was hooked. It was the beginning of an enduring love affair, many further trips, friendships and, of course, writing. From Egypt she went west into the Maghreb, an exploration which eventually led to her editing the *Insight Guide: Morocco* for Apa Publications in 1989.

Tunisia was the obvious choice for her second Insight guide. With much more to offer than the package-holiday brochures suggest and with too many first-time visitors imagining it to be next to Morocco instead of tucked like a pocket handkerchief into the broad expanse of Algeria and Libya, it was an ideal addition to the award-winning series. As well as writing a dozen chapters, Stannard, a London-based journalist, compiled the information-packed Travel Tips section.

## Panoramic Pictures

Like all Insight Guides, this book owes much to superb photography. The images here are mostly the work of **David Beatty**. Before specialising in photography and reportage on travel, geographical and environmental issues (in Africa and Asia particularly), Beatty worked as a researcher on documentaries – tough training that was to come in handy during his two months hacking round Tunisia with elaborate camera equipment strapped to his back. Brushes with Tunisian authorities were frequent, but most startling when he sought to take panoramic pictures from the roof of an advantageously situated police station, an inspired idea that resulted in virtual imprisonment. Beatty, who lives in Bath, one of England's most photogenic cities, has contributed to several Insight Guides and has been published in journals such as *Time, World Magazine*, and the *Illustrated London News*.

In assembling a team of writers. Stannard turned first to another regular Apa contributor, **Rowlinson Carter**, a widely-travelled journalist, documentary-maker and historian who "knows Tunisia inch by inch" and was sure to do justice to the country's truly rollicking history, which spans the founding of ancient Carthage to the overthrow of a compelling dictator. Carter believes history is not about dates and events, but a story about people – their glory, bravery, villainy, vanity, lechery and greed.

Tramping over Tunisian history's considerable relics, the bulk of Roman and Carthaginian sites which occupy the high plateaux known as the Tell, fell to **Robert Hartford**, a writer on travel, archaeology and music. Hartford has written books on subjects as diverse as the Wagner Festival at Bayreuth and the civilisation of ancient Egypt, and has travelled extensively in Africa and the Middle East, including two-way crossings of the Sahara and journeys to the sources of the Nile. Tunisia's Tell was familiar territory but, he said, he had not experienced the area in early spring before – "delightfully and unexpectedly verdant".

To cover the southern oases and write the features on Tunisia's wildlife and desert expeditions, Stannard recruited **Julian Cremona**, a biology lecturer and photogra-

*Stannard*

*Carter*

*Hartford*

pher from Southampton. Cremona uses the long holidays of academia to organise Land-Rover trips to North Africa and Iceland (though he confesses to preferring the comfort of his Range Rover these days). As well as contributing articles and photographs to numerous wildlife publications and being expedition consultant for *Off Road and 4-Wheel Drive* magazine, he has written guidebooks to North Africa and Europe. His most recent book is *The Handbook of Off Road Driving*, invaluable to anyone contemplating serious desert travel.

His collaborator on the *Alternative Guide to North Africa* was **Robert Chote**, who here writes the bulk of the Sahel chapters, specifically the resorts of Sousse and Port el Kantaoui and the holy city of Kairouan. Chote got to grips with North Africa while still a student, back-packing his way around the region and joining Cremona on Land-Rover expeditions. After completing a post-graduate course in journalism in 1990, he joined the staff of London's *Independent* newspaper.

**Michael Brett**, author of *The Moors* and senior lecturer in the History of North Africa at the University of London's School of Oriental and African Studies, wrote the feature on architecture. His interest in North Africa arose from a requirement to study and teach African history at University College of Cape Coast, Ghana, in the 1960s, a fact which has led him to appreciate the African dimension of the Maghreb as much as its Mediterranean and Middle Eastern aspects. In view of its history, architecture and superb situation, Brett considers Tunis-Carthage to be the outstanding city in North Africa and one of the finest on the whole of the Mediterranean (though, he admits, Istanbul probably takes the biscuit). He is currently finishing a book on the Fatimid dynasty in North Africa and Egypt.

**E. Lennox Manton**, author of the feature on the Bardo Museum's mosaics, has spent a good part of his life in the Middle East and is an expert on Roman archaeology. The fruit of his forays into the Maghreb, his book *The Romans In North Africa*, is perhaps the most entertaining work written on the subject. Now Manton, also a retired Fellow of the Royal College of Surgeons in Edinburgh and an artist who has exhibited widely, is working on a book on the history of St Paul in Asia Minor, having painstakingly retraced the Christian missionary's routes.

**Ruth Davis** writes here about the Mahlouf, the Tunisian version of a music imported from Muslim Andalusia between the 12th and 15th centuries. The modern Ministry of Cultural Affairs commandeered the Mahlouf as "Tunisia's Musical Heritage", attempting to model it on the Western symphony orchestra. Davis, a lecturer in Ethnomusicology at Cambridge University and Director of Studies in Music at Corpus Christi College, amends the record, pointing out the Mahlouf's popular role at weddings and Sufi ceremonies long before the men at the ministry ever sought to define it.

### Grumbling Officials

Thanks go to **Said M'samri**, who accompanied the project editor on her trips to research substantial sections of the Places chapters, silenced grumbling officials and helped with driving and interpreting, to **Jill Anderson** who cajoled the copy through the computers, and to **Lyle Lawson**, whose beady eye helped along the photo-edit.

Cremona            Chote            Brett

# *History*

# *Features*

# *Places*

## *Maps*

# A PRAGMATIC PEOPLE

In the mid-18th century, when most Europeans were decrying the Muslim infidels on Europe's doorstep, Thomas Shaw, a visiting English chaplain, had nothing but praise for Tunisia and its people. Whether he was a naive clergyman ignorant of Barbary Coast piracy (unlikely), or saw it for what it was, tit for tat, is unclear, but he wrote: "The Tunisians are the most civilised people who inhabit the coast of the Mediterranean; for instead of plundering their neighbours, they addict themselves to trade and commerce which induces them to cultivate the friendship of Christians." No irony was intended.

Nearly 250 years later, and with the experience of colonialism behind them, Tunisians are still taking the pragmatic approach. As well as welcoming – and not hustling – 2 million tourists a year, Tunisia hosts the headquarters of the Palestine Liberation Organisation and, since Egypt's 1979 peace initiative with Israel (the Camp David Agreement), the headquarters of the Arab League.

It is a policy that has promoted stability. Described as "habit rather than political design" by one historian, it has dictated Tunisia's history for centuries. At its most feeble, as vacillation, it contributed to the ease with which the French colonised the country in 1881 – Mohammed Bey, as effective as a cardboard cut-out of a ruler, put up flimsy resistance – but as a considered tactic it speeded the smooth exit of the French in 1956. A Frenchman, commenting on the policies of the party that led Tunisia to independence, said: "The Neo-Destour party has two faces: Western and democratic before Westerners, Islamic and xenophobic when it addresses its troops." When Habib Bourguiba became the country's first president, he managed to market himself as a nationalist hero to the electorate while befriending and emulating his old adversaries, the French.

Political moderation has been helped by the homogenous nature of the population. Save for in the Khroumir mountains, tribal revolts were never as troublesome as elsewhere in the Maghreb, not even when the bey introduced punitive taxes in the middle of the 19th century. In Tunisia, Berbers, the indigenous people of North Africa, had no great mountains to hide in when the Arabs, or for that matter any other conquerors, arrived. They quickly intermarried with the newcomers; and though countrywomen, in their bright clothes, silver jewellery and tattoos, are often referred to as Berber, they could just as easily have Arab ancestors. Distinctions are between rural and urban rather than Berber and Arab. The Berber language, alive and voluble even in the cities in Morocco and Algeria, has died out in all but the remotest Tunisian home.

The Tunisians' ability to adapt and compromise is illustrated by

**Preceding pages:** door to a hammam; the Chott el Djerid; history immured in Carthage; tiled terrace in Kairouan; market day in Douz. **Left,** cover-girl Lamia unveiled. **Overpage:** wearing your heart behind your ear.

nothing so much as the way they have embraced tourism. Like other fledgling republics, Tunisia, following independence, looked for new industries to keep its economy aloft. Shrewdly, it stressed its Mediterranean roots – Carthaginian, Roman, Andalusian – as much as its Arab and Islamic ones. Hot on the heels of the Spanish, Italians and Greeks, the Tunisians saw gold in them thar sands and built a marching line of white hotels along the greater part of them, long before the Moroccans had woken up to the fact that shovelling their sands into cement mixers was depleting their most valuable asset.

At the same time, the Tunisian government recognised the dangers of flouting traditional Islamic values. From the start, tourists were separated from Tunisia proper. The white walls and bosky gardens of the "Zones Touristiques", as the hotel areas are called, ensured that the topless sunbathing of Western visitors did not offend local sensibilities, and they shielded Western eyes from the naked reality of life for the humble poor. The bulk of tourist development is still concentrated on an affluent strip along the eastern shore, and has been joined by the luxury villas and businesses of the wealthier classes. Just 20 miles (32 km) inland lies a dramatically different country – traditional, agrarian, very poor.

Not even in tolerant Tunisia, though, can such discrepancy be ignored for ever; in 1987 members of the Islamic Tendency Movement bombed several tourist hotels. No lives were lost but it hinted at surpressed, more disturbing influences gathering in the country. How much, people began to ask, was Tunisian moderation due to coercion? Were the agreeable Tunisians in reality smiling through gritted teeth?

Certainly, when consensus has crumbled, tough measures have been taken to restore it. Divisions that emerged after independence were deftly bridged by Bourguiba. Individual and organised opposition were quashed by force and the masses manipulated by a steady diet of propaganda. In this way, Bourguiba was able to implement his own plans, incorporating "the best of the West" in what he clearly saw as *his* post-Independence state.

His sudden topple in 1987 didn't, however, release a surge of pent-up demonstrations and strikes. The most vocal demands for change come from the Islamic fundamentalists, a group currently agitating for reform all over the Muslim world. Significantly, in Tunisia, even they have little desire to reverse one of Bourguiba's earliest laws – the abolition of polygamy. As every jasmin seller in every Tunisian café will confirm, the situation is plain: a bloom worn above a gentleman's right ear means he is married; above the left ear means he is a bachelor and in the market for a wife. There is no convention for any other case.

Tunisian history begins with a sad love story, although in the more celebrated of its two versions, in Virgil's *Aeneid*, the Roman poet (70–19 BC) allowed himself a huge measure of poetic licence. The hero Aeneas, adrift after the fall of Troy, reaches the North African coast where he is courteously received by Dido, queen of a newly established Phoenician colony, Carthage. They fall in love, but the god Jupiter intervenes to remind Aeneas that he has more important things to do. Brushing aside Dido's piteous pleas, he dutifully sets sail, leaving her to kill herself in a frenzy of curses on her fickle lover.

As Aeneas's divine mission is to start the Roman race, Dido's rage is a portent of the deadly rivalry between Carthage and Rome, one which was to inspire Cato to end every speech to the Roman senate with the uncompromising cry: "*Delenda est Cartago*" (Carthage must be destroyed). The more familiar aspect of the Punic Wars, though, is probably Hannibal's crossing of the Alps on elephants.

Henry Purcell, in his opera based on the story, was no more inhibited than Virgil by a grave difficulty with dates: as Troy fell in about 1300 BC, and the founding of Carthage is usually put at 814 BC, Aeneas would have been some 500 years old when he and Dido had their night of magic in a cave, a storm erupting overhead.

**Fact, and more fiction:** Although the role of anyone called Aeneas in the actual history of Carthage and hence Tunisia may be discounted, there is some historical basis to the character of Dido who, under the name Elissa, was sister to King Pygmalion of Tyre, the Phoenician city on the coast of what is now Lebanon. When Pygmalion murdered her rich husband for his money, Dido imagined he would be after her and hers next. Collecting her inheritance, she summoned a party of sympathisers and fled in search of a new home. The fugitives stopped over in Cyprus to pick up 80 virgins – they wanted to multiply their numbers – and in due course

landed close to where Tunis now stands.

The local chieftain, Iarbus, agreed to let the settlers have as much land as could be covered by the hide of a bull. Dido's riposte to this ridiculous proposition was to cut the hide into thin strips which, when joined together, stretched around the Hill of Byrsa (i.e. "hide" in Greek). The hill was the site for the citadel of Carthage and is now recognisable by the flamboyant, though now derelict, St Louis Cathedral.

This version of events concludes with

Dido no better off than she was in *The Aeneid*. Iarbus, too, falls in love with her. Dido's quandry is that she wishes to remain faithful to her late husband but recognises that to reject Iarbus would very likely jeopardise the founding of Carthage and the lives of her subjects. She has no choice but to order the construction of a huge funeral pyre for a spectacular suicide.

**Sailors:** Trade imperatives, rather than murder, greed, lust and the usual baggage of romantic melodrama, explain why Dido sailed so far across the Mediterranean before settling on a sanctuary in Tunisia. The Phoenicians were well-acquainted with the

**Preceding pages:** Sbeitla. **Left,** the death of Dido as told in *The Aeneid*. **Right,** Tanit, the pre-eminent Carthaginian goddess.

North African coast, having already established stations at Sousse, Utica and Bizerte among other places. Phoenician sailors were intrepid adventurers, but for the routine though guarded purpose of fetching Spanish bronze they preferred to remain within sight of land and tackle the journey in comfortable daily stages of about 20 miles (30 km). Copper and tin, the ingredients of bronze, were then prized as highly as the New World's gold would later be. In both cases, the native miners had no idea that they were selling them for the proverbial peanuts.

The African coast had advantages over the more northerly European route. To begin with, Phoenician traders could sail to Egypt

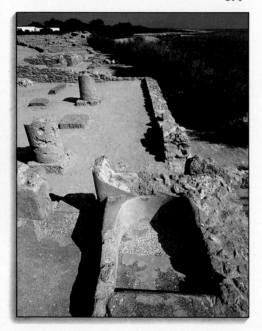

with their eyes shut, so there was no great difficulty in leapfrogging westwards from there. The northerly route invited conflict with their great rivals, the Greeks, and the Phoenicians cared more about trade than acquiring territory.

The straits between Sicily and North Africa were a bottleneck which cut the Mediterranean ("the known world") in half. The channel was about 80 miles (130 km) wide, enough to allow the Phoenicians to cede one side to the Greeks as long as they had free passage along the other. The North African route had the additional attraction of being the terminus for the gold caravans that

travelled up from the African interior.

When the Persians came along to challenge Greek supremacy in the Eastern Mediterranean, the Phoenicians recognised a potentially useful ally. If the Persians held down the Greeks in the Aegean, the Phoenicians could then take on their colonies in Sicily. In the event, the plan went seriously awry and the Greeks achieved two momentous victories, reputedly on the very same day in 480 BC. The Persian fleet under Xerxes was wiped out at Salamis; the Phoenicians were defeated at Himera.

The victorious Greek fleet constituted an impenetrable barrier between old Phoenicia in the Levant and its western interests in Carthage. The two halves of the divided empire thereafter developed more or less independently, the Carthaginian colony quickly outstripping its progenitors.

**Native residents:** The original inhabitants on the previously dark stage of North Africa seemed to have been joined at some uncharted point in their earlier history by fair-skinned strangers. As the present island of Malta is the tip of what was once a land-bridge across the Mediterranean, it is not inconceivable that these strangers were simply an overflow of the great population migrations that surged through continental Europe in prehistoric times. Very little has emerged about their true identity, but there are intriguing implications in the fact that the dolmen graves they built had something in common with the prehistoric graves found in large numbers as far north as Scandinavia.

The Greeks, notably Herodotus, had some interesting information about the tribes inhabiting the Mediterranean shores of Africa. There were the Adyrmachidae who, on plucking a tick or some other insect from their persons, "give it bite for bite before throwing it away". The Nasamones flavoured their milk with powdered locust and observed a custom whereby men who wanted to lie with a woman put a pole up to signal their needs. Among the neighbouring Gindanes, it was the women who were unabashed: they wore a leather band around the ankle for every male conquest "so that whoever has the greatest number enjoys the greatest reputation".

The women of the Machlyes and Auses tribes fought battles once a year with stones and sticks. Anyone who died was obviously "not a maiden" – not that there was any stigma attached to that condition. Sex was "casual", the question of paternity being postponed until a child was fully grown, at which point the men decided whom among them it most resembled. The Atarantes were a tribe of few words: they dispensed with names and restricted their conversation to curses at the sun for the way it burnt their bodies and scorched the land. The Atlantes "eat no living thing and never dream."

Herodotus is not one to leave a story out because he doesn't believe it either, but he usually drops a hint that a particular claim should not be taken too seriously. He is clearly unhappy with information passed on by Greeks and Romans, and neither were well-disposed towards Carthage or its inhabitants. According to Plutarch, they were "a people full of bitterness and surly, submissive to rulers, tyrannical to those they rule, abject in fear, fierce when provoked, unshakable in resolve, and so strict as to dislike all humour and kindness."

The typically grim portrait seized on the custom of child sacrifice, a practice confirmed by the discovery of tophets, the crematoriums in which their ashes were stored in urns. A child was usually strangled before being placed in the arms of the statue of a goddess, the flames licking up from below. The first-born child of a family was gener-

about men with the heads of dogs or no heads at all, in which case their eyes were located in their chests. His note of troglodytes, however, is borne out by the present day inhabitants of Matmata.

**The settlers:** As the Phoenicians invented the cursive script which is the basis of all modern European alphabets, it is especially ironic that they have left no written accounts of themselves and their achievements. What was written about them (and survived) was

**Left**, Carthaginian plumbing is still intact in Kerkouane. **Above**, *The Building of Carthage* by J.M.W. Turner.

ally reserved for sacrifice, either in infancy or at an older age to appease the gods in times of grave danger brought about by wars, epidemics and so on.

Even their sternest critics conceded that the Phoenicians were canny businessmen, and it was their commercial success which attracted lethal envy. Rome was founded, according to legend if not in reality, not long after Carthage. Its development was slower but, having first eclipsed the Greeks, Rome gradually caught up. The Mediterranean was not big enough for both of them, and to make matters worse they were face to face where the sea was narrowest. War was inevitable.

# CARTHAGE VERSUS ROME

The first Punic war broke out in 263 BC and lasted for more than 20 years. It was comparatively low-key, consisting of naval skirmishes around the coast of Sicily. As Carthaginian and Roman power were respectively on the sea and on land, the two adversaries could not properly get to grips. A captured Carthaginian ship gave the Romans the model on which they set about building a better navy, and it was thus on more equal terms that the first war was resolved in Rome's favour at the battle of Aegates.

The huge war indemnity exacted by Rome and payable over 20 years emptied Carthage's coffers, so much so that it was unable to pay the mercenaries who constituted the bulk of its army. The mercenaries could think of other ways of taking what was owed to them, the result being a rebellion so savage and protracted that it came to be known as the "Truceless War". It was put down with the greatest difficulty by Hamilcar Barca, a general who recognised that the sums of money needed to save Carthage could only come by the exploitation of Spain's rich resources. To this end he moved to Spain, taking with him a nine-year-old son named Hannibal. The message drummed into the boy's head was that Carthage's difficulties were Rome's doing. Rome's guilt must never be forgotten. Sixteen years later Hannibal inherited his father's command of the army in Spain – and didn't forget his lessons.

His plan, once he had an excuse to resume hostilities, was to take the short sea-crossing to Spain, cross the Alps with elephants and attack Rome from the least-expected direction, from the north. The famous journey cost the lives of all but one of the elephants.

Hannibal's plan was at first blazingly successful, and it is an extraordinary fact that he spent 15 years marauding in Italy without closing on his target, Rome itself. Eventually, the Romans found a young general, Scipio, who thought of ignoring Hannibal's belligerent presence in Italy in order to strike

at Carthaginian positions in Spain and Africa. Hannibal thus had to abandon Italy to meet the threat to Carthage.

The final battle of the Second Punic War took place at Zama in 202. The defeated Carthaginians were required to burn their fleet, the indemnity was colossal and, most humiliating of all, they were restricted to a corner of eastern Tunisia and were not allowed to attack any third party without Rome's permission.

Hannibal escaped the ignominy. He found

secret refuge in today's Izmir, a part of the Eastern Mediterranean which was not then subject to Rome, living anonymously so as not to embarrass his host, the king of Bithynia, who was aware of the Roman price on Hannibal's head. When Bithynia found itself at war with a neighbouring state, which was a client of Rome, Hannibal's advice was solicited. As the war was principally a naval one in boats which crews rowed naked, Hannibal hit on the idea of bombarding the enemy oarsmen with live snakes. When the fleets next engaged, his plan was executed. The Bithynians won.

The Romans learned of Hannibal's role

**Left**, engraving of Hannibal crossing the Alps.
**Right**, vines decorate the column of a Roman villa in Carthage.

and ordered that he be tracked down, in the words of Plutarch, "like a bird that has grown too old to fly, and lost its tail feathers". They discovered his whereabout and surrounded the house. Hannibal is reputed to have addressed his servants: "It is now time to end the anxiety of the Romans. Clearly they are no longer able to wait for the death of an old man who has caused them so much concern." When the Romans burst into the house, they found him lying dead. "The greatest soldier the world has ever seen," according to some, had taken poison.

Penned in by the peace treaty after Zama, Carthage concentrated on making the greatest agricultural use it could of the reduced

alive inside the walls when the siege began and only 50,000 when it ended in 146 BC. Other writers gave eye-witness accounts of the finale. Three long streets, six-storey houses on either side, led from the forum up the hill to the citadel. The Romans stormed the houses one by one, setting fire to them and forcing the defenders to throw themselves from windows and be impaled on pikes. Polybius described survivors being dragged along by hooks and thrown on to heaps of dead. He spares no detail: quivering limbs protruding from wreckage, etc.

After six days of this, King Hasdrubal appealed for mercy. It is said that his own men then turned on him in disgust. The

land available. The economy recovered over the following 50 years to the extent that a small war looked affordable. The target was Massinissa, a neighbouring king who enjoyed the protection of Rome and therefore felt at liberty to nibble away at the fringes of Carthaginian territory. Rome seized on the declaration of war with Massinissa as a violation of the Zama treaty.

**Carthage falls:** The Roman Senate, with Cato's words ringing in its ears, ordered the Carthaginians to evacuate their city. When they refused, the Romans laid a siege which lasted for three years. According to the Greek historian Strabo, there were 700,000

Queen and 900 diehards climbed the 60 steps from the public square to the temple on the summit of the hill. They set fire to the temple, and the curtain comes down on the queen standing on the roof, heaping reproaches on Hasdrubal for his cowardice. She then hurls her children into the flames and jumps in after them.

The Romans ordered the city to be ploughed over and the land salted so that nothing would ever rise in its place again. Something did, though – and it was the Romans who built it.

At first, Rome was content to mark off a coastal strip for itself with a ditch running from Tabarka to Sfax, and let Massinissa rule the rest by proxy. He was given unprecedented honours for one who was not a Roman citizen: a crown, a sceptre, and the right to wear a toga embroidered with palms. Life in his seraglio agreed with Massinissa. He fathered a child at 86, rode his horses bareback until he was 88 and lived to 90.

Massinissa's territory, which skirted the present Algerian border, was supposed to act as a buffer between the Roman province and potential unrest arising from all the mutual hatred beyond, but even so the more remote Berber kings managed to become a thorn not only in Rome's African affairs but, later, in domestic issues, notably the civil war

master of the world, and he is said to have had a dream from which he woke up to jot down plans for the rebuilding of Carthage. He was prevented from realising the dream by the Ides of March, Brutus and Cassius, and all that. Some chose to interpret his death as a divine finger-wagging for presuming to defy the curse on Carthage.

Augustus, his successor, had the prickly choice of running the same risk or falling foul of the no less binding obligation to honour an emperor's last wishes. As it happened, Carthage rose again within two centuries of its supposed destruction to become the third city of the Roman Empire.

**Roman resurrection:** Carthage was rebuilt

between Pompey and Julius Caesar, much of which was fought in Africa. Pompey, who at the time commanded Roman Africa, drew on the support of the African legions. In addition he was aided by Cato the Younger, descendant of the famous orator. Caesar eventually drove Pompey to Alexandria where, to Caesar's disappointment, Pompey was murdered, thus escaping a place in Caesar's triumph in Rome.

The subsequent surrender of Cato, who had holed up in Utica, made Caesar virtual

**Roman mosaics: <u>left</u>, Ulysses resists the Sirens; <u>right</u>, Venus is crowned by two centaurs.**

to the utmost of Rome's considerable architectural capabilities. The builders worked under military discipline, and in levelling parts of the site they heaped a protective layer of earth over the charred remains of the earlier site, creating a kind of archaeological sandwich. In 1858 a French archaeologist drilling a shaft into the Byrsa penetrated a layer of cinders more than a metre thick, which tended to confirm that Carthage did burn for 17 days, as contemporary reports stated. The cinders contained fragments of stonework, twisted metal, molten glass and calcined human bones.

The Romans built a new forum, temples,

palaces, baths, theatres, multistorey houses and market-places. A road linked Carthage with the even older Punic city of Utica. Blockhouses along the route imply a security system, probably to deter robbers. The city was supplied with water along a 90-mile (145-km) aqueduct from Zaghouan, parts of which can still be seen around Tunis.

The Romans concentrated their vast undertaking on Carthage to begin with, but the insatiable demand for grain at home, together with the need to maintain an intimidating presence among troublesome tribes, pushed the frontiers of "Africa" ever outwards. Expansion was greatly accelerated on the accession of Septimus Severus in AD

"portraits show that his nose was short and slightly *retroussé*."

He and his wife seem to have been among the first foreigners to take a holiday on a Greek island. An eminent historian was astounded as recently as 1984 to discover a stone tablet lying discarded in the mayor of Skiathos's front garden. A Latin inscription showed it to be in commemoration of their visit. Septimus spent a considerable period in Britain supervising repairs to Hadrian's Wall. He hated the damp climate and actually died in York during a particularly bad cold snap, leaving the Roman Empire in the far less capable hands of his dissolute sons.

**African rebels:** Ancient Tunisia deserves

193, who had a vested interest in the African province. He was himself an African, born at Leptis Magna in present-day Libya.

**African Emperor:** Septimus was a conscientious emperor, although his achievements almost take second place to the debate about just how black he was. African history books like to depict him as a full-blooded negro, which is a self-serving assumption based on a 6th-century Syrian description of him as dark-skinned. The same Syrian source, John Malatas, is taken to task by others for insisting that Severus had a long nose. "Unmistakably wrong," says Michael Grant's authoritative biographical guide to the emperors,

credit for a brave but futile rebellion against the monster Maximinus who succeeded the Severus dynasty. Usually reliable sources say he was eight feet tall; his treatment of critics included having them sewn up in the hollowed carcasses of wild animals. Visitors to El Djem, who usually go there only to admire the magnificent Roman amphitheatre, may wish to take a seat on an upper tier in order to imagine this now dreary town making a bid to take over the Empire.

The leadership of the rebellion was thrust on the improbable shoulders of a father and son. Gordian senior, already 80, could barely stay awake. "His love of sleep was enormous; he would doze off even at table, if he was dining with friends, and without any embarrassment." His son earned one of Edward Gibbon's celebrated epigrams in *The History of the Decline and Fall of the Roman Empire*: "Twenty-two acknowledged concubines, and a library of 62,000 volumes, attested the variety of his inclinations; and from the productions which he left behind him, it appears that the former as well as the latter were designed for use rather than for ostentation."

The rebels of El Djem, then known as Thysdrus, made what became known as a unilateral declaration of independence, with Carthage as capital. Such was the unpopular-

The defenders were routed, and it is said that more of them were crushed in the stampede to escape than were killed by the enemy. Gordian II was killed in action; his father strangled himself with his girdle.

North Africa in general, and Tunisia in particular, became the so-called granary of the Roman Empire, and the arrival of great fleets of galleys loaded with corn attracted excited crowds to the Italian ports. Tunisian oil was precious, too. Not the petroleum variety, of course, but olive oil, which nevertheless served many of the same purposes. It was fuel for heat and light and used in cooking, but never to dress a salad.

The agricultural estates took advantage of

ity of Maximinus that the Roman senate not only acquiesced but actually invited the Gordians to take over the whole empire. They wore the purple for only 22 days. Forces loyal to Maximinus, "equipped with every type of weapon and trained for battle by military experience gained in fighting the barbarians," descended on a Carthage defended by "an undisciplined mob, without military training; for they had grown up in a time of complete peace and indulged themselves constantly in feasts and festivals."

**Mosaics depicting fishing and hunting scenes testify to the natural wealth of Roman Africa.**

relatively cheap slave labour, causing Pliny the Elder to complain that six landowners in possession of "half of Africa" were the ruin of Italy. The mad Caligula, incidentally, had the six murdered and confiscated their land. Juvenal took another view, demanding respect for industrious colonists who allowed Rome "to give herself up without fear to the pleasures of the circus and the theatre".

**Decline and fall:** The price paid by latter-day Romans for so abandoning themselves to the pursuit of pleasure is still being wheeled out as a warning to hedonists. The Romans were undoubtedly enfeebled by their preoccupation with pleasure, but the actual *coup de grâce* was administered by a people who could hardly be held up as a more worthwhile example of virtue. North Africa was bedevilled by these newcomers in 429 when Count Boniface, the Roman Legate, sought an alliance through the offices of his wife. She was a Vandal, a Teutonic tribe which had been driven south as far as Spain by the rapacious Visigoths, and suggested that help might be available from that quarter. Against St Augustine's advice, Boniface invited the Vandals to North Africa.

The invitation came at a time when the Vandal settlements in Spain were under increasing pressure from Visigoths. The Vandals piled into anything that floated in the

Spanish port of Tarifa and disembarked – 80,000 of them – with all their earthly possessions. Boniface took one look at them and fled to St Augustine in Hippo, where he lay dying. The Vandals pursued him to the city walls and, after a siege which lasted 14 months, Hippo fell.

The Vandal leader was Genseric. Small, ugly, lame and laconic, he indulged in "every species of indignity and torture to force from captives a discovery of their hidden wealth". After capturing Hippo, he turned his attention to Carthage, apparently appalled by a city "polluted by effeminate wretches, who publicly assumed the countenance, the dress, and the character, of women." He unleashed his hordes on the city to put matters right, collecting all its wealth for himself, confiscating the land and distributing the nobility among his sons as slaves.

In 455 Genseric crossed to Italy and for 14 days plundered Rome, returning to Carthage with a booty which included the golden roof of the temple of Jupiter, sacred vessels originally from Solomon's Temple in Jerusalem, the dowager Empress Eudoxia and a couple of princesses. The Vandal reign of terror lasted about a century. Their occupation is marked by little more than the smashed noses on statues they did not destroy totally. Their linguistic contribution is said to have added a single word to the Berber vocabulary, a verb meaning "to drink". Worst of all, though, they demolished the magnificent Roman aqueducts. Agriculture was devasted and with it the proud profile that Roman cities like Dougga and El Djem had given to the barren land.

The Vandals seem to have been softened by life in Tunisia because when at last they were challenged militarily, they showed none of their old ferocity. Justinian, a Bulgarian by birth, had become Emperor of the Eastern (Byzantine) Empire based in Constantinople, the future Istanbul. He ruled assiduously for 38 years, expanding his domain until it contained 64 provinces and no fewer than 935 cities.

**Last breath:** Rebuilding the old African empire was always in Justinian's mind, and to this end he dispatched in 533 an army under an illustrious general, Belisarius. Within a year, the Vandal King Gelimer, Genseric's great-grandson, ran away, was captured, and taken back to Carthage as Belisarius's prisoner. With that, the Vandals disappear from the pages of Tunisian history as abruptly as they appeared.

Justinian ordered the restoration of Roman towns and constructed defences to meet the threat of Berber tribes in the interior or any sea-borne invasion. An impressive amount of Byzantine building survives to this day, but his African empire lasted only as long as that of the Vandals had done, a century or so. In 647 they suffered defeat at Sbeitla. Their victors were the Arabs.

**Left**, a smashed nose, the hallmark of the Vandals. **Right**, the Vandals invade.

The explosive spread of Islam, which, within a century of the Prophet's death, was knocking on the door of India in the east and, via North Africa, of France in the west is popularly perceived as dark strangers galloping out of the desert, a Koran in one hand and a sword in the other. They were irresistible because death on the battlefield was for them dearly to be desired, and the coincidental loss of a limb or two in the meantime could be patched up in paradise with the wings of angels and cherubim.

The Arab-Islamic invasion undoubtedly had a far greater impact on Tunisia as it exists today than any other invasion before or since, but in the words of a distinguished modern historian, Jamil M. Abun-Nasr: "The pervasive and durable influence which Islam came to have in this region was not an achievement for which the Arab rulers could claim much credit." With one exception, he says, the Muslim caliphs showed hardly any interest in the conversion to Islam of the non-Arab people over whom they ruled. Proselytisation was the work of heretical splinter groups who, prevented from preaching at home, sought converts in safer pastures abroad.

The Berbers, like the ancient Greeks before them, were quick to milk from their various political and military overlords anything that looked useful. They were adept at exploiting weaknesses, such as those which lay in the murderous schisms within Islam. The arguments were ostensibly about lines of descent from the childless Prophet or indeed whether the caliphate (the Islamic papacy) ought to be hereditary at all. If a sinful Muslim forfeited the rights of a true believer (another bone of contention), reservations about the moral propriety of overthrowing a thoroughly degenerate caliph, as some were, practically disappeared.

In Tunisia, the bewildering badges attached to Omayyads, Kharidjites, Aghlabids, Malikites and so on are rather more than distinctions between various dynasties

Left, fantasia horseman, symbol of a conquering past. Right, Arab calligraphy: a testament of the Muslim faith.

or hair-splitting theologians. They implied, *inter alia*, power struggles which took several forms: between religious and military leaderships in government, between a Tunisian-based Arab aristocracy (which, in the manner of colonists everywhere, developed independent ideas) and the caliphate, and between those who thought all Muslims were equal and others who regarded themselves as inherently superior to the most pious of Berber believers. As can be imagined, the last form converted easily into what

was tantamount to class warfare.

The Arab conquest of the Maghreb, which covers modern Libya, Algeria and Morocco as well as Tunisia, began as a series of exploratory raids by military chiefs who had conquered Egypt in the name of Islam. They became serious only with the rise of the Omayyad dynasty and its grand imperial designs which led inevitably to a struggle with the Byzantines for supremacy in the Mediterranean.

An Arab army entered Tunisia in 670 with permanent intentions. Arriving by land, it by-passed the Byzantine strongholds along the coast. As a land-based power, at least to begin with, the Arabs were at a disadvantage against targets which could be supplied and reinforced by sea. Their priority was to secure a base which would require the enemy to engage them in terrain where their cavalary would be at its best. The answer was to build a new city at Kairouan, after which they could turn their attention to individual pockets of Christian and Berber resistance. The Arabic name for the province as a whole was an adaptation of the Latin, Ifriqiya.

**Valiant Virago:** In due course the Arabs mopped up Carthage and defeated a combined Byzantine-Berber force near Bizerte. The stiffest resistance came from what must have been a surprising quarter, a Berber

kingdom ruled by a queen who is reputed to have been Jewish. El Kahina, "The Priestess", won two battles against the Arabs before a showdown at El Djem.

The legendary version of the battle is set in the Roman amphitheatre and has decidedly suspect embellishments. The amphitheatre was said to be joined by tunnel to the port of Mahdia – some 30 miles (50 km) away – which enabled El Kahina not only to defy a protracted siege but also to cause utter confusion among the enemy beneath the walls by bombing them with an apparently unlimited supply of fresh fish. It seems she escaped (by the tunnel, of course) but was pursued

and killed on the Algerian border near the town of Tabarka.

El Kahina's death was the last serious Berber attempt to oppose the Arab conquest. Her victor, Ibn el Numan, had to chase out Byzantines who in the meantime had reoccupied Carthage, and it was to deter similar revivals that Ibn el Numan resolved to create a substantial naval base. The old Punic ports had limitations. The Lake of Tunis had potential, but an isthmus separated the lake from the sea. Coptic artisans were brought in from Egypt to cut the isthmus, erect workshops and start building ships. The new settlement took its name from a nearby village known to the Romans as Thunes. It translated as Tunis.

The Berbers responded to the Arab conquest with characteristic opportunism. Many joined the colonial army, although on less favourable rates of pay than their Arab comrades-in-arms. Even deeper resentment was caused by a commander who ordered his Berber bodyguard to tattoo their own names on one arm and his on the other. The idea cost him his life. The most oppressive practice against the Berbers, though, was a kind of poll tax payable in people. Caliphs were generally entitled to one-fifth of the tribute, and one is reputed to have received 20,000 human captives by these means during his term of office. The Caliph Hisham (724–43) wrote a letter specifying the physical qualities of the Berber girls he looked forward to receiving in his next consignment.

Several generations in Africa produced a local Arab aristocracy which was as resentful of the caliphate's interference in local affairs as were the Berbers. Sufficiently remote from Baghdad to think for themselves, the scholars of Kairouan also developed deep misgivings about the none-too-pious style of life of the caliphs.

A minor rebellion which broke out in Tunis in 797 took on a more ominous nature when it spread to Kairouan. The caliph's governor was unable to restore order, but Ibrahim ben el Aghlab, a provincial leader, had a well-disciplined army and could. He thereupon suggested to the caliph, Harun el Rashid, that he be granted Africa as a hereditary fief. He sweetened the proposition by offering to pay the caliph an annual tribute of 40,000 dinars for the honour. If only because the caliph had until then been required to subsidise the province to the tune of 100,000 dinars a year, he agreed.

Ibrahim ben el Aghlab and his descendants, known as the Aghlabids, ruled North Africa until 909 in the name of the caliphs. The caliphs' flag was flown and they were mentioned in Friday prayers, but in reality the Aghlabids – who adopted the title of Emir – were all but autonomous.

**Great era:** Tunisians consider the century of Aghlabid rule as their Golden Age, pointing to the construction of the Great Mosque of Tunis and numerous splendid *ribats* (fortified monasteries) along the coast to fend off avenging Christians. The Aghlabids also pulled the economy, and especially ag-

Aghlabids; the climax of raids launched from Sicily was the sacking of the Basilica of St Peter in Rome in 846.

To some extent, however, the grandiose construction projects and military adventures were a smokescreen behind which the Arab officer class and holy men of Kairouan were increasingly critical of the regime. Wary of these undercurrents, Ibrahim moved his residence from Kairouan to a fortified palace a short distance away. He surrounded himself with troops he could trust and a bodyguard of black slaves, later augmented by European slave troops bought from Neopolitan and Venetian merchants.

The hostility in religious circles arose

riculture, out of the devastation sewn by the Vandals and only patchily restored by the Byzantines. Trans-Saharan trade with the Sudan flourished, particularly in gold and slaves. (The availability of imported slaves was a boon for the Berbers if only because they themselves had previously been the main source of supply.) Prosperity led to the development of crafts, notably those of weavers, jewellers, and leather and wood workers. Military successes abroad were intended to enhance the standing of the

**Left and above, 19th-century watercolours of Kairouan, the Aghlabid capital.**

from the contemptuous treatment of Berbers who had embraced Islam. The feeling that Muslims were Muslims regardless of race was a cornerstone of the Sunnite movement and the Malikite school of Islamic law which developed in Kairouan, and was the basis of Kharidjite opposition to Arab-caliphal rule in the Maghreb. The doctrine of equality naturally attracted the tradesmen and peasant classes to whom equality was denied and drove a deep division between what would be called, in modern language, the Establishment and the masses.

The last Aghlabid emir, Ibrahim II, at first seen as a welcome antidote to the "frivolous and extravagant" Mohammed II, king at the age of 13 and passionately addicted in equal parts to the hunting of cranes and "a life of pleasurable dissipation" (he dropped dead at 24). Ibrahim II was, in contrast, committed to justice, sincerely at first and then, alas, fanatically. His mission to defend the defenceless and poor turned into a maniacal massacre of the powerful and rich. A wealthy Arab living in a castle at Cap Bon, for example, was dragged to Kairouan for no particular reason and crucified. The serious-minded Ibrahim must have realised that his campaign to liquidate the Arab aristocracy would produce a reaction: he increased his black slave troops to 10,000 and built an-

called the state Fatimid after the Prophet's daughter was Ubaydalla Said, who at once claimed that he was not only a descendant of the Prophet (down Fatima's line) but also the long-awaited Mahdi – in Christian terms, the Second Coming. His Sunni critics offered a contradictory and obviously offensive theory, that he was actually a Jewish imposter. Ubaydalla gave an indication of how he felt about such remarks by having his critics killed.

**All the way to Cairo:** Ubaydalla planned nothing less than the conquest of Egypt and the usurpation of the caliphate. He got as far as Alexandria before being driven back, at which point he concentrated instead on

other fortified residence at Rekada, about 5 miles (8 km) outside Kairouan.

Ibrahim abdicated in 902 under pressure from the caliph. His successor was assassinated within a year by his son, who then compounded the horror by murdering his brother as well to secure his succession. Such outrages fell into the lap of the Ismailis, an austere Shi'ite sect which had long been disturbed by the relaxed Aghlabid policy on matters like drinking alcohol. They stirred a rebellion which forced the last of the Aghlabids, Ziyadat Allah III, to evacuate the palace at Rekada in 909.

The Ismaili leader who took over and

building a new capital at Mahdia, the port which supposedly supplied El Kahina with her fish bombs. All pilgrims on their way to Mecca were thenceforth required to pass through Mahdia and pay a handsome tax for the privilege. Excessive taxation to finance the leadership's wild military ambitions led to popular grumblings which the persecuted Sunnis were quick to exploit. The sound defences at Mahdia helped the Fatimids to see out the threat, and when it was over they were to gather their resources and at last achieve the ambition of conquering Egypt. The capital of the Fatimid state, which was to last until Sultan Saladin in 1171, was transferred from Mahdia to a new city, Cairo.

With the Fatimid leadership preoccupied in Egypt, their control over Tunisia slipped away. When the situation deteriorated into rebellion, they responded with what amounted to unleashing Islam's Vandals on Tunisia. The Arabian nomadic tribes of Banu Hilal and Banu Sulaym had turned up in Egypt in the 8th century and made unbelievable nuisances of themselves for 300 years. The Fatimids suddenly saw an opportunity to rid themselves of these pests: they pointed them in the direction of the Maghreb and told them to help themselves. An estimated 50,000 warriors, plus women and children, accepted the invitation.

target for Normans based in Sicily who between 1134 and 1148 seized Mahdia, Gabes, Sfax and the island of Djerba. The only credible Muslim rulers in the Maghreb at the time were the Almohads in the far west, and they responded with a counter-attack which bounced the Normans out of Mahdia and back to Sicily. Having come so far, the Almohads stayed to tidy up the mess and for the first time the entire Maghreb was under a single political authority.

The unity established by the Almohads was broken by an offshoot, the Hafsids. Their secession was recognised by Mecca, which furthermore acknowledged the ruler El Mustansir as caliph. Tunisia prospered

Historians have searched long and hard for any good that might have come out of the Banu Hilal and Banu Sulaym immigrants, and the only possible consolation may have been the spreading of the Arabic language in the countryside instead of it remaining limited to the towns. It is certainly the case that the Berber language virtually disappeared in Tunisia and Arabic as a common language may have helped diminish the gap between Berber and Arab.

Anarchy made Tunisia an irresistible

through European and Sudanese trade under El Mustansir, who used the money to transform Tunis, his capital, with a splendidly appointed palace and the Abu Fihr park. The hunting estate he created near Bizerte was said to be without equal in the world. El Mustansir's foreign policy was remarkably open-handed: merchants with whom the country traded in Venice, Pisa and Genoa were given permission to settle and do business in the Hafsid ports.

**Christian interest:** So enlightened did the country and its leadership seem to be that Pope Innocent IV crossed Tunisia's name off his list of possible destinations for

**Left**, the Zitouna in Tunis. **Right**, Islam splinters: tomb of Sidi ben Aissa, founder of a Sufi sect.

another crusade. Louis IX of France did not agree although not, it seems, for religious reasons nor because of rumours that El Mustansir was ripe for conversion to Christianity. French merchants who had also been allowed to settle in Tunisia complained that an official tax-collector executed for corruption had died owing them large sums of money which El Mustansir refused to honour. The brother of Louis, Charles of Anjou, also claimed that he was owed money. The Crusaders disembarked at Carthage on 18 July 1270 under the command of Louis.

Tunis was under attack for a month and El Mustansir was on the point of withdrawing to Kairouan when Louis died. Charles, the alleged creditor, arrived with reinforcements the same day but, finding El Mustansir ready to come to terms, ordered a ceasefire. The treaty included substantial indemnities but at least the Hafsid dynasty survived to continue, with ups and downs, until the end of the 15th century.

Some Christians never gave up hope that Tunisia could be won over to the faith. The Hafsids were not above exploiting these hopes. One of them, seeking the support of James II of Aragon, dropped various hints that he was almost ready. He reminded the right people that his mother was a Christian slave and also confided in the commander of the Christian militia in Tunis. A famous Franciscan missionary was rushed over to handle the formalities. He spent from 1313 to 1315 in Tunis waiting for a call that never came. The Spaniards as a whole had even more patience, but in the end (200 years later!) that ran out and they began to move physically into the Maghreb.

**Spanish immigrants:** The ill-advised invitation to some Vandals to come across to Tunisia had coincided, it may be recalled, with pressure on their Spanish abode by the equally dreadful Visigoths. The Visigoths duly dug in and established their capital at Toledo. In 711, a Berber army led by Tariq ben Ziyad attacked the Visigoths. Tariq had already taken Toledo when he made the mistake of requesting reinforcements from his Arab chief, Ibn Nusayr. The chief arrived with an army of 18,000, liked what he saw and decided to do the rest personally. Tariq could go home. The Berbers thus lost the fruits of their Spanish victory.

The Arab usurpers enjoyed much the same degree of freedom from the caliphate in the running of their affairs in Spain as the Aghlabids had in Tunisia. Arab families moved backwards and forwards between the Maghreb and Andalusia. The Berbers were discouraged from crossing to Spain as civilians, but many were recruited as soldiers for service there. The native inhabitants were either assimilated into the Arab-Islamic culture or were permitted to retain their Christian or Jewish identities on payment of a tribute to the Arabs.

The tables were turned in the second half of the 15th century as Spaniards gradually clawed back their country. Defeated Muslims were allowed to retain their property and practise their religion, although they were encouraged to emigrate. Most went to North Africa, mainly to Morocco and Tunisia. They did so, but at a leisurely pace – a total of about 100,000 over 350 years. Persistent preaching of Christianity at those who chose to stay behind fell on deaf ears, so from 1499 a policy of forcible conversion was put into operation. An estimated 80,000 Andalusian Muslims and Jews migrated in 1609 alone.

The Andalusians brought valuable skills to Tunisia, either agricultural in the case of those who farmed on the Cap Bon peninsula or crafts among those who settled in urban ghettos. They specialised in making felt hats, the distinctive *chechia* fez for the Tunisian market and numerous variations for export. The Andalusians worked hard at preserving their separate identity.

The archbishop who advocated forcible conversion also urged Queen Isabella to found a Spanish empire in the Maghreb. King Ferdinand, however, would have preferred an empire in Italy, so Spanish efforts in North Africa were limited to what the Phoenicians had done, in other words to the establishment of garrison posts along the coast while leaving the interior to indigenous rulers. These posts, known as *presidios*, may not have amounted to much, but they symbolised a leap across the Mediterranean in the front-line between the Christian and Muslim worlds. Alarmed Muslims appealed for help from the then dominant power in their orbit, the Ottoman Turks.

The Ottoman empire had enough trouble on its hands in the Eastern Mediterranean to take on yet more, but it was dragged into the Maghreb confrontation by a couple of renegade Greeks from the island of Lesbos, Uruj and Khayr el Din, the Barbarossa brothers. They were, of course, pirates, and they had been using Goulette in Tunis as an operational base under an agreement with the Hafsids which gave them a share of the profits. The profits were large, and in 1510 the Barbarossas were given permission to open a branch office, as it were, on the island of Djerba.

The elder brother Uruj, already minus an arm lost in battle, was killed in the course of family business in Algiers. Khayr el Din took up the reins but realised he needed help in tackling the Christians, in exchange for which he was willing to submit to the Ottoman sultan. The sultan accepted the offer and dispatched a force of 2,000 Janissary troops and artillery. Khayr el Din captured Algiers and ruled it for eight years, during which he converted the port into a formidable base for his piratical fleet. The sultan was impressed, and in 1533 offered him the job of admiral of the Ottoman fleet. His first mission was to conquer Tunis.

Khayr el Din did better than conquer Tunis. He defeated the Hafsids, his former partners, near Kairouan and thereby inherited the whole of Tunisia. Charles V, King of Spain, appeared before Tunis the following year, 1535, with an armada of 300 ships and 30,000 men. Barbarossa was ready for them, but the 20,000 Christian slaves in Tunis turned against him unexpectedly and he was forced to make a hurried escape to Constantinople. Expecting to be rewarded for their assistance, the Christian slaves opened the city gates to Charles. What followed was one of history's worst atrocities: as many as 70,000 men, women and children may have been put to the sword. Over three days, Tunis was sacked .

The politics of the Mediterranean were a tangle of secret treaties and very probably incomprehensible even to the principals involved. France had a private arrangement with the Turks against Spain, so Barbarossa was more or less seconded to the French navy. But Charles V, anxious about this freshly-minted French connection, came up with an interesting offer: if Barbarossa came over to his side, he would see to it that the popular pirate became king of the Maghreb from Algiers to Tripoli. This kingdom would have included all of Tunisia. Negotiations

HORUSCE und HAREADEN BARBAROSSA
*Könige von Tunis und Algiers und ober See Admiralen*

got no further "because of the lack of confidence on both sides". A treaty between Charles V and Frances I of France in 1544 then made Barbarossa redundant. Without an obvious future on either side, he retired and was dead within two years.

The enfeebled Hafsids had been helpless spectators in Tunisia during these labyrinthic activities. Barbarossa's short-lived conquest of Tunis in 1535 had sent the Hafsid Sultan el Hasan to Spain for help. Charles V reinstated him – not that there was anything left of Tunis to reinstate him in – but a sultanate dependent on Christian Spanish protection could not fail to displease the

**Preceding pages**: Tourbet el Bey, mausoleum of the Husaynids, Tunis. **Left**, Door of Dar Othman Dey, Tunis. **Right**, the Barbarossa brothers.

Ottoman Turks, who were a little paranoid after their humilating defeat at the epic naval battle of Lepanto in 1571. The destruction of the Turkish fleet in the Mediterranean (Cervantes of *Don Quixote* fame was a participant) was an upheaval on a par in the context of Tunisian history with the Greek victory over the Persian navy at Salamis in 475 BC. Tunisia has forever been at the receiving end of other people's problems.

Spain was only a part of the victorious side at Lepanto, but it attracted the full force of the Turkish appetite for revenge. The Turks decided that honour could best be satisfied by frustrating Spanish designs on Tunisia. A new fleet was cobbled together in record

tracting loyalties to family, friends or tribe.

The administration was manned by mamelukes, the civilian equivalent of janissaries. They, too, were kidnapped as children and brought up in the sultan's household as a pool of future talent. Many were Greeks or anyway of Balkan birth, and there are touching description of new batches being delivered still with gaps in their baby teeth. The bright ones did well and many went on to marry royal playmates.

The authority invested in the pasha appointed by Istanbul devolved to beys, who were in charge of civil matters and finance, and deys, senior army officers. The Ottoman troops were a self-perpetuating caste replen-

time and in March 1574 they set off to settle a painful score. By late August, Tunisia belonged to them.

**Beys and deys:** The Ottomans managed to rule Tunisia efficiently and remarkably economically. There were probably never more than 8,000 Turks resident in Tunisia, and half of these were Janissaries, troops of mixed nationality rather like the later French Foreign Legion. The critical difference is that janissaries were reared from childhood, having been removed from their parents in unsavoury circumstances while they were still babies, with the express purpose of forming an elite fighting force with no dis-

ished by mercenaries from Christian as well as Muslim countries, although the former were expected to "take the turban" by converting to Islam, including an uncomfortable adult circumcision. The beys, on the other hand, made sure there would always be jobs for themselves and their descendants by moulding a dynasty. The Muradists were named after their first candidate, a Corsican who had gone to Tunis as a boy and done well in the army, especially in the way he put down restless tribes.

**Above**, the bagnio still stands in La Goulette. **Right**, Khayr el Din.

# PIRATES OF THE BARBARY COAST

The corsairs of the Barbary Coast were , in plain language, pirates, but any connection between them and the chortling, rum-swilling character with a peg-leg and a parrot stops there.

The Mediterranean had always been plagued by piracy, and from the beginning of Western civilisation economic activity on Greek islands consisted of almost nothing else. Nor did it cease until France took over control of North Africa in the 19th century. In between – and especially from 1529 when Barbarossa took over Algiers as a personal fiefdom – the corsairs were capable of taking on and defeating the fleets of Europe.

Commerce in the Mediterranean became a competition to seize and hold hostages for ransom, and the exchange of 30,000 hostages in the course of a single year was by no means unusual. (In Tunis, the hostages were held in the bagnio at La Goulette, which still stands and is open to visitors.)

European history tends to portray this period as a contest between high-minded Christians, personified by the dashing Knights of St John of Malta, and odious, throat-slitting Muslims. The facts are rather different, although there was at source a religious conflict which was stirred by the zealotry of the Crusades and exacerbated by the expulsion of the Moors from Spain.

The Muslims who invaded Spain were, to begin with and in substantial numbers thereafter, not Arabs at all but Tunisian Berbers. On being expelled after centuries of occupation, they returned to the land of their ancestors and to grim economic prospects. The ports of Tunisia and the rest of the Barbary Coast were clogged by idle men with sea-faring skills running deep in their veins. The beys who reigned over these ports represented an Ottoman Empire which was effectively, if not technically, always at war with one or other of the components of still fragmented European states, many of whom, like Venice, were trying to carve out commercial empires of their own – invariably at the expense of the Ottomans. In the circumstances, nothing would have seemed more natural to the displaced Andalusians than to volunteer for pirate service.

The profits to be derived from piracy were so large that the beys, who took a percentage of the booty for the use of their ports, were happy to accommodate any pirate who looked as if he knew what he was about. This became especially relevant with the suppression of pirates who had previously made a good living off Spanish ships returning with New World gold. The hard men of the Atlantic, with more formidable ships than were generally seen in the Mediterranean, sailed through the Straits of Gibraltar in search of new opportunities. The beys took them on eagerly although for decorum's sake they insisted on the newcomers "taking the turban", i.e. declaring themselves Muslim. The first part of their initiation rites seems not to have bothered the largely Dutch, French and English recruits. They were driven around Tunis in a cart with a portrait of Christ held upside down. The second, though, involved circumcision and could come as a shock. So keen was the Bey of Tunis to secure the services of the English baronet Sir Henry Mainwaring (B.A. Oxon), who was perhaps the most accomplished pirate of his time (he had his own fleet), that the Bey offered to waive the circumcision clause. Sir Henry nevertheless declined the offer.

The courtly Sir Henry was an exception. The more typical Captain Ward was described as about 55, nearly bald, and with a fringe of white hair around a swarthy face: "Speaks little, always swearing. Drunk from morn till night. Most prodigal and plucky. Sleeps a great deal. A fool and an idiot out of his trade."

The ordinary men were even worse. "They carry their swords at their sides," a disapproving Frenchman noted. "They run drunk through the town; they sleep with the wives of Moor; in brief every kind of debauchery and unchecked licence is permitted to them." Even he, though, conceded that their services were prized. "The great profit that the English bring to the country, their profuse liberality and the excessive debauches in which they spend their money before leaving the town and returning to war (thus they call their brigandage at sea) has made them cherished by the janissaries above all other nations."

As time went by, the position of the beys with regard to Istanbul was not unlike the relationship between some of the Arab dynasties and the caliph: they paid lip service to the higher authority but were left alone to run the country as they saw fit.

The Muradist line expired at the beginning of the 18th century through assassination and war with Algeria. It was replaced by the Husaynids, a dynasty which was to last until 1957. The economy prospered, not only through vibrant trade in agricultural products, over which the beys exercised a monopoly, but also through piracy.

**Eyed by Europe:** Tunisia's prosperity put ideas into the heads of 19th-century Euro-

pean empire-builders. The continuing level of piracy after the Napoleonic wars prompted united and determined European action. A Franco-British squadron arrived in Tunis in 1819 with a document requiring the Bey's signature: he would never again arm a corsair ship. Another chip came off his autonomy with an agreement which empowered European consuls to act as judges in cases involving European nationals, a concession which resulted in endless disputes because of the ability and willingness of certain consuls to extend European nationality to individuals in extremely dubious circumstances, not least government ministers suspected of having absconded with large chunks of the national treasury.

Ahmed Bey, whose mother was a Christian-born slave – one of 150 young girls captured in a corsair raid on a small island off Sardinia in 1798 – made desperate and sometimes pathetic attempts to raise the Regency to European "standards", believing that admission to the higher ranks of diplomacy might afford protection against French (or Italian, or British) high-handedness.

Paintings of Napoleon, his hero and model, hung everywhere, and nothing was spared to expand the military from a class-ridden sinecure to a substantial army along contemporary European lines. Conscription extended to nomad "recruits" who did not have to think twice about how to fight in deserts and mountains but were mystified by the black art of parade drilling. The switch to European uniforms, particularly trousers, did not help either. Troops would roll up the trousers over their knees when off duty, claiming they could not walk properly otherwise. Worst of all, though, was the mixed bag of obsolescent weapons. An official French report declared that no more than one-tenth of the guns could be fired "without danger to the man pulling the trigger and to those close by."

In the circumstances, the prospects of the Tunisian contingent sent as a gesture of solidarity with the Ottoman Turks in the Crimean War cannot have been too good. There isn't much reliable information about the performance of the 6,600 men, 722 horses and 12 cannon that went to the Crimea. Ahmed saw them off with a stirring message, including the exhortation "For God's sake, keep your honour spotless."

An American consul wrote long afterwards, and without quoting his source, that Tunisian troops defending the redoubts at Balaklava fled before the Russian attack without firing a shot. Other reports refer cryptically to the Tunisians acquitting themselves well. A French historian said 4,000 perished "in Turkey" without having seen combat. The Tunisian Expeditionary Force undoubtedly suffered frightful losses, dying "without glory, of sickness and misery in the Black Sea camps". It must have been awful for men not yet comfortable in trousers.

**Left**, Ahmed Bey. **Right**, ceiling of the Bardo.

Ahmed Bey, by all accounts an intelligent and well-meaning ruler, was not alive to see the survivors return from the Crimean War. The dynasty limped along for almost a century after his death. Chaotic finances brought about the downfall of his successor, Mohammed Bey. About 30,000 Frenchmen were left holding worthless Tunisian government bonds and they put pressure on the French government to intervene.

The Congress of Berlin in 1878, confronted with the infamous "Sick Man of Europe", cheerfully set about carving up the Ottoman Empire. Britain agreed to let France have Tunisia in exchange for keeping quiet about British ambitions in Cyprus. Bismarck agreed too, hoping that Tunisia would take French minds off their recent loss of Alsace-Lorraine. Italy was fobbed off with Tripolitania, the future Libya.

France presented the Bey with a draft agreement providing for a French protectorate over Tunisia and occupation of strategic points. He declined to sign it, so France looked around for a pretext. It presented itself in the form of a rather meaningless raid by a Tunisian tribe into Algeria, already a French *département*. The Bey offered compensation and to deal with the tribesmen himself, but that was not good enough. A French cavalry detachment crossed into Tunisia from its base in Algeria and headed not for the culprits but for the capital. A few days later a sea-borne French force occupied Bizerte. Other French forces were soon in Tunis without opposition, and on 12 May 1881 Mohammed el Sadiq Bey signed a treaty which recognised that he was still head of state. The concession could hardly disguise that he was left with little else.

Herbert Vivian visited Tunis a few years later to see how the Bey was getting along. Vivian was the sort of Englishman who was still cross about Napoleon. The administration of Tunisia in 1899, he concluded, "is as rotten as that of the French Republic". But what of the Bey? "A visit to His Highness

**Preceding pages**: early tourists in Nefta. **Left**, Avenue Jules Ferry in 1905. **Right**, Cardinal Lavigerie, Christian empire-builder.

Ali, Bey of Tunis, is like a visit to an extinct volcano," he wrote. "You may spend weeks in the Regency and remain unconvinced of his existence... Should you chance to be near the Italian railway station of Tunis on a Monday morning, you may witness the arrival of a portly old gentleman, who hurries into a ramshackle medieval carriage with a beflagged escutcheon on the door, and drives off to Dar el Bey as fast as his pair of white mules can carry him."

Other visitors, even English ones, were

more complimentary about what the French were achieving. "Thousands of miles of roads and railways, harbours, and manner of works of public utility have been constructed," wrote W. Basil Worsfold in one of a series of "Studies of Colonial Administration." He was generally optimistic about the future of French North Africa. "France... has made up her mind that if Africa Minor is to be won back to civilisation, it will be by the efforts of the European, not the native, population. And to the building up of this young neo-Latin nation she has lent, and given, of her best."

World War I saw 63,000 Tunisian troops

doing their bit for France. They cannot have adjusted to life in the trenches any more easily than their predecessors to conditions in the Crimea. More than 10,000 were killed or missing in action. The end of the war was all about President Woodrow Wilson and the doctrine of self-determination, and that found a ready audience in Tunisia, particularly among the elite group calling themselves the Young Tunisians, in imitation of the Young Turks.

**Nationalism stirs:** The aspirations of the Young Tunisians at first disturbed the conservatism of the religious leadership more than the complacency of the French. The tactics of the party that evolved from the

suited his political purposes to lament a poor and deprived childhood, his family were reasonably well-off and able to send the Bourguiba brothers to the esteemed Sadiki College in Tunis.

Habib later went to the Lycée Carnot, which was a grade above a college serving the Muslim elite in that the majority of pupils were French. He read law in Paris and returned to Tunis in 1927 thoroughly Frenchified and with a French wife. Not completely acceptable either to the traditional Muslim elite or to the French colonials, he did what people in that dilemma were doing in colonies, protectorates, etc all over the world, not just French

group, the Destour Party, founded in 1920, reflected its elitist origins. Rather than working for mass support, it sponsored a couple of professors at the Paris Faculty of Law to produce a Cartesian argument which attempted to deduce from impeccable hypotheses that a new constitution would not be incompatible with the definition of a protectorate, the official term for French rule.

The man-in-the-Kasbah (and there were a great many as a result of the post-war urban drift) was not going to get his teeth into that kind of thing, which no one understood better than young Habib Bourguiba. He was born in Monastir in 1903. Although it later

ones. They gave up whatever they were doing to become full-time political activists determined to change the status quo.

Bourguiba skilfully manipulated popular indignation about the submersion of Tunisian culture. In an article published in 1929, he defended the veiling of women as a form of cultural identity – not that the first Mrs Bourguiba ever wore a veil (he might have argued that she was French) – yet he was soon to pick up where Ahmed Bey left off, pushing Tunisia towards Europe and the United States and away from the Islamic tendencies which, towards the end of his long career, posed the greatest threat to it.

Religion was nevertheless Bourguiba's springboard. He saw incongruity in the holding of the (Roman Catholic) Eucharistic Congress in Carthage in 1930 and also wondered whether Tunisia really needed a statue of Cardinal Lavigerie, zealous 19th-century Christian empire-builder, peering into the Tunis medina. The Destour Party split on burial practices: specifically, whether Tunisian Muslims who had taken French citizenship belonged in a Muslim cemetery. Had they not ceased to be under the jurisdiction of Islamic law and in so doing lapsed from the faith? A conciliatory Malikite jurist ventured that they might decorously squeeze in if they repented on their death beds.

next clash with the authorities was sparked by the sacking of an Algerian workman in Bizerte (112 dead, 62 wounded) and resulted in imprisonment in France in 1938, which was where he was in 1939 when the war broke out.

**War games:** World War II had peculiar repercussions in Tunisia. In the period leading up to it, Mussolini's Fascist agents had been very active in Tunisia. The bald dictator could happily envisage Tunisia as part of a resurgent Roman Empire under himself. Tunisian nationalists could not escape the security blanket the French used to stifle such activities, but the fall of France in June 1940 soon threw the whole apparatus of

The Destour Party was in the thick of the controversy and deeply divided. The executive committee censured Bourguiba for supporting a demonstration in Monastir against the burial of a naturalised Franco-Tunisian child in a Muslim cemetery. He resigned to form the Neo-Destour party.

The party was banned six months after its foundation and remained illegal for 20 years. Bourguiba first went to prison, for two years, because of a brawl between Destour and Neo-Destour supporters in the Sahara. His

**Left**, demonstration of the Neo-Destourians in 1954. **Above**, Europeans in the Porte de France.

government in Tunisia into grave doubt.

Moncef, latest of a line of almost forgotten beys, edged into the political arena as the surprise champion of Tunisian nationalism. He no longer required his hand to be kissed, he entertained Destour and Neo-Destour politicians alike, he went on what were later to be known as walkabouts and started sending demands to the Pétain government for constitutional changes. German troops who happened to occupy the country from November 1942 would have been fascinated if they had understood what was going on. Moncef Bey, sometimes accused of pro-Nazi sympathies (a charge that was also

# A DESERT WAR

Half a century after the event, memories of the Desert War tend to be of tanks storming through sand, thunderous artillery barrages, the escapades of special units like the Desert Rats, Montgomery and Rommel, and, in Alexandria, ice cold beer and small boys selling dirty postcards. Tunisia may not have the same evocative impact – for those who were not there – as places like Benghazi, El Alamein and Tobruk, but it is nonetheless where Germany entered the North African campaign in earnest, where American land forces were blooded, and where American and Allied forces first linked up for the big push whose momentum carried across the Mediterranean and began the bitter battle for Europe.

Tunisia's technical status was a bit of a conundrum at the outbreak of war and particularly after the collapse of France. Although the country was a French protectorate, the nominal ruler was still the Bey, a distant Ottoman, and he was not averse to Fascists who, by removing France from contention, put a silver lining on the otherwise poor prospects for his geriatric dynasty. The local French administration was torn between support for Vichy, which would have entailed cooperation with Germany, and the Free French then rallying under General de

Gaulle. When both Germany and Britain moved to secure a foothold in Tunisia, the French sank ships at the entrances to Bizerte and Tunis, thereby denying access to both and postponing the need to declare which side they were on.

As things turned out, the Germans entered Tunisia through Bizerte, Tunis, Sousse and Sfax. In so doing, they coincidentally answered a difficult question for Roosevelt's military planners who, in August 1941, were given one week by the president to specify where American troops could most usefully go into action against Germans. Tunisia looked ideal, and Churchill was enthusiastic. Anxious to accelerate direct American involvement, he offered to put British troops into American uniforms if that would help.

When Germany won the Race for Tunis, the Allies were forced to think again. Under the codenames "Gymnast", "Super Gymnast" and ultimately "Torch", the Allies planned to move in force from Algeria. If the British Army could then push forward from the east, the Germans would be cornered in Tunisia and could be finished off.

That is what happened in the end, but not without desperate fighting. Among numerous difficulties was the nature of the terrain, the perils of which had been hard lessons for the Romans and dozens of subsequent armies. Tunisian mountain ranges are not the Himalayas, but they are laid out in parallel rows which, for modern military purposes as for the ancient trade caravaneers, put the utmost value on the defensible passes running east-west between them. The Americans had their first bloody taste of German panzer capability as they fought for the pass at Kasserine in central Tunisia. The Tunisian campaign was really a matter of infantry forever battling for the high ground, capturing one "djebel" and then, without respite, trudging onwards to tackle the next.

The classic example of history repeating itself was at the Gabes Gap, a narrow corridor with the Mediterranean on one side and, on the other, the Chott el Djerid salt flats and the Matmata Mountains. For invaders from Egypt and Libya, as the British Army now found itself to be, the Gabes Gap was the only way through to Tunisia's vital ports. An Egyptian army once tried to skirt around the gap and was lost (at the wrong time of year) in the treacherous chott. The British Army arrived at the wrong time of year, too, the winter of 1942–43, and was forced to sit out the winter months.

On 8 April 1943, British units which had at last forced their way through the gap had their historic meeting near Gabes with American troops who had been working steadily eastwards since their grim initiation at Kasserine. Within a month, the combined Allied forces had taken Tunis and Bizerte, which left pockets of German resistance only at Zaghouan and Cap Bon. The former fell on 11 May, and the following day Indian troops captured General Jurgen von Arnim, his well-laid plans for the protracted defence of Cap Bon failing to materialise. The Axis surrendered the very next day, on 13 May.

levelled at the Neo-Destour party), was a re-vivified volcano, his national standing out-shadowing that of any other political leader.

The Allies entered Tunis in May 1943 at the end of the epic battle with Rommel in the desert. A week later Moncef was deposed by the Free French.

Bourguiba, occupying a prison cell in Marseilles, never wavered in his opposition to collaboration with the Axis. He smuggled out a message urging his party colleagues to put political differences on ice for the duration of the war and assist the Free French. The Germans transferred him to a prison in Rome, and there the Italians tried in vain to coerce him into saying he supported the

Bourguiba went off on secret missions to Egypt, where the Arab League was being formed, and to any part of the globe where he thought he could usefully drum up support for the Tunisian cause.

**French response:** France dabbled with various schemes which would have given Tunisians a certain amount of representation in government but, as England discovered with its troublesome American colonies in the 18th century, co-operation in such schemes by ambitious nationalists could too easily be misconstrued as acceptance of, or at least acquiescence in, an overall scheme of things which was fundamentally repugnant. The Tunisian position was further complicated

Axis. Eventually the Italians gambled on his presence in Tunisia being detrimental to France and the Allies and let him go. They were wrong: on his return he issued a proc-lamation denouncing his recent captors and calling on Tunisians to support the war against them.

The French were in no mood at the end of the war to rush headlong into change in Tunisia. Moreover, their hands were full in Algeria. Probably a little disillusioned,

**Left, Allied marines examine evidence of the hasty German retreat. Above, Bizerte, prized French naval base.**

by the fact that authority rested nominally not in Paris but in a bey.

Despairing of a political solution, Tunisian nationalists had an example to follow in neighbouring Algeria. From 1952, they took to the mountains and commenced guerrilla operations against French settlers. The settlers responded with the Red Hand, which hunted nationalists who were not in prison and assassinated them. Tunisians to suffer at their hands included an activist named Farhat Hached, a famous trade unionist. The violence and killing were not remotely on the scale of Algeria – the strength of the *fellagha* guerrillas never exceeded 3,000 – but it was enough to persuade the Mendès-France government in 1954 to ask the Bey (not the Neo-Destour party) to choose a new government to negotiate independence. The appointed negotiators turned out to be Old-Destourians.

The rules were changed with the fall of the Mendès-France government and, next time round, Bourguiba was allowed to take part. Bourguiba agreed that France should retain control of foreign affairs, the army, the police and the economy, and these concessions were the genesis of a long-running feud between him and Ahmed ben Salah and Salah ben Youssef. This rift, in the years after independence when the rhetoric of the

murdered in Frankfurt in August 1961.

**Independence at last:** Tunisia won its independence on 20 March 1956. El Amin Bey, then 76, had to wait more than a year to learn what would finally happen to a line of beys which went back 240 years and which a bad-tempered English visitor had pronounced extinct 60 years previously. A constituent assembly dominated by Neo-Destour members voted unanimously to abolish the monarchy, declared a republic, and invested Bourguiba as head of state. His leadership was soon tested. In the Bizerte crisis of 1961 (over French reluctance to evacuate the naval base of Bizerte), deliberately precipitated by Bourguiba but which resulted in 1,365

struggle was quite redundant, revealed Bourguiba's natural habitat to be among a new aristocracy of power-brokers (whispers of the "Monastir Mafia"), whereas the other two relied on the quasi-socialist trade union movement and idealistic notions of pan-Arab unity.

Salah was in and out of government and eventually charged with high treason in 1970. He was sentenced to 10 years' imprisonment but managed to escape after three. Youssef formed a guerrilla army in southern Tunisia and resorted to terrorism. His military days lasted until 1956, after which he sniped at President Bourguiba from exile. He was

Tunisians being killed, he managed to ride severe public criticism and unite his party into the bargain (*see page 174*).

History will need a breathing space before final judgement is passed on Bourguiba personally and his direction of independent Tunisia. Westerners wise in the ways of Third World despots could not help recoiling at a personality cult in full cry: the main street in every city, town and village named after him, statues and portraits everywhere, interminable homilies to El Mujahid el Akbar (The Supreme Combatant), the modest title he chose for himself, even re-runs on television of his favourite speeches when he went a day or two without making a new one.

The colossal, gilded mausoleum in Monastir could never be officially completed in his life-time; to have done so would have been tantamount to expediting the sad event. Towards the end of his career, when the most natural question was to ask who would succeed him, it was political suicide to be mentioned as someone who might.

Bourguiba was sometimes within a hair's-breadth of qualifying as a despot, in that he was in a position to indulge every whim had he chosen to do so. In the event, he exercised commendable restraint, and many, perhaps even most, of his achievements were real. He believed there was a huge job ahead – nothing

education produced a younger population with rising expectations – rising faster and farther than could be met by an economy without a windfall of oil.

"The octogenarian Bourguiba still has enough prestige to prevent the system he has built from completely disintegrating," Abun Nasr wrote, "but he has lived long to see its decline which his successors are not likely to be able to arrest." Before the print was dry, it was announced that Bourguiba, who had hardly been seen in public for months, had quietly consented to step down. In fact, in a bloodless coup, on the night of 6 November 1988, Bourguiba's prime minister, Zine el Abdine Ben Ali, assembled seven doctors

less than a social and economic revolution – and probably believed he was the only person who could properly get it done.

He was in some ways the victim of his own success. By demoting the role of Islamic law so that all Tunisians, regardless of religion, could look forward to equality under a unified legal code, he gave hard-line Muslims a grievance to fester over. The same quarters would have found fault in abolishing polygamy and granting the sexes equal rights when it came to divorce. Health services and

**Left, Bourguiba and his second wife Wasila. Above, the Bizerte crisis, in which 1,365 died.**

who certified Bourguiba as senile. Ben Ali assumed power the following day.

The Roman poet Virgil might have found a postscript to Dido and Aeneas in one of the twists to Bourguiba's consistent, pro-Western stance in international affairs. When Yasser Arafat's PLO fighters were expelled from their bases in Lebanon in 1982, none of the hard-line Arab states would consider for a minute giving them a refuge.

After a voyage from old Phoenicia, Arafat and his band landed at a spot within catapult range of an old Carthaginian settlement. Waiting to give him a friendly reception was the second Mrs Bourguiba.

When Zine El Abidine Ben Ali was sworn in as president on 8 November 1987, the day after Habib Bourguiba's unceremonious demise, he promised a new age of greater democracy. It was the usual boast of new presidents the world over, but in Tunisia's case it couldn't be treated as mere rhetoric to be consigned to a corner and quietly forgotten until the next president needed something to pack his credentials in. Tunisia was ready for democracy. It had had a dictatorship for 30 years.

Change was long overdue, as a brewing sense of unrest in the country warned; but it had to be implemented carefully. Waiting to step in at any sign of going too far were the army and the police force, and poised to turn an inch into the proverbial yard were the fundamentalists.

By the end of that November Ben Ali's government had already passed laws suggesting he meant what he'd said. Newspapers critical of the state were permitted to publish, the length someone could be held on remand was limited to six months and detention without the authority of the public prosecutor was limited to four days. By the following March over 5,000 political prisoners had been released.

Soon afterwards, the post of President-for-life, an invention of Bourguiba when he felt his presidential grip slipping, was abolished and replaced by multi-party free elections by universal suffrage every five years and a maximum of two consecutive terms of office for any president. To quash any chance of another bath-chair president, the age of presidential candidates was limited to 70 (Bourguiba having been 84 when he was forcibly retired).

In reality, the impact of such reforms is modified by numerous safeguards. No changes have been made to the electoral system – under which all seats in each multi-member constituency goes to the party that gets the most votes, unfailingly the ruling Rasemblement Constitutionel Democra-

tique (RCD) party – and political parties which pursue "purely religious, regional or racial objectives" are not officially recognised and therefore unable to stand as a party in an election, a clear attempt to cull the activities of the Islamic fundamentalist movement En Nadha (the renaissance). In an attempt to lessen ill-feeling over this last point, Ben Ali has conceded various trifling demands: prayers are once again broadcast on television, the Zitouna University was established as a tribute to the university

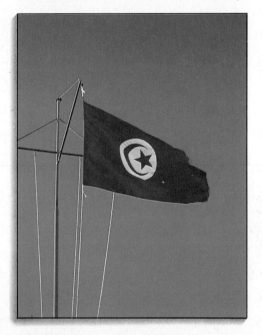

status of the Zitouna Mosque, and Hegira dates now head offical documents.

But the fundamentalists cannot be so easily silenced, mainly because their strength is drawn from the country's mosques, which – as all visitors soon notice – are the visible and audible mainstays of every town and village. The imams are in direct contact with the people, especially the discontented poor to whom secular life offers little hope of improvement. Bourguiba was always replacing one imam or another, and Ben Ali's regime, too, is keeping a sharp ear on the *fatwahs*. According to En Nahda, over 70 imams have been removed by the new government,

**Preceding pages: puppets; jasmine seller. Left, the under-20s account for 60 percent of the population. Right, flag waving, a national sport.**

either because they are politically active or because they associate with someone who is. As Ben Ali's difficulties have grown, so have the number of presidential portraits in public places.

**Fools rush in:** The president's reaction to the 1991 Gulf War exposed the government's delicate position. Even before war broke out, Ben Ali refused to associate himself with the Allied build-up in Saudi Arabia, in spite of the facts that the Gulf States (meaning Saudi Arabia and Kuwait), France and the US are the biggest donors of financial aid to Tunisia, and his nextdoor-but-one Maghrebi neighbour King Hassan of Morocco quickly dispatched 1,700 troops to the

the American bombing of Libya in 1986 (for reasons outlined below). He also spotted the inconsistency of suddenly condemning Saddam Hussein as a malevolent dictator when for years Arabs everywhere, not least in Tunisia, then led by an Iran-phobic Bourguiba, had been subjected to Pro-Saddam/Iraq propaganda in order to sustain support for the Iran-Iraq war. Ben Ali sat tight, banned French TV coverage of the war, expressed sympathy for Iraqis, and went only so far as closing schools and universities to curb civil unrest.

He didn't have much to be happy about, however. Even without unsettling influences at home, the repercussions of the war

frontline. Ben Ali was a wise man to do nothing. When Desert Shield turned into Desert Storm and the Allies started their relentless bombing of Baghdad, pro-Iraqi demonstrations resounding to slogans such as *"Mitterrand assassin"* (Tunisian anger fixing on the role of the French as usual) and "Saddam, we will sacrifice ourselves for you!" marched through Tunis without any restraint from government forces.

Ben Ali shrewdly realised that, should he be seen to side with Western infidels, the fundamentalists could gain not just inches or yards out of the crisis, but mileage, as they had done when Bourguiba failed to condemn

were bad enough for Tunisia. Tourism, accounting for one-fifth of foreign earnings and employing 800,000 people, collapsed and exports to Iraq – worth $100 million – were indefinitely suspended. The danger was that hardship would push more people into the arms of the militant mullahs.

Ben Ali's stance was a surprise to Western diplomats, as, like Bourguiba, he has generally pursued a moderate pro-Western foreign policy. But, from the start, Ben Ali was also keen to strengthen his Arab ties, particularly within the Maghreb, which save for the period when most of it was French had been plagued by territorial disputes. In 1987 full relations were restored with Libya, with whom the Tunisians had been on shaky terms since 1985 when Gadaffi, accused of attempting to undermine Bourguiba's regime, expelled 30,000 Tunisian workers and dealt a blow to Tunisia's economy.

As a gesture of their renewed friendship both countries agreed to let the International Court of Justice determine borders in the oil-rich Gulf of Gabes, and embarked on a joint exploitation of the 7 Novembre oilfield. Amicable relations proceeded, with agreements to allow Tunisians and Libyans to work or live in either country. In no time at all, Libyans were pouring into Tunisia for their holidays (a new motorway to Sfax was

proved. One obvious obstacle is the fact that the states still don't officially recognise one another's currencies. Any Maghrebi travelling between the countries must have hard currency, preferably dollars or francs.

Restoring relations with Libya helped offset the shrinking of Tunisia's traditional markets for emigrant labour, France and Italy. France, which now has approximately 3 million Maghrebi immigrants, has been closing its gates for some years, and in 1989–90 Italy, after granting an amnesty in the form of a *permesso di soggiorno* (work permit) to any illegal immigrant already living there, introduced quotas for non-EEC guest workers and required visas from all

purpose-built) and 30,000 Tunisians were toiling in Libya's service industries.

Having resolved its differences with Libya, Ben Ali was instrumental in reconciling Morocco and Algeria, who had been at odds over the Western Sahara. In 1988 the latest version of L'Union du Grand Maghreb, an attempt at a North African common market composed of Mauritania, Morocco, Algeria, Tunisia and Libya, was ratified in Algiers. How successful this is in actually achieving anything has yet to be

**Left**, exhibition marking L'Union du Grand Maghreb. **Above**, the much-pictured Ben Ali.

North African visitors. One of the EEC's biggest headaches is what might happen when its internal borders are abolished if one country cannot control immigration.

**Power of patronage:** With more and more young Tunisians unable to seek their fortunes abroad, employment opportunities at home become crucial. Apart from being dependent on a fragile economic development – thrown by the vagaries of tourism and the price of oil, the victim of droughts and even locusts – when one year seems so promising and the next on the verge of ruin, recruitment is corrupted by patronage. Bourguiba was the supreme weaver of the mesh of ties based on kith and kin which incarcerates industry.

Before independence, egalitarian ideals were spurred by the common aim of ejecting the foreign power; once this had been achieved people turned to the customs of the past, to absolute rule by one man. The president played much the same role as a sultan. Nearly all Bourguiba's closest advisors were from the same area of the Sahel and many belonged to his own family. Ben Ali has made some attempts to change matters, though he has been hampered by old Party members, who suspect they may lose their privileges; his new government after the 1989 election was drawn from the whole country (a third from the deprived south) and

West) deprived of the fruits of their scholarship – a job – can be a danger rather than an asset, and possibly easy prey for the dreaded fundamentalists.

The government is therefore fearful of the influence of fundamentalism in universities and schools, particularly as the student union, L'Union Générale des Etudiants de Tunisie, is fundamentalist-dominated. It believes that the union deliberately exaggerates complaints about facilities, lodgings and transport in order to whip up support for wider aims. Within three years of rehabilitating the Zitouna University, Ben Ali was forced to split it into three faculties to avoid repeated student clashes. The Sharia faculty

for once included real technical experts.

But patronage has a long tradition in the Arab world and cannot be easily dissolved. Therefore education, in theory the key to the success of a country emerging from colonialism, does not necessarily lead to "executive posts necessary to economic and social development," as the Ministry of Information would have it. Secondary schools have multiplied 13 times since independence, their teachers have increased 18-fold, there are now six universities attended by a total of 44,000 students and a further 12,000 students based abroad. A large educated population (some of whom have studied in the

(teaching Islamic law) was moved to different buildings and isolated.

Fundamentalism in Tunisia shouldn't, however, be overestimated or confused with ordinary expressions of Islam – which, according to En Nadha, is precisely what the government does when public employees caught praying at work are earmarked as religious zealots. Even in the absence of politicising fundamentalists, Islam plays an important role in most Tunisian lives right from birth. Koranic school, a kind of religious kindergarten, where children from the age of four are taught to recite the Koran, is still popular among parents – if not their offspring – who see a solid grounding in the Koran as the best guide to life there is.

Non-practising Muslims never forget their religion, posssibly because, like Catholicism, it has such terrifying visions of hell, and they usually return to it at a later age. The speech of even the most ardent sinner is liberally sprinkled with supplications: *Bismillah* (in the name of God) is said before consuming food or drink, *Insh'Allah* (God willing) is always contained in any statement of intent and *Hamdullah* (thank God) can occur almost anytime.

Religion goes hand in glove with the traditional way of life. The most important annual festivals, such as Aid es Seghir (the end of

by a small proportion of Western-influenced youth, though the ageing Bourguiba did make his birthday an annual holiday, a piece of Bourguiba vanity which was soon abolished by Ben Ali.

Independence spawned various festivals based on nationalism. The great day itself, 20 March 1956, is marked by a national holiday, now coupled with National Youth Day to symbolise Ben Ali's dynamic new era.

Tunisia isn't, perhaps, as famed for its cultural heritage as Arab countries such as Egypt or Syria, but it scores high for being the birthplace of Ibn Khaldoun (1332–1406), considered to be the greatest Arab historian, the home of *mahlouf* music (*see*

Ramadan), Aid el Kebir (in commemoration of Abraham's sacrifice of a lamb instead of his son), Mouloud (the Prophet's birthday) and Ashoura (celebrated 10 days after the beginning of the Muslim New Year), are all religious events. Family celebrations, with the exception of marriage, are similarly grounded in religion – for example, the circumcision of boys at the age of two or three and the return of a family member from the *hadj*. Personal birthdays are celebrated only

**Left**, Western-influenced wedding in Hotel Majestic, Tunis. **Above**, Koranic school, a type of religious kindergarten.

*page 88*) and for producing the writer Aboulkassem Chabbi (1909–34), a towering name in Arab literature. These days, however, vigorous local arts and cultural festivals notwithstanding, the most enthusiastic expressions of national pride are reserved for sport, particularly volleyball, football and track and field events.

In 1978 Tunisia qualified for the World Cup, no mean feat when only two African teams are allowed to qualify, and performed creditably. But a decade earlier Tunisian pride reached its zenith at the 1968 Olympic Games in Mexico. Mohammed Gamoudi won the gold medal for the 5,000 metres.

Until 1957 Tunisian laws relating to the status of women were firmly based on the Sharia, the code of Islamic laws drawn from the Koran and the Hadith (the sayings of the Prophet), which evolved within 100 years of the Prophet's death. In view of the time and place, 7th-century Arabia, and what was on offer in the way of women's rights in the rest of the world, much of the Holy Law was enlightened. It laid down certain rights for women, including rights of inheritance and rights to maintenance.

But as time passed, so different, selective interpretations of the Koran evolved and theologians responsible for defining the law extrapolated only what suited their purposes, which in the case of women was to restrict their freedoms as much as possible. And there was much in the Koran and Hadith to aid them (and modern-day feminist detractors of Islam), especially in what Mohammed had to say on the subject of women. "Those who entrust their affairs to a woman will never know prosperity," he warned. His advice to husbands was: "Ask your wife's opinion, but do the opposite." In a court of law a female witness was considered inferior to a male one. What's more, and Mohammed's own catalogue of wives far exceeded what was tentatively suggested as a reasonable quota in the Koran: "Marry of the women who seem good to you, two, three, or four, and if ye fear that ye cannot do justice, then one," it said. The Prophet had 14 wives in all, and during the last years of his life 10 at the same time, many in marriages motivated by sexual attraction. His comment on his own grandson, Hassan Ibn Ali, who married a total of 200 wives, was: "You resemble me physically and morally."

In view of such contradictions, it is all the more amazing that the Sharia's guidelines on female status should survive intact for 1,300 years in every Arab and Islamic country, especially when its laws relating to other spheres of life – for example, usury (un-

Islamic, according to the Sharia) – were adapted to meet modern needs. The reason, the feminists would argue, is that the Sharia's stance on women is in the interests of men; they are hardly likely to change it.

But in the case of Tunisia it was a man who did just that. Ex-president Habib Bourguiba introduced his Code of Personal Status for women in August 1956, just five months after independence. It was not just daring, it was revolutionary. At a stroke, it abolished polygamy in Tunisia and introduced a for-

mal court procedure for divorce, which for the first time could be initiated by a wife as well as a husband, and it set a minimum age for marriage, which from then on demanded the bride's consent, previously considered a mere technicality. No longer could men marry up to four wives, nor divorce by simple repudiation – a thrice-repeated statement along the lines of "I divorce thee" uttered in front of the *adil* (religious judge) – and no longer could fathers sell off young daughters to bring in a tidy income.

It was an attempt to accelerate modernisation at a rate not even talked about by the French, and the more extreme religious

**Preceding pages:** choosing clothes; Souk des Bijoutiers, Tunis; traditional wedding. **Left,** applying henna to a bride's hands. **Right**, bikini-clad girl, epitome of east coast youth.

sheiks were furious. But Bourguiba had anticipated that. He installed a moderate imam in the Zitouna University Mosque, appointed one of his relatives, Abdelaziz Djait, as Mufti of Tunisia (religious legal expert) and reshuffled the sheiks who sat on the Sharia courts. In so doing he managed to delay a confrontation with the religious establishment for several years, by which time it was up in arms about something else. Thus did Tunisia come to be the first Arab state to outlaw polygamy. To date, only Algeria has followed suit.

Other measures in favour of women followed Bourguiba's new law. He encouraged the formation of the Union Nationale des

got well under way during the colonial era. He used various methods, including referring to it as that "odious rag".

"It is unthinkable," said Bourguiba, not mincing his words, "that half the population be cut off from life and hidden away like a disgraceful thing."

Unveiled faces were given a shining example in the elegantly coiffured Wasila Bourguiba, the president's second wife whom he married in 1955 after his marriage to a French war widow ended in divorce. The second Mrs Bourguiba, considered to be the Arab media's answer to Jackie Kennedy, constantly made news throughout the Arab world. At home she was a feisty figure in the

Femmes de Tunisie (UNFT) to pursue female emancipation, and in 1957 women were given the vote. By 1960 the UNFT had 40,000 members. Its main achievements were to educate women in their new rights, set up kindergartens and promote female education and work opportunities. In addition, a continuing policy of birth control was introduced in 1961, and abortion was legalised in 1967 – not that it hadn't been common practice before, special potions and massage usually doing the trick.

**Veiled threats:** Throughout this time Bourguiba tried to dissuade women from wearing the veil, a derobing that had already

UNFT and believed to be an important influence on her husband (though in the end not even she was excluded from Bourguiba's vision of treachery at every turn, and shortly before his fall from power he rewarded her with a divorce).

Inevitably all this liberation took a lot longer to take effect than to implement, particularly among the lower, poorer classes. Such women didn't seize their new rights with any great fervour. A few years after women's suffrage, statistics showed that the number of women registering for elections had declined. For Berber women in particular, who have always shouldered a great deal of agricultural work (they are under those walking bundles of esparto grass that you see on the plains near Kasserine) greater work opportunities have little relevance. Nonetheless, the government claims that the number of women working in non-agricultural sectors has risen by over 800 percent since independence.

This means, of course, that Tunisian women are now working harder than ever. The types of jobs women tend to undertake are light factory work and carpet-weaving, the latter often done at home, and for the better educated, nursing, teaching or office work. With the exception of shopping, which men have traditionally done (origi-

household appliances are luxuries. Wives face the same kind of pressures that were borne by Western women in the 1960s.

**Living doll:** That said, married is what most girls want to be when they grow up. A traditional wedding celebration lasts up to 15 days and consists of a long prelude of sexually-segregated parties which culminate in a feast. The bride is literally the centrepiece, a painted, plucked (superfluous hair removed, please), puffed-up ornament who for the most part sits ensconced in a pack of ululating women. Her hands and feet are decorated with lace-like patterns of henna, painstakingly applied by a woman hired to enhance the beauty of the bride and instruct her in

nally so that women would not have to leave the home), domestic chores are almost without exception the responsibility of women, though it is common for better-off families to employ a maid (male or female) to help.

The daily grind is made worse by the obligatory long break for lunch, which still tends to be eaten at home. Invariably working women have to prepare a meal in advance, rush home to cook and serve it and get back to their job within two hours. Convenience food hardly exists in Tunisia and

**Left**, taking cover under wraps. **Above**, uncommonly bold.

conjugal duties for up to two months before the wedding; often she ends up looking like Coppélia, a walking, talking doll.

Weddings are huge celebrations in Tunisia, as they are in every Arab country, but they are not given a religious framework and the marriage ceremony itself is a simple civil procedure. Islam is quite matter-of-fact about marriage; above all it is a practical measure to provide a stable environment for children and guard against promiscuity, hence the practice of arranged marriages, still common in Tunisia but no longer the rule. Love of a spouse should never come before love of God.

# MUSIC TO TRANCE TO: THE MAHLOUF

*Mahlouf* means familiar or custom. In Tunisia, it is the name given to the musical tradition which was originally brought over by Andalusian refugees: Muslims and Jews fleeing the Christian reconquest of Spain from the 12th to the 15th centuries. The tradition can be traced back to the early 9th century when the outstanding musician Ziryab was ousted from the court of Baghdad by his jealous teacher and rival, Ishaq el Mawsili. Turning westward, Ziryab eventually found refuge in Cordoba where he sowed the seeds of a distinctive Andalusian school of Arab music, which blossomed in the rich artistic and intellectual environment of Moorish Spain.

Today, Andalusian music is represented in Morocco, Algeria, Tunisia and Libya by four distinct national traditions, each reflecting a different path of development in its country of adoption. In Tunisia, musicians tend to underplay the *mahlouf's* Andalusian origins, maintaining that it has since evolved into an authentic Tunisian tradition. During the struggle for independence it became a symbol of the national identity, and in publications by the Ministry of Cultural Affairs it is designated "the Tunisian musical heritage".

The *mahlouf* is essentially a vocal repertory with instrumental pieces serving as introductions and interludes. The song texts belong to the poetic forms of *muswashshah* and *zajal* and use both literary and Tunisian dialectical Arabic. Unlike the music, which until recently has survived solely in oral tradition, the poems were traditionally recorded in special collections called *safain*, literally meaning vessels. Their themes are mostly romantic descriptions of love and nature with frequent references to wine and its intoxicating effects.

In general, the music reflects the strophic rhyme scheme of the poetry: each line of verse is set to the same melody with a different though often related tune for the refrain. Like all Arab music, it is a highly developed melodic tradition based on a complex scale system which, in addition to the tone and semi-tone intervals of Western music, contains a variable neutral interval in between.

Most of the pieces of the *mahlouf* are divided into 13 repertory groups called *nubat*, each representing a particular melodic mode, or *maqam*.

Within each *nuba* all the pieces apart from the instrumental introduction are based on one of five characteristic rhythmic patterns, which are performed in a conventional sequence. With its repetitive melodies and rhythmic-metric patterns and its lack of tonal contrast, the *nuba* is static rather than dramatic, meditative rather than explorative, comparable in effect to the repetitive orna-

mental patterns of the Arab plastic arts.

A performance of a *nuba* normally includes only a selection of its total repertory, and lasts about half an hour at most.

Until Independence the *mahlouf* was concentrated in the towns of the northern and coastal regions. It was a genuinely popular tradition in the sense of belonging to the people as a whole rather than to any particular social group. Its chief patrons and practitioners were Sufi brotherhoods – classless, communal, religious organisations whose ceremonies included music and dance to induce heightened spiritual states culminating in trance. Some brotherhoods cultivated the *mahlouf* in addition to their religious repertoires, as a recreational activity, either interpreting the profane texts allegorically or substituting sacred ones. It was normally performed after the public Sufi ceremonies, in order to calm the participants; the atmosphere was informal and everyone present would clap and sing along.

Outside the lodges, professional musicians performed the *mahlouf* in coffee houses and in communal celebrations for religious and family festivals, especially weddings. The

kettle drums) or *tar* (tambourine), the exact format depending on the tradition of the lodge. Elsewhere, notably in more refined environments, the *mahlouf* was performed by small solo instrumental ensembles, traditionally comprising a rabab (two-stringed bowed fiddle), *oud* (Arab lute), *naqarat*, *tar* and solo vocalist. In the 20th century Middle Eastern instruments such as the *qanun* (trapezoid plucked zither) and the *nay* (bamboo flute) were sometimes added, as were European instruments of fixed pitch

musicians were invariably either Jews or members of the lower classes, since Islamic social taboos obliged all others to confine their musical activities to the lodges or to the privacy of their homes.

In the lodges, melody instruments were generally banned and only the songs were performed. The typical Sufi ensemble comprised a unison male chorus accompanied by hand-clapping and percussion instruments such as the *bendir* (frame drum) *darbuka* (vase-shaped drum), *naqarat* (pair of small

**Preceding pages: musicians near Nefta. Left,**
***Mezhet* player. Above, a Sufi entranced.**

such as the harmonium and the mandolin. Each soloist interpreted the melodies in an individual way, improvising embellishments.

Today, the *mahlouf* is more likely to be performed by a large instrumental and choral ensemble, typically comprising several violins, perhaps one or two cellos, a double bass, even an accordion, an arbitrary smattering of traditional Arab instruments and a mixed male and female chorus. The original model for this format was the Rashidiya ensemble (named after Mohammed el Rashid Bey) which was founded in Tunis in 1934, the same year as the Neo-Destour party. The new ensemble aimed to preserve and promote

Tunisian music – effectively the *mahlouf* – in the face of the increasing influence of Egyptian and other foreign trends popularised by visiting celebrities and the media.

Ironically, the Rashidiya ensemble was modelled both on the Western symphony orchestra and on contemporary Egyptian ensembles, with the reservation that instruments of fixed pitch, which could not produce the neutral interval of the Arab scale, were excluded: a condition not always respected by the ensemble's imitators. The *mahlouf* was transcribed into Western musical notation in order to standardise its interpretation, and improvisation was virtually abolished. Finally a conductor was introduced to co-ordinate the large numbers of players and singers. Subsidised by the government both before and after independence, the Rashidiya ensemble became the official bastion of the *mahlouf* and the training ground for Tunisia's leading musicians.

Following independence, the Sufi brotherhoods fell into official disfavour. Their activities were suppressed, and their role as patrons of the *mahlouf* was commandeered by the Ministry of Cultural Affairs. As the musicians abandoned their lodges, so the government established amateur *mahlouf* clubs throughout the country along the lines of the Rashidiya ensemble. Its notations were published and distributed to the new ensembles, effectively overriding regional interpretations. Now an annual cycle of residential courses, competitions and festivals culminates each summer in the International Festival of the Mahlouf in Testour, in which the best Tunisian groups perform alongside musicians from other countries of the Maghreb, the Middle East and Spain.

Despite the government's discouragement and neglect, the former types of *mahlouf* ensemble may still occasionally be heard, whether in traditional communal contexts such as weddings or, under the unlikely guise of tourist entertainment, in modern ones such as hotels. As the official attitude towards the Sufis has become more lenient, so certain brotherhoods have partially resumed their activities, even recruiting new members. And in Tunis, some of the best establishment musicians continue to perform the *mahlouf* at home, among their family and friends, in small solo ensembles, improvising their personal embellishments.

Everyone has surely seen, although they may not know it, Tunisia's earliest kind of dwelling, the cave. At the very beginning of the film *Star Wars* Luke Skywalker returns to the farm where he grew up to find it burnt by the Empire. The farm is, in reality, a pit dwelling in Matmata, a troglodyte village in the hills bordering the desert in the south of Tunisia. It is one of several hundred holes, each perhaps 30 ft (9 metres) wide, in the sides of which comfortable living quarters have been excavated.

Let no-one think that because the people themselves are simple peasants making the most of a barren landscape this is a primitive way of life. These artificial caves are ideal for the climate, keeping an even temperature in a land of hot days and cold nights.

The pits themselves serve as substitutes for the region's hilltops, where villages such as Chenini were built out of lines of caves in the horizontal strata. At Ghoumrassen, most cave dwellings have been abandoned for modern houses on the valley floor, boxes which sacrifice the advantages of life underground for the sake of accessibility, their need of defence against neighbours and nomads no longer applying. The nomads' herds of camels and peaked brown tents no longer represent a threat.

Like all perpetual conflicts, the battle between nomads and villagers was normally governed by an uneasy peace, which found architectural expression in *ksour* or fortified granaries, such as Ksar Ouled Debbab or Ksar Haddada. These are in effect laagers comprised not of waggons but of cells or *ghorfas*, which turn their backs to the outside world and locate their entrances inward upon a cul-de-sac entered through a gatehouse.

The *ghorfas* are rectangular, built out of mud and stone and set side by side and one on top of another, with an inner and outer room and a tunnel-like roof. So much do they resemble caves that at Medenine, where they are piled to heights of six storeys, precariously reached by unprotected stairs, their

**Preceding pages:** ghorfa architecture. **Left,** distinctive brickwork in Tozeur. **Right,** Tamezret, hill village near Matmata.

original function as storehouses for the grain of peasants and nomads has disappeared, and they have been colonised by people.

The tunnel or barrel vault of the *ghorfa*, crudely constructed upon a core of earth overlaid with mats, is one of the basic elements of traditional Tunisian architecture, together with the flat roof laid upon beams and the pitched roof with tiles. The flat roof and the pitched roof divide the country, the former spreading up from the dry south, the other spilling over the border from Algeria

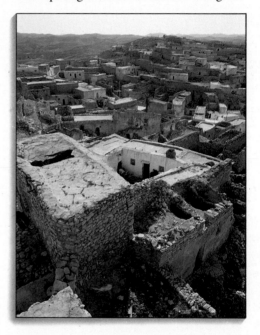

into the rainier hills of the northwest. The climatic divide represents a cultural difference in more ways than architectural; it also divides the traditional ways of life that vary from the oases to the steppes and to the Mediterranean-style lands of the north.

But the battle of the roofs is also historical. The flat roof dominates the medinas as far north as Tunis, symbolising the dominance of an ancient Arab urban civilisation whose style it is; yet Tunis, too, has its pitched roofs, reflecting the influence of Morocco from the 13th century onwards. At Sidi Bou Said and inland at Testour pitched roofs derive directly from Muslim Spain. There is the clue. Although it originates with the climatic conditions prevailing at the time of the Carthaginians and the Romans, the battle was fought out under the aegis of Islam.

Islam is a religion that underlies a civilisation. In Tunisia as elsewhere, the Islamic influence on architecture is not simply upon the mosque or upon the house, with its concern for privacy and seclusion, but on the way in which these buildings are grouped together. The earliest and most revered of the mosques in Tunisia, the Great Mosque of Kairouan, was designed to meet the needs of the first Muslim capital of the country. In the case of the Great Mosque of Tunis, however, the city gradually evolved around it.

The great court within is a place of refuge for the populace, with its own water supply in the cisterns underneath the pavement fed by the marble drain in the centre. With its colonnades, it is at the same time a place of assembly, where the *cadi*, or judge, might hold court, and the doctors of holy law teach their pupils. The huge pillared prayer hall opposite the tower is for a mode of worship resembling a military drill, not directed, as in a Christian church, from west to east along the length of the building, but from north to south across its width; what would have been the transept of a cathedral has become the nave, running from the dome over the entrance to the dome over the *mihrab*, the blank

Kairouan was established in the 7th century as a camp for the invading Arab army. The Great Mosque that was built in the 9th century was the final reconstruction of the area in the middle of that camp. The massive brick wall that surrounds it, although built for prestige in the caliphal style of Samarra in Iraq, is a reminder of its military origin. The mosque is, in fact, a huge fortress dominated by the tower at one end. Ignoring the cupola on top, which is a later addition, as well as the name "minaret", suggestive simply of the call to prayer, we can see that this tower is equipped with battlements and arrow-slits for defence.

recess that in a pagan temple would have contained the statue of the favoured deity.

To all these purposes the architecture is subservient: the great castle walls enclose a delicate structure of endless colonnades around the court, and inside the hall, row upon row of arches springing from innumerable Roman columns re-employed by a new community for a new faith. Free-standing, the colonnades are bound together only by the painted beams that bear the weight of the great flat roof. Such fragility, to such effect within so mighty a shell, is the stamp of early Arab architecture, as it is in Tunis and as far away as Cordoba in southern Spain.

Kairouan was abandoned as a capital in the 11th century. Only at Tunis and at Sfax can such a mosque be appreciated in its context at the heart of the city it was meant to serve. The minaret of the Zitouna, the Great Mosque of Tunis, dates from the end of the 19th century, but the building itself is contemporary with the Great Mosque of Kairouan. Conspicuously, it is surrounded by the city's souks, the centre of the commercial life which overtook the militarism of the early years. The scholarship which turned the Zitouna into one of the great traditional universities of the Muslim world went hand in hand with the mercantile interests that sustained the civilisation of Islam beneath

wouldn't have compared with Mahdia, built as the second Muslim capital of Tunisia in the 10th century by a monarch who claimed to be the Mahdi, the Messiah of Islam.

An entire city was built upon the headland at Mahdia. It was to be the centre of the Muslim world. As with the Great Mosque of Kairouan, a massive wall surrounded the refinement of the city's interior, but here there was no call to preserve the buildings of men and the luxurious palaces have disappeared. The great gate, the Skifa el Kahla, has been rebuilt to take cannon, but only the original mosque survives intact. This was not simply the royal place of worship but the bastion that defended the most vulnerable

the glitter of caliphs, emirs and sultans.

**Palatial ruins:** The Muslim rulers of Tunisia have left little of their palaces to posterity. Only the Bardo, the Versailles of the Husaynid dynasty deposed in 1956, which houses on the one hand the National Assembly and on the other the National Museum, survives to give an impression of the Whitehalls and Westminsters of the royal cities. The most colossal ruin is that of Mohammedia on the road from Tunis to Zaghouan, but this 19th-century monstrosity

corner of the enceinte. A similar arrangement is to be found at Sousse, where the Great Mosque of the 9th century protected the harbour, which it once overlooked.

The walls of Sousse enclose a rarity, the *ribat* or guardcastle for the holy warriors who defended the North African coast at the end of the 8th century. It is a small, simple fortress rendered superfluous by the major fortifications built 60 years later, but of seminal importance. It is square, on two floors, with battlements facing both outwards and inwards upon the central court; the chimney-like tower, the *nador*, was added as a look-out.

**Left**, the Ribat in Sousse. **Above**, Dar Ben Abdallah, Tunis.

With its well in the middle, it served all the military purposes of the Great Mosque of Kairouan, and the religious purposes as well, for there is a prayer hall on the first floor above the gateway; the dome above the *mihrab* looks like a gate tower. But it was too much of a castle to develop as the great mosque of the growing city, and since it was not built into the new city walls, it lost its military significance as well. The *murabatin* or guardsmen who garrisoned it became instead a community of hermits who fought battles of the spirit, not the sword.

At Monastir the original *ribat* was enlarged into a purely military fortress in the 11th century; elsewhere along the coast, the

ribats are mere ruins. But the *murabatin* lived on as holy men to adopt the tradition of Islamic mysticism, or Sufism, when it arrived from the east in the 12th century. On the strength of the Sufi tradition they came back from the margins of society to take up a position at the centre. The *zaouias*, the niches in which they ensconced themselves, grew into the equivalent of monasteries, typically built around the tomb of the founder, equipped with mosque, school, refectory, living quarters and accommodation for guests. All this was paid for by pious gifts. Sidi Kassem Zilliji, a maker of painted tiles in Tunis, founded a *zaouia* alongside his

mausoleum in the 15th century. More prestigious were the foundations of princes, who sought in such works a more lasting monument than their palaces. Tunis is full of them, but the best to visit is the Zaouia of Sidi Sahab at Kairouan, reconstructed by the Bey of Tunis in the 17th century. Nefta, in the south, is also full of *zaouias*; their social and political influence was once enormous.

More often than not, however, the domed tombs of the holy men stand alone, places for women's prayers and offerings and serving, like crucifixes and wayside shrines in a Catholic country, to bless the locality and its people. Such tombs are known as *marabouts* (that is, *murabits*, from the holy men themselves), and they range from the primitive construction at the entrance to the valley of Ghoumrassen to elaborate structures like those at Menzel Temime on Cap Bon.

They draw attention to the dome itself, the *koubba*, introduced from the east along with the *mihrab* as long ago as the 8th century, but which came into its own in the Ottoman period from the 16th century onwards. The Mosque of Sidi Mehrez in Tunis is in the style of the huge domes of Istanbul, but elsewhere the dome is allied with the tiled roofs of the Moorish tradition, crowning an attractive domestic as well as religious architecture of slender columns, graceful arcades, intricate woodwork, stucco and marble. Most characteristic of all are the composite tile pictures elaborated out of motifs of foliage and arches.

From the 17th century onwards the Italian baroque and rococo influences became fashionable, as in the Dar Ben Abdallah and the elegant mosque of Hammouda Pasha in Tunis. The mosque's slim, octagonal minaret contrasts with the Zitouna's square tower which, with its latticework panels, is a latterday copy of the minarets of Algeria, themselves deriving from the Koutoubia at Marrakesh and the Giralda at Seville; but the style is popular. It carries on the eclecticism best summed up in the Bardo, where the palace is a museum in its own right. Built in the middle of the 19th century to represent the arts and crafts of all the provinces of Tunisia, it is architecturally as fascinating as the Roman mosaics it so admirably displays.

<u>**Left**</u>, **a courtyard in the Bardo.** <u>**Right**</u>, **the ceiling of an old mansion in Kairouan.**

Sunset over the Grand Erg Oriental marks the beginning of a nocturnal conflict. Darkling beetles, like miniature tanks, push their way across the dunes, leaving tiny tracks in the sand. Small mammals emerge from burrows wary of the fennec, a fox whose large ears can pin-point the slightest sound. When dawn breaks, only myriad tracks, peppered with discarded shards of beetle and droplets of gerbil blood remain. By mid-morning all traces will have disappeared under the Sahara's shifting sands.

But beetles, if they can avoid predators, stand a good chance of surviving life in the apparently barren sand dunes of the Grand Erg. Their hard wing cases harbour pockets of air, and they eat almost anything. The fact that they can survive for up to two years without food makes them one of the insects best adapted to desert conditions.

**Adapt or die:** For such a small African country, Tunisia boasts an exciting variety of habitats. In summer, when the lowland steppes bake, the northern forests are rich in nectar, attracting displays of rare butterflies and hovering humming-bird hawkmoths. Wild boar and deer roam among tree heathers. In contrast, a good day's travel south takes you through salt steppes and the scrubby vegetation of semi-desert to the oasis habitats of the true Sahara around Tozeur or Douz.

Invariably, extreme conditions lead to extreme specialisation. The most deadly poisonous scorpions can be found in Tunisia, although the chances of seeing one are remote. Arachnids, which include scorpions, are adept at surviving heat and dehydration because of the thick waxy cuticles that cover their bodies. And most desert mammals are nocturnal: they not only avoid the heat of the day but also desiccating winds, at their most intense in the afternoons. Likewise, the leaves of plants have been reduced to spines so that water loss is minimal. The reason why desert oases are dominated by the date palm is because it can stand being partially covered by sand and has extensive root systems

reaching deep into the desert's water table.

When rain does come it usually arrives suddenly, filling the *oueds* with flash floods and washing most plants away. Like the palm, oleander bushes, with their mass of pink flowers, cling on with deep roots. For many species a sudden drenching is an opportunity to be seized. Reproduction may have to be squeezed into these short periods. Seeds which have lain dormant for years will germinate overnight and within a few days the barren, lifeless plateaux become a blaze

of colour, making spring one of the most rewarding times to travel.

Aridity is not the only problem which plants and animals have to face. Salt impregnates the steppe regions. Soil water evaporates rather than drains away, drawing dissolved minerals to the surface where the salt forms crusts. Much of Tunisian plant life is therefore halophytic, able to tolerate large concentrations of salt. Salicornia has such high levels of salt in its stems that it was once collected and used in the manufacture of glass. Also known as glasswort, this leafless plant can be seen growing around the southern chott lakes, though where the salt levels

**Preceding pages:** darkling beetle at large. **Left,** tower-head grasshopper. **Right,** canny survivor.

become exceptionally high it too disappears.

The poor soil will not tolerate complete colonisation by plants – witness the tussocks of tough esparto grass – and competition for minerals and water is fierce. Tamarisk and broom bushes are the largest plants of the steppe but the longest living is the tough choufleur. As the name suggests it looks like a cauliflower, with compact woody branches. Small mammals, such as jerboas, like to burrow into the sand and dust that accumulate around their bases.

Some species have been introduced from Australia to alleviate conditions in the steppe. The roots of acacias, trees noted for their pea-size, fluffy yellow flowers during

habitat. Inland, drier conditions discourage many of these plants, so lower growing species like herbs, typically sage, thyme and rosemary, abound, and other plants change their pattern of growth. The Kermes Oak, for instance, attains heights of several metres near the coast but becomes low and spreading around Le Kef.

During spring the maquis is alive with flowers, particularly bulbs. Easter is the time for orchids. By mid June the flowers will be burnt to below ground level.

**Lions, tigers and dragons:** Insects, perhaps the least popular wildlife, are a fascinating part of the Tunisian fauna. The larger butterflies and moths are best seen in the north of

spring, possess nodules containing bacteria that helps put nitrogen back into the soil. At one time eucalyptus or gum trees, distinguished by their peeling bark, were reputed to ward off the malarial mosquito. This is now thought to be a myth, but extensive stands of eucalyptus can be seen shading roads throughout Tunisia.

All the coastal areas were once densely wooded. Only a few semi-natural areas remain, such as those around Tabarka in the north. The vegetation that has taken over is a tangle of shrubs and low bushes, like broom, tree heathers and the aromatic myrtle, which are ideal cover for animals. This is maquis

the country in late spring and early summer. When the desert is at its hottest, tiny Tiger Blue butterflies flutter around thorn bushes, and blue, green and red flashes of darting dragonflies can be seen hawking up and down the shady irrigation ditches of the palmeries.

Wherever there are sandy, dusty conditions look out for small, symmetrical pits in the ground. They contain the larvae of the ant-lion. The adult looks like a dragonfly with clubbed antennae but the larvae are oval and flattened, with huge sets of jaws. Any small animals unfortunate enough to fall into their pits are encouraged to continue their roll by the ant-lion flicking sand on to them. Once at the bottom, their body fluids are slowly sucked dry.

Stony desert is the typical haunt of grasshoppers, which merge into the background with their drab upper parts when on the ground but, on taking flight, display brightly coloured wings to disorientate potential predators such as the desert mantis. A superbly camouflaged beast with long, narrow running legs, the desert mantis is very different from the usual varieties (common in lush vegetation) which move slowly over flowerheads in search of nectar-feeding insects. At midday it can be seen running down insects as large as locusts.

years ago lush vegetation would have covered the country and as desertification occurred so the frogs and toads became stranded in the oases. Like island populations these amphibians have evolved their own distinct races. Reptiles are probably more at home in these conditions than any other vertebrate. Over 80 different species are represented in Tunisia.

Chameleons are common "pets" of young children, while the magnificent spiny-tailed lizard, which can grow up to half a metre in length, is hunted for food by the people of the northern Sahara. This latter beast has a thickset tail which stores food. It is unusual in that it eats both vegetation and insects, unlike the

For at least one stage in Tunisia's past the country formed the bottom of the sea. As the geological plates of Africa and Europe collided, so the land was pushed skywards and the ocean floor formed mountains. Northern Tunisia is therefore rich in fossils of early life forms. Ammonites, bivalves and brachiopods all imply marine origins, and the hills around Kasserine are notably rich in these fossils.

It may also seem strange to find amphibians in the desert regions, but thousands of

Left, hovering humming-bird hawkmoth. Above, Lake Ichkeul, wildfowl haven.

large desert monitor, which reaches over a metre in length and feeds on lizards and small mammals on the firmer parts of the dune hollows. Finding snakes requires considerable searching. The poisonous horned viper tends to remain buried under sand by day, especially under tamarisk bushes, so beware...

**Bird life:** Tunisia is on many of the migration routes for birds passing between Africa and Europe. They cross the sea at the tip of Italy where the waters narrow. These migrants add to a wealth of birds which breed in this part of North Africa. At over 50 sq. miles (130 sq. km), Lake Ichkeul, near Bizerte, is one of the top three waterfowl grounds of the western Mediterranean (the others being the Camargue in France, and the Coto Doñana in Southern Spain).

During the winter months 150,000 wildfowl arrive. Rafts of widgeon, pochard and coot cover the water's surface for as far as the eye can see and the skies are filled with the cacophony of grey lag geese in V-flight formations. Other wildfowl include the white-headed duck, teal, marbled teal, shoveler, pintail and gadwall. Wading around the edge of this permanent lake, little egrets, herons, flamingos, redshank, avocets, pratincole, little stints, stilts and black-tailed godwits feed, whilst in the

reedbeds skulk little bitterns and the secretive but spectacular purple gallinule.

The shallow waters provide a rich diet of invertebrates, pondweeds and seeds. Water levels fluctuate during the year and in spring the surrounding meadows come alive with wild gladioli and marigolds. The area around the lake is almost as rich in bird species as the lake itself, especially in the variety of falcons and vultures.

The scrubland is a good place to see the red, black and white Moussier's redstart, although the population extends southwards over much of Tunisia and Dougga is another good place to see this rarity. The dry steppe

lands are low in bird diversity because of the harshness of the habitat. Here, predatory species, particularly kites and shrikes, predominate. The crested lark is often the only resident species to be seen, scuttling across roads and desert.

In the oases many birds fly in to feed on the ubiquitous alfalfa, especially the desert sparrow. Here, migratory species include the chiffchaff, bee-eater, wagtail and flycatcher.

**Boar and more:** Other than a fleeting glimpse of a jackal in the northern forests or a puff of sand as a jerboa disappears down a hole, mammals are easily overlooked in Tunisia. Wild boar are common in forested areas but usually sightings are of shot individuals on minibus roof racks. Hedgehog, hare, gennet, wild cat and the European fox are also found in these forests. The fennec may wander this far but is more at home in the desert regions, its large ears radiating heat away from the body.

Rodents, like the many species of gerbil, jirds and bipedal jerboas, are the most successful of mammals in the dry areas. By day they remain underground and survive without drinking, relying on the water they have metabolised in their food. Moisture in their breath condenses on the rocky walls of their burrows, only to be licked and reingested.

The wild and deep waters of the north coast are rocky; the extensive, shallow waters in the Gulf of Gabes are sandy and more akin to those of the tropics. With water temperatures averaging 57° F (14° C) in February and 75° F (24° C) in July, the seashore fauna and flora is rich. The tidal range is approximately 18 inches (46 cm) and a variety of seaweeds and animals is left when the tide drops on a rocky shore. There are delicate sea anemones and sponges, and deeper waters hold the massive bath sponge. Where softer rocks are present purple sea urchins live in crevices.

The north coast is termed the "Coral Coast", and, though some natural corals are present, there is extensive growth of a coral-like red algae. Molluscs, such as cowries and the beautifully coloured sea slugs, are in great abundance. Snorkelling is recommended. Scuba diving centres operate around the coasts.

**Left,** the fritillary butterfly. **Right,** wintering flamingos.

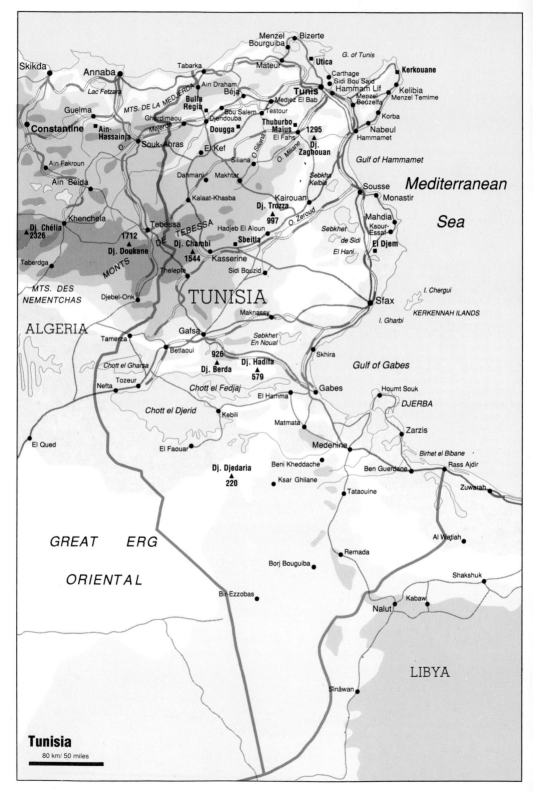

116

A fine coastline has earned Tunisia a reputation for a sun and sand resort, beloved by Europeans looking for a family destination or those in need of a fortifying but not too expensive dose of vitamin E before winter releases its annual bouquet of germs. In the main it attracts holidaymakers whose idea of exploring beyond the beach is some golf or snorkelling arranged through their rather good hotels.

But the beaches, running the length of the east coast from the sandy coves of Cap Bon to the opal-coloured lagoons off Djerba close to the Libyan border, are only the gilded edge of what Tunisia has to offer. Those with the slightest urge to venture further experience the best of the country – the people, the scenery, its character – seldom meeting many other tourists along the way.

Just 50 miles (80 km) from the seaside resorts stand the world's least visited but most extensive Roman ruins; a little further in a northerly direction are the rugged Khroumir mountains and the well-watered valleys of the Medjerda Valley, ideal territory for hiking holidays; and the same distance south lies the palm-fringed edge of an entirely different sea, the Grand Erg Oriental of the Sahara desert, starting point for trans-African expeditions. For such dramatic shifts in scenery, distances are slight, and in a week it is possible to sample all of these different terrains.

When it comes to historic cities, Kairouan has a special claim, being the country's first capital and next to Jerusalem in Islam's league of holy places, but Tunis has most to offer non-Muslim visitors. The medina, dating from the 9th century, still has a toe-hold in the Middle Ages, while the new town with its handsome colonial architecture, is a mixture of contemporary Arab and old-style French with a hint of Italian dash.

Tunis restaurants are excellent, the hotels come in all shapes and sizes from the skyscraping Africa Meridien to the V-shaped Hôtel du Lac, and transport is efficient. But, perhaps uniquely for a capital city, the centre is eclipsed by its suburbs: within a few miles of the tree-lined boulevards lie the Bardo, housing the best collection of Roman mosaics outside Italy, the ruins of ancient Carthage, and the steeply-raked village of Sidi Bou Said, as picturesque as any to be found either side of the Mediterranean.

**Preceding pages:** Sousse viewed from the Ribat; Mahdia's busy port; across the Chott el Djerid; on the beach.

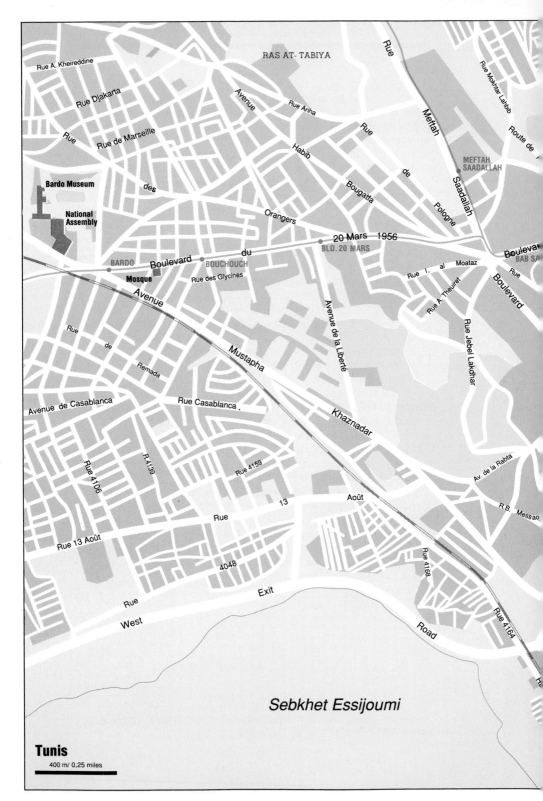

Tunis

400 m/ 0,25 miles

# TUNIS

Poor Habib Bourguiba. The capital's statue of the one-time hallowed statesman has been removed. Place d'Afrique, which the bronze statue of an equestrian Bourguiba for so long graced, is now **Place du 7 Novembre**, the date in 1987 when the octogenarian president who had orchestrated independence and led Tunisia for 30 years was certified as senile and ousted from his job. Bourguiba on his horse has been moved to the suburb of La Goulette, the statuary equivalent of being put out to grass, and a plain clock has been erected in its place. The implication, perhaps, is that the coup was timely.

Officially, the name of the city's main artery running from the clock to Bab el Bahar and the medina has undergone a similar re-alignment: formerly Avenue Habib Bourguiba, it is now **Avenue 7 Novembre** – demonstrating that the new regime has much in common with the last when it comes to blowing trumpets. But the people who work and relax here still refer to this pleasant thoroughfare as Avenue Habib Bourguiba, and not even those officials seem able to remember to forget.

The avenue's central column of bushy trees shades florists' stalls and Parisian-style newspaper kiosks strung with *Elle* and *Jeune Afrique* and piled high with copies of *Le Monde* and *Es Sabah*. Its character is definitely Arab, but many of its expressions are French. The major banks, the offices of Tunis Air, the well-guarded Ministry of the Interior and the sky-scraping Africa Meridien Hotel are headed by the Catholic Cathedral, the French Embassy and an old French theatre that looks like a badly-iced wedding cake.

Packed between these imposing buildings are fragrant rotisseries, *casse-croûte* outlets and old-fashioned *pâtisseries*. Their lack of tables and chairs obliges customers to stand, an arrangement aggravating to weary sightseers but entirely suited to the evening *passants* whose prime concern is to see and be seen. On either side of the avenue, streets of shops, restaurants, hotels and a few low-key nightclubs finger north and south. Nowadays the pulse of the city definitely beats louder here, but it was in the medina that Tunis developed into an important Mediterranean power.

**The making of a capital:** Tunis is a large conglomeration containing one-fifth of the country's 8 million people – far larger than second-city Sfax and dwarfing Sousse. The spit of land to the north, running from La Goulette to Gammarth, has become a wealthy suburb and Hammam Lif, under the wooded Bou Kornine hills to the south, an untidy backyard.

During Tunisia's earliest history the city was insignificant. As Thunes, it was one of a string of North African ports established by the Phoenician traders who plied this coast, and after 814 BC it operated as an outlying village of the great city of Carthage. The backbones of a capital didn't emerge until well after the Arab invasion. The

Aghlabids finished its Great Mosque in the 9th century, and in 1237 the Hafsids, realising that future prosperity lay in trade with a newly booming Europe, decided it made a more sensible capital than Kairouan, a city whose importance had been founded on Divine associations rather than natural assets.

After just a few years of Hafsid rule Tunis was a centre of Mediterranean commerce. They enlarged the town, constructed souks around the Great Mosque and built its ramparts. Following successive religious persecutions in Spain, later culminating in the Spanish Inquisition, Andalusian Muslims and Jews, renowned for their refined culture, fled to North Africa, not least to Tunis where they added to an already cosmopolitan population – merchants from Venice, Pisa and Genoa had also begun to settle in the town – and enhanced agriculture, architecture, arts and crafts.

But when the Hafsid dynasty expired at the end of the 15th century, a weak Tunisia lay vulnerable to invasion. The seas off Tunis became the frontier between Turkey and Christian Mediterranean powers and the city was repeatedly occupied by the Spanish. In 1574 Turkey, who already governed Tripoli and Algiers, placed Tunisia under Ottoman rule to put an end to such incursions, and settle some old scores in the process (*see page 52*).

Faced with more pressing concerns in the Balkans and Asia Minor, Turkey left Tunisia much to its own devices, and Turkish rule quickly became nominal. Ottoman culture, however, exerted greater influence. In Tunis the beys and deys were keen to outdo one another in terms of architecture, hospitality and modish dress. New mausoleums, mosques, palaces and houses incorporated Turkish rather than Moorish features – even if they pre-dated the Turkish era, chances are they were renovated or rebuilt in accordance with Turkish fashions, which by the 18th and 19th centuries were becoming increasingly European. When Mohammed Bey had the Bardo rebuilt in 1882,

**Avenue de Carthage at night.**

124

Moorish, Turkish and Italianate styles were combined.

The French arrived in 1881 and established their infrastructure outside the old city, between the medina walls and the "**lake**", the depressing landlocked water fronting the Gulf of Tunis, which then, according to Alexandre Dumas, thronged with birds of every species including flamingoes. In contrast to the sinuous alleys and impasses of the medina, what the French town-planners designed were straight avenues and boulevards radiating from Avenue 7 Novembre, then Jules Ferry, and intersecting like a grid. Administration was transferred here and the medina's role in Tunis diminished.

**The Medina:** Following independence an attempt was made to restore at least symbolic importance to the medina by housing the prime minister's office and the ministry of foreign affairs in the **Dar el Bey** (a former beyical palace) behind the Great Mosque. Other palaces and great houses were turned into museums or used as headquarters for bodies set up to protect the Tunisian heritage, a policy the French had already initiated. **Dar ben Abdallah** in the south of the medina was converted to a museum of popular arts. Dar Hussayn, close to the Great Mosque, is now the **National Institue for Archaeology and Arts** (not exactly a museum, but the Institute's employees don't mind people wandering into the courtyard to look at their palatial offices).

Most importantly, **l'Association de Sauvegarde de La Medina** was set up in Dar Lasram, a late 19th-century palace in Rue Tribunal, to direct the restoration of the medina's historic monuments, calculated to number more than 700. After years of neglect, the task was huge. Families had moved into the mausoleums and *medersa* or, coveting their excellent stone, incorporated bits of them in their homes. The **Sidi Bou Khroussane museum**, in Rue ben Mahmoud off Souk Sekkajine, is typical of the problem. The courtyard of the 12th-century mausoleum of the short Khrousssane dynasty is strung with

As in Italy, you stand in most Tunis cafés.

washing and populated by chickens. The resident family have been made its custodians, but it's a shy eye that peeks at any tourist determined to enter.

Gradually, the Association is acquiring all the architecturally important buildings and restoring them (with varying levels of applause). What a preservation society cannot do, however, is revive medieval trades and practices when there is no demand. Streets in the medina can still be identified by their souks, but only just. Although the medina is busy, cheap international goods swamp traditional products, and craftsmen are usually knocking out tourist tat. A tour of Tunis medina is not, therefore, as exciting as exploring Fez. There are no mules loaded with pungent cargos of mint or newly tanned hide and cries of "*Balek!*" (move out of the way) to let them pass. But, *Hamdullah*, although attractions are less obvious, unlike in Fez there is not a hustler poised on every corner to help you find them.

From **Bab el Bahar**, the marooned Hafsid gate in Place de la Victoire over-looked by the British Embassy, two thoroughfares strike into the medina: **Rue de la Kasbah** and **Rue Djemaa el Zitouna**. The former heads straight for the Dar el Bey and the Place du Gouvernement; the other, after diving through a phalange of souvenir shops, emerges at the Great Mosque, or Mosque of Zitouna (meaning olive tree, and thought to refer to a giant olive tree that once grew there).

The **Great Mosque** was begun by the Omayyads in 732, completed by the Aghlabids in 864 and enlarged and adjusted during almost every century since – architectural amendments typifying a Great Mosque in a capital city. Who did what is recorded in its domes. In terms of age and reverence, it is second to the Great Mosque of Kairouan, though to an untutored eye Zitouna's less pristine restoration may make it appear more ancient. In fact, in spite of brand-new pointing, Kairouan's Great Mosque is archetypal early-Arab architecture: it is very simple, functional and, above all, obviously

**Perfumier Khaled Trab in Souk el Attarine samples his goods.**

defensive. Non-Muslim visitors to the Zitouna must make comparisons from the courtyard as, unlike at Kairouan, they are not allowed even a glimpse into the prayer hall, which is situated on the left-hand side.

During the Hafsid dynasty (1228–1535) the Zitouna flourished as a centre of Islamic studies. At independence 15,000 students from all over Tunisia studied here, though by then the capital's elite favoured Sadiki College where their children received a broader education. But the Zitouna's *imams* remained a powerful influence on public opinion and Bourguiba didn't benefit from repeatedly incurring their disapproval. President Ben Ali has been careful to accommodate some of their demands. Shortly after coming to power he re-established Zitouna's status as a theological university, which had been revoked by Bourguiba in his secularisation moves of the 1960s.

As in all the Arab cities that developed during the Middle Ages, streets around the Great Mosque contain souks dealing in luxury goods (heavier and smellier industries, such as dyeing and leather tanning were banished to the outskirts of town). Old and wealthy families always settled around the Great Mosque and the souks; not only were they then at the heart of things and a touch nearer Allah but they also imbibed the sweeter air and water that the elevated site enjoyed. The Andalusians, who arrived in the 13th and 14th centuries occupied streets further south (witness Rue des Andalous to the southwest) or much further to the north. When the Turks arrived they tended to take over the properties around the Great Mosque.

The monied classes have long since moved out to Tunis's suburbs, but vestiges of this arrangement can still be traced. To locate the diferent souks and former palaces, study the tiled map of the medina on the wall in front of the Zitouna Mosque.

On one side of the mosque, **Souk el Attarine** (perfume), dating from the 13th century, still contains one or two

**Carpet making, a painstaking craft.**

# ORDER OF THE BATH

If one thing links all the civilisations that have colonised Tunisia previous to the French occupation it is a fastidious sense of cleanliness. The Carthaginians had some grisly primitive practices – including child sacrifice – but when it came to sanitation their methods were enlightened (mainly by the Greeks). Among the most surprising Carthaginian remains in Tunisia are the well-appointed bathrooms in the houses of Kerkouane, a modest settlement on Cap Bon. The baths are roomy, comfortably-shaped and handsomely lined with waterproof red cement, a design not unlike the type of slipper bath found in old-fashioned Tunis hotels to this day.

It was the Romans, though, who elevated bathing to a social occasion. Master plumbers, they devoted great time and energy to solving problems of water supply, heating and drainage, and were the first to exploit the health-promoting thermal springs at Korbous on Cap Bon, Hammam Bourguiba near Ain Draham and Gafsa and Kebili in the Djerid. Their public baths became ever more elaborate complexes, with changing rooms, hot and warm rooms, swimming pool, cold plunge pool, *palaestra* (gymnasium), and sometimes, in their anxiousness to cater for every taste, a library and/or brothel close by (witness, for example, the layout of ancient Dougga).

The invading Arabs had a similarly strong sense of hygiene, mainly because the Koran has so much to say on the matter. It stipulates that a person must wash (all orifices, hands, feet, and hair) before praying – five times a day – and before reading or reciting its verses. Otherwise prayer is of no value in the eyes of God. Nowadays this washing is usually done at home, but as this wasn't always the case and as the slightest attack of flatulence on the way to the mosque can invalidate the whole procedure an essential feature of every mosque courtyard is a water fountain. In some circumstances, for example, if water is unavailable, a person is permitted to mimic the actions of washing by using sand or a stone, hence the common sight of a man nursing a stone on a long bus journey. He is simply making contingency plans, not about to club his neighbour.

The Arab answer to the municipal baths of the Romans was the hammam, or steam bath, still an essential amenity in every Tunisian medina where fully-equipped household bathrooms are rare. It was perfected by the Turks, who introduced all kinds of luxury accoutrements, such as special platform clogs called *nahn*, worn by refined women until quite recently.

Larger towns have numerous hammams, a few modern with signs in French and English, but others Stygian places marked only by the fuel piled outside their doors. Villages may have just the one, open to men and women on alternate days. In all cases, like the Roman establishments, the hammam is also a social club where friends meet. Before a wedding it is common for a family to hire their local hammam for the evening and invite friends for a pre-nuptial steam. For women, the hammam is the equivalent of the café.

A visit explains why Arabs view Western-style bathing as little short of disgusting. Once entrance has been successfully negotiated – men-only establishments next to mosques may not admit non-Muslims – you will find a changing area leading into a series of dim, misty chambers of varying temperatures, and be given a bucket for sluicing down. Women take all sorts of other paraphernalia, including something resembling a wall-paper scraper for exfoliation, and red henna and black soap preparations. More often than not, these are happily shared with ill-equipped foreigners.

The mood in the female hammam is animated (for one thing most women have a small child in tow), and sober in the men's, where the only sound may be the intermittent clicking of bones – an essential part being a rigorous physiotherapy administered by the masseur; but in both a strange mixture of abandonment and modesty prevails. You may lie in the arms of a semi-naked masseuse (masseur for the gents, of course) who scrubs you mercilessly and examines your every pore and hair follicle, but at no point in the hammam are underpants removed. It would be considered most impolite.

original shops, delicately painted in gold and green and stocked with stoppered bottles and jars of incense, though most have been edged out by stalls of cut-price toiletries and cosmetics.

Beyond is **Souk el Trouk** (souk of the Turks, where Turkish weavers and tailors used to operate), headed by the 17th-century Youssef Dey Mosque, which with its octagonal minaret reflects the early Turkish influences in the city. Souk el Trouk intersects with **Souk des Etoffes** (drapers), one of the oldest souks in the medina and distinguished by elegant red and green striped columns, and beyond this is **Souk des Femmes**, where women still come to buy lengths of white or cream fabric to make their *sifsaris*.

On the opposite side of the mosque, intersecting with Souk des Etoffes, is **Souk de la Laine**, originally the wool market but now accommodating an overspill from **Souk des Orfevres** (goldsmiths) where business is still thriving (gold jewellery being a measure of prestige even today, and many tradesmen still preferring to put their wealth in gold rather than dollar bills).

In **Souk de Leffa** (just beyond Souk de la Laine), now sporting carpets, foreigners are likely to encounter their only Tunis hustler. He entices prey with promises of a panoramic view. The fact that this is to be had from the terrace of a **carpet emporium** should alert even the most naive to his aim, but so long as it doesn't cost a carpet or rug – large numbers of which are unfurled when you descend – it's worth venturing up, and not just for the view of the Zitouna.

The terrace is a pastiche of Tunisian history. Arches tiled in a mish-mash of designs have been wedded to scraps of Roman columns to make a sort of Arab-Roman ruin. Well-placed urns add to the effect. It looks inventive, if not authentic, until you look at the much vaunted view. Similar terraces are dotted round about.

**Rue des Libraires**, a turning to the left off Rue Djemaa Zitouna before the Great Mosque, has only a couple of bookshops these days. But it does con-

tain three small 18th-century *medersa*, where students of the Zitouna once lived and studied. The **Palm Tree Medrassa** (at number 11 behind a yellow studded door), so called because of the large palm tree occupying most of its courtyard, is especially attractive. The cells off the courtyard are all open to view, some containing desks, blackboards and boxes of chalks – aids to the imagination rather than the original fixtures and fittings. The nearby **Bachia Medrassa**, number 27, opposite an agreeable café and undergoing extensive renovation, and the **Slimania Medrassa** on the corner were both commissioned by Ali Pasha I in the middle of the 18th century.

On the opposite side of Rue des Libraires, at number 30, there's **Hammam Kachachine** (men only), which along with the bookshops and the National Library (situated on the Rue Djemaa Zitouna) would have fulfilled the students' needs.

**Souk des Chechias**, a vaulted souk between Souk el Bey and Rue Sidi ben

Arous, is one of the most atmospheric spots in the medina. Each outlet off the tall, shadowy souk is a shop cum workshop with a wooden counter for sales and a group of intent crafsmen at work – shaping and trimming the red felt hats. Now worn mainly by older men, *chechias* were at one time the favoured headwear of the refined classes throughout North Africa and the Middle East and consequently one of Tunisia's biggest exports.

In the 19th century the industrious Souk des Chechias surprised English writer G.A. Jackson so much that he was forced to admit: "The manufacture of caps in Tunis is upon an establishment which would do no discredit to an European country." Bourguiba, during his most fervent wave of Europeanisation, tried to discourage their use, but to no avail. Many men still wear *chehias*, though their advanced ages suggest the industry may die before long.

Bisecting the souk is a café which is a haunt of dignified businessmen and traders alike. They come to smoke *hookahs*, read the daily news papers and drink *café turc*.

At the bottom of Souk des Chechias, Rue Sidi Ben Arous, named after the 15th-century holy man who introduced Tunisians to the mystical branch of Islam known as Sufism, contains a cluster of minor *zaouias* and mosques, including the **Hammouda Pasha Mosque**, unmistakable because of its pink marble facade. Hammouda Pasha el Mouradi, to give him his full title, was Tunisia's third bey. His mosque (built in 1655) and mausoleum (added later) are notable for their fancy but superfluous features, such as blind arches, geometric motifs, and a concern for decorative symmetry. The mausoleum inspired the design of the Bourguiba family mausoleum in Monastir.

Round the corner, in a cul-de-sac off Souk Belagh Jia, is the **Medrassa Eshammaia**, the first *medrassa* in North Africa, founded in the 13th century and rebuilt in 1647. It contains the **Tourbet of Princess Aziza Othmana**, a revered local lady who died in 1646 leaving a reputation for good works and

**Door of Dar Othman, palace of Othman Dey.**

generosity. The main hospital in Tunis, next to the Dar el Bey, is named after her. Again, this site was occupied by families until l'Association de Sauvegarde de La Medina commandeered it. The richly embellished tourbet contains 24 tombs of the Othman family.

At the other end of Souk des Chechias and left of Souk el Bey is **Souk el Berka**, the original site of the Tunis slave market, stocked in the 17th century by the Christian victims of Barbary Coast piracy (who could not raise a ransom) and by black Africans brought from the Sudan via Tunisia's south. The slaves were kept in stalls until they were ready to be auctioned, when they were placed on a stand known as "the cage". The market and the office of the *caid el berka*, its administrator, were finally closed in 1841 by Ahmed Bey, who at the time was so keen to be liked in Europe that he was prepared to forgo the fat tax levied on slavery. His rashness accelerated his bankruptcy.

Beyond the Dar el Bey and Place du Gouvernement a hill leads up to **Place de la Kasbah**, once site of the original Hafsid Kasbah and now overlooked by the headquarters of the ruling RCD (Rasemblement Constitutionel Democratique) party. The road to the right hugs the medina to Bab Souika and contains several tributes to Tunisia's struggle to escape colonial shackles and the first years of independence. In the shadow of the United Nations building lies the **tomb of Farhat Hached**, a militant trade union leader murdered in 1952. The inquiry into his death was quietly dropped by the French: it was generally assumed that the Red Hand, a terrorist group comprising French settlers, was to blame.

The white, colonial-looking building just behind the UN is **Sadiki College**, founded in 1875 by Kher el Dine, a modernist prime minister who, a forerunner of Bourguiba, thought the way forward for Tunisians was to adopt European methods and culture. The college later became the Tunisians' means of access to administration and increased social success. It was attended

**Medrassa of the Palm Tree.**

by children of the middle classes from all over Tunisia, generally young people with ambitions. Nationalism was fomented here, and many of the leaders who emerged at Independence were past students of Sadiki, including Bourguiba.

The **9th April Museum** on the other side of the Place de la Kasbah and along from the 13th-century **Kasbah Mosque** is a tribute to Tunisia's progress in education. The date commemorates Martyr's Day, the date in 1934 when violent nationalist demonstrations resulted in 122 deaths after government forces fired randomly at the crowd. The museum, housed in an old prison, used to chronicle the career of Habib Bourguiba, who was once interned here by the French. Never a vital stop on an itinerary, the museum is still not really worth a visit.

**Southern quarters:** More rewarding is the **Dar ben Abdallah Museum**, devoted to the "daily life of Tunis in the 19th century", in the south of the medina. It occupies a 19th-century palace just off the Rue des Teinturiers (dyers), demonstrating all the features of Italian-influenced architecture typical in Tunis at the time. The entrance leads into a stone hallway, which in turn opens into a colonnaded marble courtyard complete with Italianate fountain. The walls are colourfully tiled and surmounted by intricate stucco.

Heavy wooden doors lead into T-shaped rooms containing the exhibits – costumes, household furniture and implements, children's toys, jewellery, bathing accessories, etc. Some of the costumes and furniture are moth-eaten and the life-size models sporting the costumes are a touch lurid, but they still manage to convey an idea of the refined comforts of domestic life. For those keen to try a Turkish bath, there is a detailed map of the medina, pinpointing even the hammans, inside the entrance to the museum.

Nearby, on the corner of Rue Tourbet el Bey and Rue Sidi Kacem, is **Tourbet el Bey**, which remains open to visitors despite interminable restoration work.

**The esteemed Restaurant M'rabet in the Souk el Trouk.**

It contains row upon row of marble tombs housing most of the Husaynid dynasty, which ruled Tunisia from the 18th century until Independence in 1957 (albeit for the last 75 years under the auspices of the French). Even until 1945, members of the family were buried here. It was founded by Ali Pasha II in the 18th century. In recent years it has hosted the living as well as the dead, and following the recent evacuation of resident families some of the tombs were found desecrated, others to have disappeared altogether – including the one containing the, in his day, not to be trifled with Ali Pasha.

At the opposite end of Rue Sidi Kassem, on Rue des Teinturiers, is the Dyers' Mosque, also known as **Mosque Djedid** (new), commissioned by Husayn Ben Ali, founder of the Husaynid dynasty, and finished in 1726. It was the first of the surge of lavish building projects which flaunted the city's prosperity in the 18th century.

**Café as social club.**

Round the corner, in Rue El Mbaza, is the most splendid door in Tunis, that of **Dar Othman**, the palace of Hafsid ruler Othman Dey (father of the gentle Aziza). It was built at the end of the 16th century, and is now being restored.

**Going north:** From the southern quarter it's possible to cut right across the medina, via Rue Sidi Ali Azouz, to the northern sites. The route threads through the main shopping souks and at one point picks its way across the **Hafsia**, currently a wasteland devoted to second-hand clothes' stalls, once the Jewish ghetto. In the early 19th century the Hafsia was enclosed by vast walls, and the rights of its inhabitants were restricted by the bey.

Repression lifted in the middle of the century, when an influx of rich Maltese and Italian Jewish merchants began to settle in the more salubrious areas of Tunis. In 1857 equal rights for Jews were enforced by law. The catalyst for reform was an incident involving a Jew who had insulted a Muslim, been imprisoned for his crime, then decapitated and thrown to the crowd. The fact that the bey had sanctioned such punish-

ment provoked international accusations of savagery.

Conditions for Jews continued to improve under the French (at least, until the Vichy Government) and those Jews who could afford it moved out of the Hafsia into the new town. The Hafsia, declared insanitary in 1933, was gradually demolished, though poor migrants from the countryside continued to settle in its shell. L'Association de Sauvegarde de La Medina is overseeing the redevelopment of its land.

Across the Hafsia, the tunnel of kaftans and cheap Western clothing continues (just inside, there is a hygiene-forsaken café for the market traders that serves some of the best *briks* in Tunisia), opening out near the white multi-domed, but obscured, **Mosque of Sidi Mehrez**, built between 1657 and 1692 when pure Ottoman influences were at their height in Tunis. It was commissioned by Mohammed Bey, but was not finished in his lifetime. Had it been, no doubt it would be named after him instead of Sidi Mehrez, whose *zaouia* lies on the opposite side of the street.

The *zaouia* of Sidi Mehrez – entrance through the cluster of sweet stalls – is the busiest in the city, rivalling the Zaouia of Sidi Sahab in Kairouan in its popularity among women. Female pilgrims flock to pray at the ornately embellished tomb and sip the holy water ladled from a well in the ante-room. Sidi Mehrez, the patron saint of Tunis, was a 10th-century hero who oversaw Tunis's recovery following rule by the Kharidjite zealot Abou Yazid. The original *zaouia* was rebuilt in 1862.

Place Bab Souika marks the northern exit from the medina. **Place Halfouine**, just beyond, is a convivial place to sit in a café and revive. From here you can walk up Souk Djedid and Rue Sidi Abdessalem to Boulevard Heidi Saidi and catch a bus to the **Bardo**. Alternatively, pick up bus number 42 at the station at Habib Thameur gardens. If you're heading to the Bardo from Avenue Habib Bourguiba, catch the number 3 from outside the Tunis Air building just down from the African

**Straw hats: business takes off in summer.**

Meridien hotel. By now, a tram service should also be operating from Place de l'Indépendence. The important thing is to get there somehow; it's one of the most impressive archaeological museums in the world.

**Brilliant Bardo:** Described as the Bey's "fairytale residence" by Alexandre Dumas when he visited it in 1846, the Bardo, a beyical palace complex, was regarded by some as more of an architectural horror story after its rebuilding in 1882. It is now split between the museum and the Tunisian House of Representatives, an arrangement at odds with the government's usual paranoia about privacy – though notices strictly forbid nosy tourists to take photographs from the museum's windows.

Rooms are labelled according to the period and excavations they cover. Most ancient are the Punic remains – pots, lamps (single-lip versions are the oldest), stelae (headstones), masks and sarcophagi – dating from the 7th to the 3rd centuries BC. Much of the material was recovered from the tophets, the communal graves of the victims of child sacrifice, which best survived the destruction wreaked by the Romans and succeeding civilisations. Compared to the wealth of Roman mosaics, the Punic material may seem meagre, but it's from such bits and pieces that archaeologists have pieced together an idea of Carthaginian society (*see page 146*) and what it owed to the civilisations of the Egyptians and Greeks.

The extent to which Carthage suffered economically from Greek domination of the Eastern Mediterranean from 480 BC has been proved by the fact that excavations have yielded large numbers of black-figured vases made in Corinth and Attica prior to that date but very few of a later red variety. Egyptian amulets (examples in this collection) also appear to have vanished from Tunisia after then. Archaeologists believe Greek supremacy hampered Carthaginian trade routes and recession ensued.

The Bardo's most celebrated exhibits, however, are the Roman and Byzan-

**The vegetable market in Rue d'Allemagne.**

# THE STONES SPEAK

Following the devastation wreaked by the Vandals and the decline of the Byzantines, North Africa's Roman heritage fell into oblivion, at the mercy of wind and weeds and intermittent plundering by Arab builders for over 1,000 years. In the 18th and 19th centuries, it was rediscovered, often by lone and intrepid travellers such as James Bruce, a Scot, who reported the existence of Timgad in Algeria in 1765.

The systematic exploration and rehabilitation of the ancient sites did not begin until the French arrived in North Africa. Archaeology was still a relatively new science, owing much to the pioneering work of Amelia B. Edwards, a journalist and author who travelled extensively in Egypt in the 19th century. She was the first to realise that the preservation of ancient monuments (many of which had already been pillaged from Egypt) depended upon a scientific approach to their excavation and recovery, not one motivated by the prospect of finding treasure.

"To collect and exhibit objects of ancient art and industry," she wrote, "is worse than idle if we do not also endeavour to disseminate some knowledge of the history of those arts and industries, and of the processes employed by the artists and craftsmen of the past."

North Africa's ruins speak volumes, and in the case of inscription and graffiti sometimes very directly. Though there is nothing to match the wit and wisdom found in Pompeii where the ash from Vesuvius proved such an effective preservative, an amusing example is found carved on the standing arch in the ruins of Hammam Zouarka. "Those who urinate here will incur the wrath of Mars," it warns.

It is, though, the multitude of fine mosaics that have been removed to the Bardo that tell the most vivid stories. Designed and prefabricated in workshops, they were laid down in sections at their respective sites, for the most part floors of villas, temples or municipal buildings.

Some were imported or copied from famous prototypes, but many were made locally in a more naturalistic style than was common elsewhere in the Empire. They present a composite picture of urban and rural life. Themes include agriculture (harvesting, ploughing, hunting and the farming calendar); the flora and fauna of the time (including elephants, lions and tigers); popular gods (commonly a goblet-brandishing Dionysus, the Greek god of wine), action-packed scenes of events in the amphitheatres and touching cameos of family life.

Fishing and seafaring scenes were popular inland as well as in coastal towns, suggesting that rich landowners may have owed part of their wealth to investments in shipping. The Bardo's mosaic of 23 different types of fishing vessels was found at Medina (Althiburos) in western Tunisia, as far as one can get from the sea.

Occasionally the mosaics incorporated captions, usually pompous mottos in dog Latin, but sometimes a good joke. One mosaic from El Djem depicts a party of gladiators enjoying a riotous banquet on the night before they fight. In the centre is written *"Silentium dormiant Tauri"* (Silence, let the bulls sleep).

Some of the most impressive African mosaics came from the large country estates that prospered in the 2nd and 3rd centuries AD, when many small farms were swallowed up by richer neighbours and absent landlords returned to their country seats to avoid the worst of iniquitous taxes. The best artisans, also evading the taxman, sought a new market for their work and joined them.

A telling example is the Bardo's Signor Julius mosaic originally found near Carthage. It shows how well-endowed the country estates were. At its centre is a handsome turreted farmhouse with first-floor living quarters (to provide defence) and, behind it, a multi-domed bath house. The master is seated proudly in his chair, with all the industry of his estate going on around him – servants tending to the crops and animals – and his wife, elegantly coiffured and fashionably dressed in spite of her peasant audience, is taking a necklace from her maid, who clasps a large jewel box.

The mosaicist has excelled himself in capturing the mistress's expression: one of complete and utter smugness.

tine mosaics taken from sites all over Tunisia. Whole floors and walls are paved with mosaics, many virtually intact, from the 2nd century BC to the 7th century AD. Subject matter includes Greek and Roman myths and gods; simple scenes of domesticity, husbandry and celebration; and mottos festooned with birds and animals. Agricultural scenes roll over whole walls, evidence of North Africa's main function in the Roman Empire.

Particular highlights include the 3rd-century mosaic of Virgil writing *The Aeneid* attended by two muses; a mosaic of the Greek myth of Andromeda being delivered from a sea monster by Perseus, again 3rd-century; and a depiction of Ulysses and his sailors resisting the Sirens' songs. The Palaeo-Christian room is covered in mosaics on Christian themes, notably a mosaic illustrating Daniel in the lions' den. By the 2nd century Christianity had spread throughout North Africa.

The **Mahdia rooms** contain the cargo of a 1st-century BC shipwreck discovered in 1907 by sponge divers off Mahdia. The haul took six years to raise. Some of it has suffered a sea-change for the worse but the bronze figures are still in excellent shape. Various theories attempt to explain where the cargo might have been heading. One suggests that the Grecian bronze and marble figures were bound for the home of Juba II, Roman Africa's Client King, who had a collector's interest in *objets d'art*, and certainly bought similar pieces for his home in Volubilis in Morocco. But, more probably, the statues were destined for private villas, and are yet another indication of the great wealth of the Roman cities in North Africa.

The Bardo also includes a well-displayed Islamic section, with examples of early Koranic scripts, faïence tiling imported from Iznik, jewellery, antique costumes, Jewish religious accoutrements, weaponry, and 16th-century prints of Tunisia.

Behind the archaeological museum there's a lively display of regional costumes and crafts, though it must be said

**Famous Bardo mosaics: <u>Left</u>, Perseus rescuing Andromeda from a sea-monster. <u>Right</u>, Virgil attended by the Muses.**

that at this point most people, satiated by Roman mosaics and the Bardo's extravagant decor, forego it and head for their hotel.

**The New Town: Avenue du 7 Novembre** boasts the biggest hotels. The Africa Meridien dominates the Tunis skyline. It attracted much criticism when it was built in the 1960s, but if nothing else it serves as a useful landmark to newcomers lost on the city's outskirts. It offers a better than usual cinema, restaurants and pavement coffee shop, but don't expect a comfortable late-night bar – apart from the nightclub (open until 4 a.m.) the hotel is dead by 11 at night, when the bar (downstairs) closes. (Other than in discotheques, late drinking in Tunis is confined to the downbeat bars around the station.)

On the other side of the Avenue is the vast International Tunisia, favoured by Gulf Arabs; and at the very end of the avenue, beyond Place du 7 Novembre, is the V-shaped Hotel Du Lac, which looks more like a social benefits office than somewhere you would pay to stay.

The streets dissecting Avenue Habib Bourguiba are full of restaurants (see *Travel Tips*) and modest hotels dating from the colonial era; many of these offer excellent service, crisply laundered linen, huge *en suite* bathrooms with noisy plumbing, and ornately caged lifts – all bathed in a 110-volt gloom.

The colonial architecture is now of sufficient vintage to be of interest in its own right. Avenue de Paris is lined with some of the best examples: particularly Hotel Majestic. The French Embassy on Avenue 7 Novembre was built in 1862, and the neo-Gothic **Cathedral of St Vincent de Paul** opposite was constructed 20 years later. The cathedral doesn't really merit the description "splendid" awarded by the kindly travel writer Eric Newby; its heavy, stolid architecture embodies the spirit of colonialism rather than anything holy.

To indulge the senses, visit the **food markets** on Rue d'Allemagne and Rue D'Espagne. Even after the main markets – for meat, fish, vegetables, live

**The social kiss.**

poultry, spices, olives, cheeses, snails – have been cleared away, bright stalls of dates and honey remain open until well after dusk.

**Escapes:** For those wanting to flee the summer heat, **Belvedere Park** is the nearest option. A pleasantly rambling, hilly expanse containing the city's **zoo** and contemporary **art gallery** (not very exciting) near its gate, it rises in the north of town at the far end of Avenue de la Liberté, and commands some impressive views. At weekends, the cafés by its lake on Place Pasteur are packed with Tunisians *en famille*; the number of pushchairs, prams and small children clutching balloons suggests that the government's policy on population cannot yet be called control.

Alternatively, people take the TGM, the light railway operating from just beyond Place du 7 Novembre to ancient Carthage; the attractive, cliff-top village of Sidi Bou Said (popularly known as Sidi Bou), which the French writer André Gide described as bathing in a fluid, mother-of-pearl sedative; the sea-side town of La Marsa or the once fashionable beach of Gammarth. Even as early as the 18th century, the ruling classes and richest merchants of Tunis were building property in these salubrious suburbs.

The original railway was built by a British company in the late 19th century when an ambitious consul called Richard Wood was trying to extend British influence in Tunisia. Its features included a bell connected to the British Embassy which would ring before a train was due to depart, just in case Wood needed a ride. The railway proved unprofitable and was later sold to Italy.

To venture further afield, perhaps north to Bizerte or south to Sousse, take a train from **Gare SNCFT** in Place Barcelone. For day trips to the Roman sites of Thuburbo Maius (nearest town El Fahs) or Zaghouan, or the rural backwaters and beaches of Cap Bon, catch a bus or *louage* from Bab Alleoua, situated beneath the picturesque cliff and cemetery to the south of town.

**Navel gazing.**

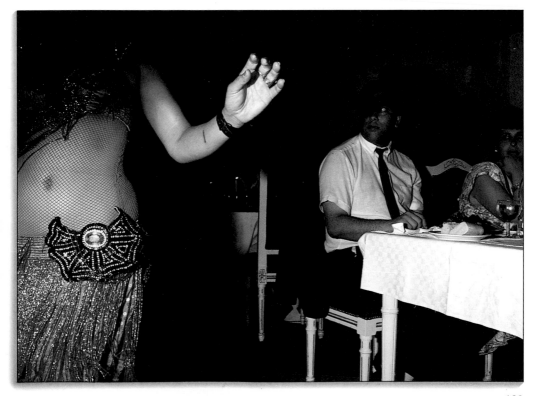

## THE ANCIENT SUBURBS OF TUNIS

It comes as something of a shock to see a name so full of historical resonance as Carthage adorning an international airport and a seaside suburb of Tunis. Knossos as a bus destination on Crete has nothing on Carthage with its railway stations called after Salammbo, Amilcar and Hannibal. When Virgil wrote his epic poem *The Aeneid* – a bit of political propaganda intended to endow the budding Roman Empire with a history in keeping with its aspirations by linking it with the glories of ancient Greece and Troy – he cast his hero, Aeneas, ashore at Carthage and so gave the city a romance and glamour hardly borne out by its ruins.

Carthage (its name comes from Qart Hadasht, or New Capital) was founded around 800 BC by people from the Eastern Mediterranean known as Phoenicians after their homeland. The Phoenicians had established a trading empire throughout the Mediterranean Sea with a wide scattering of bases. When their country was invaded by Assyrians many left to settle permanently in their trading outposts, turning them into quite elaborate city states with substantial ports.

Legend, with reference to Phoenician wiles, has it that their Queen Dido (in some versions of early date she is Elissa) arrived in Carthage and traded with the local ruler Iarbus for as much land as might be enclosed by an ox-hide. She proceeded to have her biggest bull slaughtered and its hide cut into the thinnest of strips, which she strung out to mark the boundary of her city. Hence the Hill of Byrsa (*byrsa* being Greek for hide) which dominates the ancient ruins. Iarbus tried to take Dido as his queen but, rather than betray her people, she opted for death on a funeral pyre.

Virgil, writing his version of the legend around 40 BC, substitutes Aeneas for Iarbus. He tells, memorably, of the love between Dido and Aeneas and how she chose to perish when he obeyed his destiny and went off to found Rome.

However, to meet Virgil's scenario the Trojan warrior would have been some several centuries old when he met Dido.

Historically, and from the archaeological record, it is known Carthage flourished for centuries. Carthaginian cities proliferated along the coast and inland, bringing an Eastern Mediterranean system of terraced agriculture to the Maghreb that survives today. They defended these settlements against marauding Greeks; and fought off early Latins in the series of conflicts called the Punic Wars (Punic comes from the Greek for Phoenician, synonymous with Carthaginian) that led to the Carthaginian general Hannibal's famous attempt to take Rome from the north, crossing the Alps with elephants.

The Romans looked upon Carthage as a thorn in their side. In 149 BC they ordered the Carthaginians to evacuate their city and, when they refused, the Romans laid siege for three years. The sacking of 146 BC and the attendant pillage and slaughter of many hundreds of thousands ended only when the

**Preceding pages: Carthage, salubrious suburb. Left, figure of Baal. Right, lions were common in Africa then.**

Romans pulled down every building that remained standing and – the final devastation – ploughed salt into the soil.

Yet the location of Carthage beckoned Rome. Some 24 years after the conquest an attempt to establish a North African base there was abandoned only when the auguries proved inauspicious. In 46 BC, after Julius Caesar had defeated Pompey's cohorts in the area and put down the Berber tribes, the city was rebuilt and ruled directly from Rome as its nearest African province.

Later pages of the Carthage palimpsest show conquest by Christian Vandals who, living up to their name, left nothing but destroyed much; the passage of the cruel, disputatious Byzantines who contended with a whole century of Berber harassment; and, in the 7th century, the arrival of the Arabs. The city then became a quarry: columns and marble were carted off for use in mosques all over Tunisia.

The remains of Carthage are not impressive; the sites are to be visited for the memories they evoke rather than the marvels they reveal. Much was encroached upon by the building of smart modern villas and tourist hotels. Ex-president Bourguiba once said that if ever Tunisia struck oil on a grand scale he would order their demolition and reconstruct Carthage. In 1972 UNESCO, alarmed at the potential losses, embarked upon a scheme to rescue and record what was left of the ancient remains before they fell victim to mechanical diggers and the pouring of concrete. Teams from archaeological institutes in Europe and the US joined with local forces to excavate, assess and record the widely-dispersed sites.

Bearing in mind that archaeology is itself the ultimate destruction and that its sole purpose is not to dig up objects for display in museums but to record and publish, this venture has been no more than partially successful. There are plenty of excavated artefacts but little literature on them.

**Along the way:** The sites are strung out 3 or 4 miles (6 or 7 km) along the coast and the best way to visit them is to begin

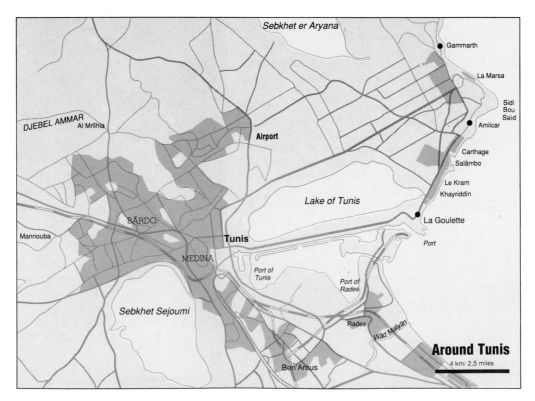

Around Tunis
4 km/ 2,5 miles

at one end and work to the other, crossing the railway track and the main road as necessary. The suburban railway (TGM) runs from Tunis with trains every 20 minutes. To get there by road, take the causeway across the Lake of Tunis towards **La Goulette**, the city's port. The massive Kasbah here, built in 1535 by Charles V of Spain but falling to Arab forces in 1574, is worth a quick look. The unfortunate victims of Barbary Coast piracy languished in its vast dungeons until either a ransom was raised for them or they were carted off to the slave market and auctioned.

La Goulette is also worth a fish lunch or supper, though choose your restaurant (the main street is lined with them) with care – prices and quality don't necessarily tally. Beyond, the busy road runs straight to Le Kram and then to Carthage proper.

Begin with the harbour of Carthage; it is reached from the Byrsa or Salammbo stops on the TGM and is signposted **Les Portes Puniques** down a lane off to the right of the main road. The sole cause

for marvel is how such a modest pair of lagoons, now stagnant and grown over with weeds, could be the base for a great maritime power like Carthage; the lesser port to the south was for mercantile use. A British contingent investigated the Punic Ports for UNESCO; some perfunctory works are taking place still. Between the ports is a Museum of Oceanography that merits only a passing visit.

Inland from the southern harbour, on a corner of the Rue Hannibal, is the **Tophet**, or *Sanctuaire Punique*, tastefully signposted in mosaic. This is the location of the temples of the Carthaginian gods, Tanit and Baal (the latter from Asia Minor). It is the site of human sacrifice of the cruellest sort, which was practised here for more than half a millennium. In times of trouble Carthaginians would bring their young children to the altars of these deities, strangle them as offering and appeasement, and burn their bodies. Burial pits and funerary urns were unearthed here in profusion; commemorative stelae are

Tales of child sacrifice.

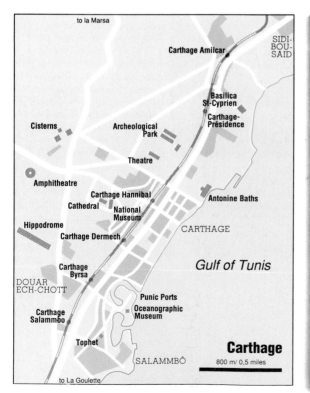

# PEOPLE OF CARTHAGE

It is one of the great ironies of history that the Phoenicians, inventors of the cursive alphabet which revolutionised writing and produced the modern European alphabet, left behind nothing in writing about themselves. The total destruction of Carthage would of course have taken all the existing paperwork with it, but Carthaginian influence spread wide and there were outposts that did not fare so badly. Historians tend to think that, having gone to the trouble of inventing a marvellously versatile alphabet, the Phoenicians made only sparing use of it.

Nor did the Carthaginians leave behind the kind of Roman mosaics and Greek vases which show ordinary people going about their daily lives. The most comprehensive information about furniture, dress and even their appearance is gained from the contents of tombs as the Carthaginians, no less than the Egyptians or for that matter the Vikings, liked to take the trappings of prosperous lives to the grave and hoped to make use of them in the next world. A reconstruction of life in Carthage is also assisted by the recovery of stelae, or tombstones.

The knowledge derived from archaeology is not evenly distributed; we know a lot, relatively speaking about child sacrifice and plumbing but almost nothing about Carthaginian emotions or their sense of humour, if they had one (their Roman critics thought probably not). It does seem that in spite of their Semitic origins many had African features. Their tightly curled hair required double combs and, in the belief that it contained supernatural properties, was carefully arranged. Hairstyles evolved, men of one period favouring hair combed forward and fixed in front with an amulet, others opting for a middle parting with a fringe over the forehead and coils around either ear. The women consistently grew their hair very long, which came in useful during the final siege of the Punic Wars when it could be cut and used in catapults reputed to be capable of killing a man at 400 paces.

Fashions in dress fluctuated too. One of the

styles inherited from Cyprus could hardly have been ideal in the African climate. It included a hat like a bishop's mitre and four layers of clothing, the outermost (worn by men and woman alike) resembling modern tails – open in front and a knee-length flap at the back. Men and women evidently drenched themselves with scent and women, at least, applied rouge to their cheeks and kohl to their eyes. Both sexes went in for tattoos as they did for rings, not only in their ears but also through their noses. Bracelets and anklets were substantial and numerous. A Greek comedy by Plautus pokes fun at the Phoenicians, particularly a Carthaginian merchant whose dress earns a derisory shout of "Hey, you there without a belt!". Scholars who pore over such slender threads have decided that his stage costume must have been the kind of long straight woollen robe which Phoenicians from Tyre wore without a belt. Had the merchant in question been in the full regalia of tattoos, hair parted in the middle and coiled around the ears, nose and ear rings, a bishop's mitre, tails etc, it is improbable that a critic's attention would have been fixed on a missing belt.

The rich lived in houses with elaborate bathrooms; the poor got by with an enormous jar standing in the centre of their only room. Smaller jars were used instead of cupboards for storing food and clothes. Like the Greeks, they scraped their bodies with a crescent-shaped device after bathing and applying oil. Men who shaved at all, a minority, used razors like elongated axe-heads. Their diet, also like the ancient Greeks, seems to have consisted of nothing but porridge. Cato gives the recipe for one of them: "Put one pound of coarse-ground cereal in water and allow to soak thoroughly; pour into a clean trough; add three pounds of fresh cheese, half a pound of honey and one egg. Stir well and cook in a new saucepan." Lovely.

Carthaginian medicine seems to have been rudimentary – a reasonable deduction from what is known of their veterinary care. Horses with bladder problems had filings from their hooves mixed with wine and forced up their nostrils. Some medical prescriptions had to be mixed specifically in the presence of a dog which had been kept indoors for 10 days.

piled up to one side. Hideous practices were carried out on this spot, and the Roman propaganda vilifying the Carthaginians for such acts was fully justified (even if it went to mitigate their own unholy butchery).

A pleasant guest house, Le Residence Carthage, adjoins this site. With scant regard for historical susceptibilities, it chooses to call its rather pricey, pretentious restaurant after the god Baal, and appears not to worry how this might affect a delicate appetite. Indeed, this entire leafy suburb seems quite untroubled by ghosts. Imagine a neat residential area located, say, in the neighbourhood of Auschwitz. But time has dulled sensibilities and only the rows of pollarded trees and their bare arms raised in supplication bear witness to what went on all those centuries ago.

Across the main Avenue Bourguiba (TGM Carthage Dermech) is the **Hill of Byrsa**, with the derelict **French Cathedral**, a copy of the one in Tunis, and the **Archaeological Museum**, as yet in the course of arrangement, with its un-

paralleled collection of Punic artefacts. Roman material is scattered about the garden: capitals of columns, pillars, bits of statues and some entertaining carvings. Worthy of attention are the stone sarcophagi and, on the southern side, an excavated settlement.

Down the hill to the west lie the sketchy remains of an amphitheatre and, a little to the north, a group of huge cisterns that formed part of Carthage's fresh-water system. Retracing the road back towards the shore and past the crossroads dedicated to a couple of international oil giants leads to the site of the **Antonine Baths**. The foundations, for the most part all that remains, cover some 9 acres (3.5 hectares); an area of this size, directly related to the population, demonstrates the vast extent of Roman Carthage. The entrance gives on to a Schola (a school-cum-club for the children of the wealthy – the Roman equivalent of a public school) and a ruined Basilica, and elsewhere are stores for fuel and remnants of the pipes that carried heated water and steam.

Left, funerary stella. Right, mosaic *in situ*.

Hard by the Baths is one of Tunisia's several Presidential Palaces (TGM Carthage Presidence).

For the final leg of the Carthage trail, moving landward along the Avenue du 7 Novembre, there are the **Baths of Gargilius** on the left and, to the right, the heavily-restored **Theatre of Hadrian**, now used during the months of July and August for a modern festival of the arts that guarantees events less scandalous than those of antiquity. Beyond is the Parc Archaeologique des Villas Romaines, an assemblage of basements, columns and statues making up a site valued most for its setting, with views of the Gulf of Tunis, and a few mosaics *in situ*. For those who have to see everything, basilicas either side of the central route round off the sprawling area of Carthage.

**To Sidi Bou:** Standing as a goal at the end of the Carthage trail, like the prow of a great ship jutting out proudly to the sea, is the cliff-top village of **Sidi Bou Said**. Its gleaming houses and stunning location commanding the Gulf of Tunis make a rewarding destination after the arduous string of historical sites it somewhat disdainfully overlooks.

This air of hauteur strikes casual visitors to Sidi Bou Said: they wonder if they really have any right to be here beyond picking up tourist souvenirs – themselves with an edge on the quality of what prevails elsewhere – taking an almost obligatory drink up on the terrace of the **Café des Nattes** and wandering the maze of lanes and alleys that resolutely guard their shuttered ambience, bewildered by the blazing whiteness of the mute walls and the ever-so-carefully selected blueness of the studded doors and the *masrabias*, with glimpses of seas below and beyond.

The secret of Sidi Bou Said is the secret of Mdina on Malta and regrettably few places around the Mediterranean: it copes with its tourist influx by largely ignoring it. Smart people live in Sidi Bou Said and behave like those with old money everywhere, by putting up a blank wall to the intruders and, at the most, treating them as a passing

**Doors and windows of Sidi Bou Said.**

wave. After the call of group suppers takes away the trippers, Sidi Bou Said lives its quiet, cat-patrolled life as it has done for ages. Ages? Well, nine-tenths of a century is a venerable age as far as tourist resorts go, isn't it?

Yet there is history in Sidi Bou Said. It takes its name from the 13th-century holy man whose tomb and *zaouia* were built here on the site of an earlier Arab *ribat* and lighthouse. Fanciful legend has it that it was, in fact, Saint Louis who, escaping the sack of Carthage, set up here with an accommodating local girl and established a reputation for the curing of scorpion bites. True or not, Saint Louis gave way to a tide of Islamic mysticism; eventually Sidi Bou Said became the patron of the coast's marauding pirates. The Spanish held sway here during the 16th century then, mindful of religious antagonism and the dissolute ways of the unbelievers, their successors forbade all but Muslims to enter Sidi Bou Said until as late as 1819.

Rather self-consciously developed since the beginning of this century, Sidi

Bou Said has attracted generations of European artists and writers; nowadays it is to be appreciated as something of a living museum. There is certainly no cleaner spot on the Mediterranean littoral. It is a delightfully romantic place to wander under the stars. Stay at the magnificently-located Sidi Bou Said Hotel (where the terrace is the place to be seen on a Saturday night, at least for the capital's well-heeled youth), or the several guest houses, but make sure of a room with a bay view in return for their premium rates.

**La Marsa**, sprawling along the coast to the northwest, is something of a comedown after Sidi Bou Said. It is not even a port, although port is what its name means. La Marsa, according to one John Ogilvy who visited Tunis in the 17th century, "is adorned with a Royal Palace and pleasing places whither the rulers of Tunis go in the summer… and keep their Court". Some of these summer residences of the beys remain standing today: there is the dismal Abdulaya behind the post office on

Courtyard of the convivial Hotel Dar Said.

the Gammarth road for one, and the British Ambassador's residence out on the Tunis road for another.

Predominantly, La Marsa's seafront is lined with French colonial villas and seasonal bars and restaurants, a product of its summer trade. However, now that it is a stop on the convenient, comfortable and reliable TGM, La Marsa is rapidly becoming yet another dormitory suburb of the capital.

For a curiosity, it is worth seeking out the Café Saf Saf, not far from the TGM station by the Place Saf Saf. There is a Hafsid mosque here but the café offers a more singular sight: it is built around a well of some antiquity from which, during the tourist season, water is raised by a camel treading in tight, endless circles and blinkered to stop it falling down dizzy.

Being the newest and farthest out of Tunis's northern suburbs, **Gammarth** has claim to be the smartest (always excepting the unparalleled Sidi Bou Said). The modern two-domed mosque with its square Maghrebi-style minaret

decorated in blue and white filigree designs is an attractive feature.

**Naked bathing:** Leaving La Marsa, the road divides. To the right, the coastal branch leads past a chain of impressive hotels fringing what became known to the locals as the *Baies des Singes* (the Bays of the Monkeys), said to be because of the habits of the uninhibited Europeans who disported themselves naked here during the 1950s. Needless to say, nude bathing is a practice no longer encouraged by the government. The shingle beaches, littered and polluted, are not inviting and would-be bathers are advised to travel to the much better beaches of Cap Bon.

The left-hand fork of the road rises up to the heights above Cap Gammarth and from here pleasing vistas make this an altogether classy location, something endorsed by the substantial villas immaculate in brilliant white set off by azure blue doors and window grilles. The trees that line the streets are carefully manicured and it is a cause of little wonder that this is an area favoured by foreign legations, that of Spain most advantageously located of all.

Towards the summit of the Djebel Khawi – or Hollow Mountain, so named because it was riddled with ancient burial shafts – lies, appropriately enough, the French Military Cemetery, beautifully tended but largely deserted. Opposite, on the lower side of the road, is the *Complex Cinématographique Tunisien*; the tops of a few classical columns can be glimpsed from the road. Real or fake?

The mountain road drops to join the coastal road and thus forms a loop to take the visitor either back in the direction of Tunis or further along the coast to where it begins to peter out in a track across the sand dunes flanking the salt marshes. On the way, there are signs of development with a vast new hotel complex rising in relative wilderness, a venture that ignores the fate of the nearby Jardins de Carthage, a sprawling village of holiday homes built with money from Saudi Arabia but seemingly deserted even before any of them were occupied.

**Left**, most clothes are bespoke. **Right**, evening view from the terrace of Café des Nattes.

# CAP BON

Frank Lloyd Wright called George Sebastian's house in **Hammamet** "the most beautiful house I know". Others liked it too. Sir Winston Churchill favoured the guest room on the right by the fountain; Anthony Eden often cut an elegant figure on its terrace; during World War II Montgomery planned military strategy beside the colonnaded swimming pool.

These days the former home of the royal Roumanian millionaire and his American wife is doing community service – as Hammamet's **International Cultural Centre** and the venue for weekly gatherings of the Lions Club. Fortunately, outside the months of July and August when an annual festival takes place, Hammamet isn't culturally vigorous, and the members of the Lions Club confine themselves mainly to the kitchen, where banners proclaim greetings from branches in exotic places – such as Sunderland in northern England.

The interior of the villa has been left with some ornaments and furniture still in place. You can peer through the windows, wander about the grounds and explore the open-air theatre (active during the festival) without meeting anyone, but if you are lucky you will find an old retainer who shows visitors around the rooms, pointing out relics such as the black marble dining table on the terrace, the period refrigerator Sebastian's wife insisted on importing from America, the modest guest rooms and Sebastian's device for telling which of them were occupied. The bathroom is the *pièce de résistance*: it contains a four-seater sunken bath in grey marble, served by ingenious plumbing.

The house, which under its immaculate white exterior, is made of mud bricks, was designed by a Sicilian architect living in Nabeul and built by a local builder. Sebastian and the architect added Art Deco references to classical Andalusian forms. The house was such a success that other homes were com-

missioned along the bay. Later, some of the hotels tried to copy the work of the Sicilian.

The wild gardens on the far side of the swimming pool and terrace lead towards the **beach** and a tiny domed building like a *koubba*. This was where Sebastian made the decision to build his villa. Looking through the latch-gate separating the garden wilderness from the white powder sand, it is clear why Sebastian chose this incomparable spot folded in the green headlands of Hammamet at the base of Cap Bon.

Sebastian, Madame Schiaparelli, painter Paul Klee, French writers André Gide and Georges Bernanos, to drop just a few names, discovered Hammamet when it was a fishing village. After the war it became popular with other discerning tourists and in the 1960s the town's hotels were built. It was in great danger of being completely spoilt, but somehow the rapid building programmes couldn't quite ruin Hammamet: lush vegetation quickly engirdled the low-rise hotels and, with package

**Preceding pages: Hammamet's villas are bijoux. Left, a Cap Bon falcon. Right, café mural.**

tourism centred in these comfortable white playgrounds, local entrepreneurs realised that the town could support only a modest number of restaurants and bars (see *Travel Tips*).

Souks, though, were a different matter. Tourists always shop. The bazaars were tucked inside the medina en route to the 13th-century kasbah overlooking the beach – a shrewd bit of town planning, as this is the only historic sight in Hammamet and every tourist visits it. The kasbah was attacked repeatedly by Christians in the 17th century. On one occasion in 1602 it fell victim to 300 Knights of Malta disguised as Muslims who landed unchallenged on the shore then took the town.

The **kasbah** has been restored to pristine condition, thus robbing it of much genuine age or interest (unless a long-promised museum finally materialises here), but the ramparts offer views over the white domes and terraces of the medina to the rear and a silver scalloped coastline to the fore. Early evening viewing is best. From here, it's hard to believe hotels are strung all the way to Nabeul.

**Pottering about:** Though white and abundantly sandy, the beach at **Nabeul** is less appealing. With its clutch of large hotels, it is divorced from the town, reached down the purpose-built, tree-lined Avenue Bourguiba. The centre's position away from the sea reflects Nabeul's development as a community of potters and farmers rather than as a fishing village, though the seafaring Phoenicians, whose traces were found when Nabeul's first hotel was excavated and now lie in the small **archaeological museum**, did manufacture the culinary fish paste garum here.

Its economy is nonetheless now dependent on seaside tourists. The local pottery has been adapted: tea-pot stands and mantelpiece accessories are more in evidence than well-made household earthenware; the town's shops – large gutted emporiums fantastically tiled – are overflowing with gift-priced items.

The **Friday market** (follow Avenue Ali Belahouane or drift with the

**Sebastian's colonnaded pool.**

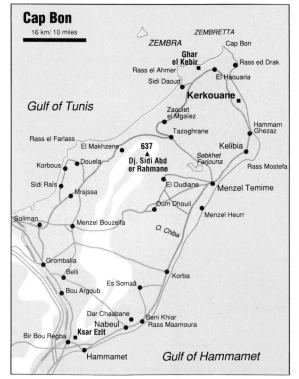

crowds) is an open-air extension of these snares: jewellery, copper, rugs, drums, leather pouffes and jackets, Moroccan babouches, live tortoises, Egyptian papyrus, dead scorpions in boxes and outcrops of desert rose carpet the streets in a pan-Arab bazaar. One word of warning: the so-called "**camel market**" is an outright con. The fenced-off enclosure is for very staid camel rides, and only very small children will be impressed.

But not all of Nabeul is engaged in meeting the insatiable demand for souvenirs and camel rides. Bricks are made and fired on the outskirts of town and in **Dar Chaabane**, just under the mountain of that name to the northeast, stone-masons carve neo-Moorish stucco friezes, pillars and cornices from locally-quarried stone. Civic buildings, hospitals, hotels and mosques all tend to incorporate traditional motifs and forms rather than break new architectural ground, so artisans still thrive – though quality is compromised by economic considerations. The masons

Fishing village origins.

trace their designs on to the stone with charcoal and then tap out the three-dimensional form with chisels.

**Remoter beaches:** So far, only Club Méditerranée at **Korba** has colonised the white and silky flank of Cap Bon. The coast road to Kelibia via Menzel Temime runs just inland from the shore. In parts wide ribbons of crops or salt flats intervene between road and sea, impeding approaches (and hotel development), but in other spots you can leave your car or bus and reach a fine, deserted beach. Access is easy and worthwhile at the bridge over Oued Chiba. A path cuts through wheatfields and low sand dunes.

From **Menzel Temime**, a busy market town, roads twist west through the intensely-farmed heartland of Cap Bon. Meadows have existed here since the Carthaginians realised that farms could provide better pasture for livestock than nomadic grazing and started organising the land into well-run agricultural estates. Together with those of the Medjerda valley, Cap Bon's farms

supplied food for the whole of ancient Carthage. Clearly, the landowners were wealthy men; tombs from this region contained more expensive Grecian artefacts and jewellery than those in Carthage itself. Cap Bon agriculture was the envy of Rome. Cato the Elder (he who closed every speech with the resolution "Carthage must be destroyed") is said to have brandished some Cap Bon figs at the Senate in Rome in order to resuscitate flagging aggression.

When the Romans did get their hands on Carthage, the area made a substantial contribution to the tables of the Roman Empire – though at first, so that they would not compete with Italian agriculture, African territories were allowed to export only cereals. When Hadrian acceded such trade barriers were removed and tax incentives were introduced which further encouraged Cap Bon farmers. Later, Andalusians settled here, bringing with them sophisticated new farming methods from Spain. Most recently the French established vine-yards, re-introducing a wine industry that had been dormant in Tunisia for 12 centuries. The French nurtured the vines so successfully, producing a fine muscat wine, that after independence the Tunisians put aside strict Islamic principles and adopted the industry as their own.

**School of fish:** The coast route runs straight on to **Kelibia**, a workaday place with an important harbour, modest beach (surrounded by a few hotels) and a splendid fort, all situated about a kilometre from the unremarkable centre of the town. Its Techinical School of Fishery trains fishermen from all over Tunisia, and at the end of each day flotillas of various-sized fishing vessels nose out of the harbour and head to sea, a spectacle best appreciated from the battlements of the **Byzantine fortress** overlooking the port (entrance fee: 500 millimes). This sandstone fort, which seems luminous even on dull days and glows deeply when the sun sets, is well worth the climb. It dates from the 6th century, but Punic and Roman remains

**Seaside villa in Kelibia.**

# WINE

The first surprise about Tunisian wine, if one were mindful of Islamic taboos, is that it should exist at all, the second that the tradition of wine-making is as old as any in the world, and the third that it is really quite good. Long memories may recall the odd bottle of Vin de Tunisie on European shelves before there were supermarkets, i.e. between the world wars, but it has hardly been seen abroad since and even then, as we shall see, it was probably not Tunisian wine but some shameful poison to which French-Algerian wine producers – for it was they – wisely declined to attach their names. History reveals 2,000 years of conspiracy to deprive Tunisian wine of a fair trial in the market place.

In view of the undeserved obscurity, if not cynical vilification, one or two guidelines may be in order. The best Tunisian wines are generally medium dry (red and white) and on a par with, say, the lower-middle order of French wines. The worst a visitor is likely to encounter, which is to say one which has nevertheless squeezed on to a wine-list, is never so poor as to hurt when swallowed or require an ambulance. Tourists who routinely sample local firewater – Portuguese agua dente, say, or the explosive grades of Greek ouzo – will find their Tunisian challenge

in fig brandy, called Boukha. It doesn't hurt either, but the ambulance could usefully be held within hailing distance, especially if it is downed in a gulp by people who, unequal to the subtleties of Arabic pronunciation, thought they had ordered Boga, a popular lemonade.

The wines tend to be produced and labelled by co-operatives with a wide catchment rather than localised growers (Kelibia being a notable exception), so there is no great profusion of names and vintages. The moderate imbiber could easily and cheaply sample all of the standard varieties within a two-week stay and still have time to let a relationship develop with personal preferences.

The discovery of a cheap wine surpassing all others is immensely satisfying but, of course, deeply subjective (Haut Mornag and Carthage crop up in this context); without or before that moment of triumph, price is as reliable a general rule as any, rather more so in Tunisia than elsewhere. Drinkers who wish to get their bearings right away could start with Vieux Thibar and then work up or down from there.

The pedigree of Tunisian viticulture goes back to the Phoenicians, who taught practically the whole world how to grow vines and what to do with them, including the Romans who in turn took over all their vineyards. While there were always parts of Tunisia which could match the Mediterranean conditions most conducive to wine production, the local efforts seem not to have equalled those of the competition. The Carthaginians apparently sold their domestic production to the Barbarians in order to buy better wine from Rhodes.

The Carthaginians took more pride in a kind of sherry, which even their implacable enemies the Romans liked. A Roman writer provided the recipe: "Gather well-ripened grapes early in the morning, removing those which are mouldy or damaged...", the first step towards a fermentation period of 20 or 30 days, after which the liquid was decanted into jars and covered with a skin. Jews around Bizerte were said still to be following the recipe in this century.

While the strictures of Islam, first under the Arabs and then the Ottomans, advanced the idea that grapes were divinely intended for eating, not drinking, a steady demand for drink was maintained by all sorts of intruders – Byzantines, Normans, corsairs and so on – who did not share this belief. Whatever it was they were drinking, English pirate crews based in Tunisia were not constrained by their "taking the turban" (i.e. contractual conversion to Islam) from drunken hooliganism next to which 20th-century football fans could not hold a candle.

As a French protectorate, Tunisia attracted immigrants from France as well as French-ruled Algeria, and they set about resuscitating the vineyards. The competition was not welcomed by the more established producers in Algeria. It seems that they bought up the best of the Tunisian wine and shipped it off to European markets as "Made in Algeria", while the worst of their own they blamed, as we have seen, on Tunisia.

found on the site indicate earlier settlements and it has performed defensive roles on many occasions since; in the 16th century it was sacked by the Spanish and repaired three times. It has been undergoing thorough restoration for some years; one hopes this won't ever infringe upon the vegetables, cow and chickens (belonging to the guardian) which flourish in its crown.

North from the ramparts, a string of tempting **beaches** are visible. These, approached via the road to the wealthy enclave of **Mansourah** running behind the fort, are vastly superior to the town's bran-tub sands. On weekdays outside school holidays, it's possible to have a whole beach to yourself. To reach them, follow the road through Mansourah to where it peters out in front of an orchard. A short walk through acacia and olive trees leads to the sands. Just a few kilometres further along the coast is the Punic settlement of Kerkouane.

The site of **Kerkouane** spreads over low cliffs above a rocky shore. It is prefaced by a herb and flower garden tended by a guardian, who will endeavour to show you around. As the ruins are low and spreading and you can easily miss the more interesting points, for once this is worthwhile; afterwards you will probably want to spend time alone, absorbing the rural peace of the spot.

Kerkouane was discovered in 1952 and first excavated in 1953. Although a modest site, it was considered an important find, as unlike other Punic villages and cities it had not been rebuilt by subsequent civilisations. The Romans did sack the town during the Punic Wars but they were so preoccupied with the destruction and then reconstruction of Carthage that they never returned to it.

An immediate clue to the purpose of this community was found in the great number of broken sea shells littering the area: they were left by fishermen and workers engaged in extracting a purple dye from murex, a shellfish with a colourless gland that turns purple on exposure to light. This was an industry practised all round the Mediterranean at the time. The dye was in great demand, first

**The Punic village of Kerkouane.**

in Carthage and later in Rome, where it was used to colour the togas of the Imperial family. (Modern scientists have calculated that it would have taken 12,000 murex shellfish to produce enough dye for one garment.) The flesh of the fish was put into vats hollowed out of the rocks and left to decompose. Naturally, the murex works were situated down-wind of the town's houses.

The fact that this was a working community helps account for the absence of public buildings. The **residential area**, denoted by a network of partially-restored walls of about a metre high, comprise the most extensive and interesting ruins of Kerkouane. Houses are surprisingly well appointed. Most remarkable is the number of private bathrooms – many with baths and wash basins. The red water-proof cement that lined the baths is still intact, and it is possible to trace the sophisticated drainage sytems.

The guide will point out the city's walls, gates and harbour (by no means obvious) and lead you to the image of the Punic goddess Tanit inlaid in a floor.

Tanit and Baal are the gods usually associated with the Carthaginians, though it is thought that they didn't achieve pre-eminence until the 5th century BC, when serious defeats against Greece prompted the Carthaginians to simplify their religion and prune their range of deities. Tanit's origins are uncertain: many say she evolved from the Great Mother worshipped by the pre-Hellenic people of the Aegean Sea; certainly she was associated with fecundity: her appearance on stelae is often wreathed by images of flowers and fruit or sandwiched between two wheat sheaves.

**Ancient sport:** Cap Bon also provided ancient Carthage with limestone for its buildings. When closer supplies were exhausted, stone was brought from El Haouaria, the backwater village at the peninsula's tip.

**El Haouaria** has a remote aspect, even for Cap Bon. It is at the northernmost point of Tunisia, 80 miles (130 km) from Sicily. It is where the white sandy underbelly of the peninsula takes

To El
Haouaria
Festival.

cover under a dark and rocky shell. One of the best beaches on the coast, **Rass ed Drak** (signposted from the town) lies just to the south. The encompassing hills are covered with fern and bracken; from autumn until late spring, damp sea mists settle on the minarets and in the hotel beds.

The rugged coastline makes appropriate breeding ground for falcons, and falconry is traditionally associated with the town; the one classified hotel is called l'Epervier (the falcon). The birds are taken from their cliff nests in spring, used for hunting quail, hare and partridge in the early summer and then set free again. Providing there are falcons and enough game birds, a festival of falconry is held in the town in mid-May.

Other than the dubious attraction of a cave full of bats up on the mountainside (*grotte des chauves-souris*; ask the children to show you), the **Carthaginian quarries** are the only other "sight" in El Haouaria. The fact that they draw twice weekly coachloads from Hammamet reflects the tour operators' desperation to sell excursions rather than the quarries' special fascination, but for the independent traveller the location is rewarding in itself.

**Cave man:** Known as **Ghar el Kebir**, the quarries are reached after a 40-minute walk along the unmade road heading directly north of town. The road climbs a short way uphill then slowly descends, making for a shack (a welcome café) perched on the cliff's edge, and what gradually emerges as the erect and saluting figure of a man. This is Mohammed, the octogenarian *Guide des Grottes*.

Mohammed claims to speak most languages. Indeed, each of his sentences is composed of at least five, and therefore unintelligible to anyone. His only English is the admonition "Mind your heads!", helpfully repeated every few yards.

It is thought that at one time the only access to the caves was by sea and that the chambers were jails as well as work places for the prisoners of war, convicts and slaves who laboured here. The rock in the shape of a kneeling camel, which the guide will point out, is probably owed to the ingenuity of the incarcerated rather than natural erosion or the magic attributed to it by a local legend that claims it is guarding treasure and springs to life every night.

The ease with which the stone could be shipped by barge from here to Carthage meant that huge blocks could be transported intact, without being broken into more manageable sizes. As the stone would have been too friable for exterior use or to take decoration, it was often covered with a stucco facing. (The poor quality of locally-available material is blamed for the primitive level of Carthaginian sculpture.) El Haouaria limestone was used in the wall joining the shore to the island in the Punic Ports, and often used for building tombs. Archaeologists have found Cap Bon tombs made of El Haouaria limestone dating from the 6th century BC.

El Haouaria has one hotel, one pension, a few cafés and nothing other than L'Epervier's dining-room that you could really call a restaurant, but it is a **Young birds are captured and trained in March.**

busy town populated by farmers (market on Friday) as well as fishermen working at nearby Sidi Daoud.

Opposite the rocky islands of Zembra and Zembretta – sanctuaries for birds and hooded seals – **Sidi Daoud** is a desolate place with a few dilapidated buildings, including a tuna-canning factory. It has a ghostly air for most of the year; a heavy shroud of white lime dust gusts up at the slightest wind, the few fishermen eye suspiciously any outsider who approaches. But from May until early July it is the busy centre for the slaughter of tuna fish, an event known as the *mantanza*. The black barges in the port then shudder into life, like the stirring of the undead.

The Roman writer Pliny the Elder recorded in his *Historia Naturalis* vast schools of tunny swimming west to east in the Mediterranean during the breeding season, and fishermen in Spain, North Africa and Sicily have profited from the migration to warmer waters for centuries. The first tuna reach the Straits of Gibraltar in April; they must then negotiate a labyrinth of nets all the way to Sicily. The fishermen's method is to lay a net at right-angles to the shore, stretching for several miles; this blocks the path of the fish and forces them into tapering corridors of further nets.

When the fish reach the final catch net called "the chamber of death", the circle of fishing vessels supporting the net close in and haul it to the surface. The great surge of thrashing fish is then slaughtered with batons, harpoons and knives. As the very biggest tuna can be 14 ft (4.3 metres) long and weigh 800 lbs (350 kg), the killing is frenzied and the water soon incarnadine.

At one time the Italians controlled the Tunisian tuna fishing, but nowadays the money behind the industry throughout the Mediterranean is Japanese. Animal rights pressure groups are protesting about the trawler method of tuna fishing, mainly because of the large numbers of dolphins that also get trapped in the nets.

It used to be possible for tourists to witness the *mantanza*. Then it was de-

**Falconers display their art.**

cided that a bloody massacre wasn't very suitable entertainment for visitors, and now only specialists can obtain permission to join a boat.

**Healing powers:** More salutary diversions are available in the spa of Korbous, the only settlement large enough to be called a village before the road reaches Soliman. The cliff-top drive from Sidi Daoud is spectacular; Korbous eventually comes into view, in the base of of a sharp ravine.

The Romans discovered the thermal waters of **Korbous** (then called Aquae Carpitanae) and travelled to them regularly from Roman Carthage – their underground sweating rooms are still in evidence. Seven springs, each reputed to have different healing properties, gush out of the cliffs at temperatures of 50–60° F (10–16° C). Like many spas, the village has a slightly faded look in spite of the face-lift given to the Etablissement Thermal, the former beyical palace on the shore, which was converted to a spa clinic in 1901. Approaching rack and ruin on the cliff face

is a former presidential residence – Bourguiba was a great believer in thermalism and used Korbous as an alternative to Hammam Bourguiba, the spa retreat near Ain Draham.

On Korbous's one street are a few cafés and the Restaurant Bar Les Thermes. The hotels, which commandeer the springs, all look like hospitals and are only likely to appeal to the seriously arthritic or bronchitic who go in for thermal cures. Hotel des Sources is the most exclusive establishment; half-board lodging costs from 15.5D in summer (treatments extra), but the afflicted poor can do as the locals do and visit the village *hammam*.

The spring of **Ain Oktor**, a kilometre further south of the village is the source of a popular mineral water, bottled on the spot. A free sample can be obtained from the water fountain in the forecourt of the Oktor Hotel.

**Sidi Rais**, a little further down the coast, truly has seen better days. Such painted wooden houses on stilts, *bit el bahr* (there is another example on the

Cap Bon is the main area for market gardening.

shore below Sidi Bou Said), were popular in the 19th century when they functioned as holiday homes for the richer artisans and merchants of Tunis. During the hottest summer months families would take off to the beach for a day, a week or even several months, depending on whether they rented or owned their *bit el bahr*.

From here, the rugged scenery of Cap Bon's north coast mellows to become like the cultivated farmland of its interior; enclosed olive orchards and market gardens replace heath and moorland. If you are seeking the scenic route wind inland to **Menzel Bouzelfa**, for its orangeries and multi-domed *zaouia*; in springtime the town is fragrant with orange blossom. From there, make for **Grombalia**, the main wine-growing area, and approach Tunis via the autoroute; it cuts a broad swathe through the wooded Bou Kornine hills.

All too soon on the coast road, at **Soliman** the landscape opens out to embrace the urban blight of south Tunis: pylons, billboards and industrial wasteland. Across the polluted Gulf of Carthage, a white crust on the horizon marks the city's suburbs of Carthage, Sidi Bou Said and Gammarth.

The beaches along the southern strip are not recommended. Venturing hopefully down a road marked "Zone Touristique" is a complete waste of petrol, unless you are unfortunate enough to be staying in one of the few hotels to which it leads. The refuse tips are almost as high as the sand dunes. Cranes swing into view over **Soliman Plage**, suggesting that there are still hopes of reviving this depressing suburb resort which used to be smart.

A little further on, **Hammam Lif** isn't much better, despite its pleasant position under the eastern side of the Bou Kornine hills (containing the PLO headquarters at Bordj Cedria). Though Hammam Lif has some history – Roman origins, crumbling colonial architecture – it is now in a state of flux. Spotting a finished building is an event on this stretch of road; they don't seem to make them like that any more.

**Thirty-two percent of Tunisia's workforce labour on the land.**

# THE NORTH

The Mediterranean-style farmhouses built by the French in the Medjerda Valley were described by one writer on the protectorate, Jacque Berque, as "the most provocative symbol of the colonial epoch in the Maghreb". It is easy to imagine what he meant. To the Tunisian labourer, a cheerful terracotta-tiled roof nestling on neatly cultivated slopes must have made him see red in more ways than one.

The French knew what they were at when they carved up the north of Tunisia and introduced new concepts of property with the Land Registration Act of 1885. In summer the region is warm and dry, in winter it is wet; it has valleys that are fertile and the only perennial river in the country. What's more, there was potential for vineyards, and boar-stuffed forests that promised good sport. In short, it had much in common with Provence – only, unlike back in France, labour was plentiful and cheap.

When independence came the *colons* were reluctant to abandon the good life they had built, and many left only when land nationalisation in 1964 forced their feet; but the area remained an old favourite with Gallic holidaymakers. Unbeknown to most other nationalities, it has beaches, scenery, unspoiled towns and ancient sites. There are family-run hotels and restaurants, and no package tourism – yet.

Only in World War II did the British and the Germans come here in any numbers. The region experienced the most bitter fighting of the Tunisian campaign, and few of those who survived – plenty did not, as is evident from the war cemeteries – bothered to come back. A British traveller's cheque presented at a rural bank north of Tunis is rare enough to summon the manager. Invariably, he will study the cheque cautiously, make motions of purposefulness, and then come to an unshakeable decision: "*Je regrette…*"

Bizerte is 40 miles (65 km) from Tunis, along a road which, once beyond the wastelands on the city's outskirts, wends through agreeable rural scenery. Car drivers can make an interesting day of it by taking in the Roman remains of Utica, the old pirate lair of Ghar el Melh and a quiet beach – Rass Sidi Ali el Mekhi or Raf Raf are hard to beat. Bus travellers can hop off at the turning for Utica (18 miles/30 km from Tunis) and walk the short distance, slightly more than a mile to the site.

**Utica**'s remains are mainly Roman, but its origins are Phoenician. When the site was first excavated in the 1940s, a typical Punic floor – red cement inlaid with small fragments of white marble – was found under a 1st-century Roman floor of black and white marble, which in turn was under a handsome 2nd-century flower-patterned mosaic.

According to Pliny the Elder, Utica was founded in 1101 BC, some 300 years before Carthage – though there is no archaeological evidence of a settlement earlier than the 8th century BC. In either case, it was long before the Medjerda river had deposited so much

**Preceding pages: Raf-Raf, a beach worthy of superlatives. Left**, private lives. **Right**, pausing for a breather.

alluvium that the sea was forced to retreat. Utica, situated about halfway between Tyre and Cadiz, was a vital Phoenician port; now it is 6 miles (10 km) inland.

Despite its proximity to Carthage, it showed little allegiance to the great city and probably competed with it. In 310 BC, during recurring hostilities between the Carthaginians and Greeks, Agathocles of Syracuse used Utica as a centre for ship-building and a base for raiding Carthaginian estates. Later, in 149 BC, under the influence of Massinissa, a Numidian chief who was keen to annex Carthaginian territory, the town sided with Rome against Carthage, and Roman legions landed at Utica before going on to win the Third (and final) Punic War. As a reward, Utica was made capital of Roman Africa five years later.

As Pompey's North African headquarters in the Roman Civil War, the town found itself on the losing side. In 43 BC, Caesar's one remaining opponent, Cato the Younger, committed suicide in Utica by falling on his sword when news filtered through of Pompey's accumulating defeats.

Utica's excavations are disappointingly small, but scrupulously cared for; they are signposted, swept, and brightened by a garden which the custodian is usually busy tending. His concern for its irrigation is such that – unlike his colleagues on other national sites – he makes no moves to act as guide. If he is preoccupied, lift the wooden planks on the pavements to see the small collection of *in situ* mosaics (receptacles of water are provided for brightening, not to say ultimately ruining, their colours), the most impressive of which are the fishing scenes in the **House of Cascades**, thought to date from approximately AD 69–96.

Several villas remain but this large, obviously wealthy house is the only ruin that really testifies to Utica's importance in Roman Africa. Its doorway, with notches where roof beams would have been supported, leads to an extensive complex of reception rooms paved

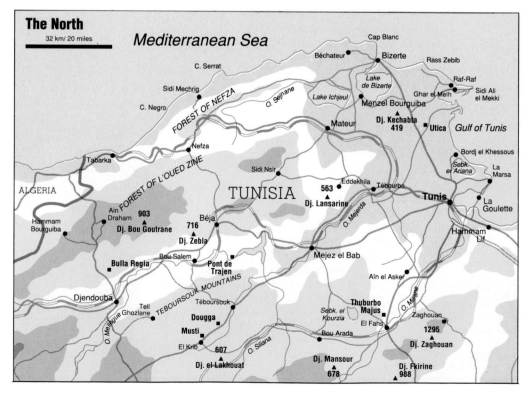

with varicoloured marbles, the pink and orange brought from Simitthu, the modern Tunisian village of Chemtou near the Algerian border, and the green imported from Greece. The room with the U-shaped floor decoration was the dining-room, or triclinium, formerly lined on three sides by banquettes.

The Punic necropolis to the northwest of the villas was the source of some of the material in the **museum** just along the road to the site; though important finds have been removed to the Bardo, leaving mainly mundane household items. Punic sarcophagi, found 12 ft (6 metres) below the Roman level, held amulets bearing Egyptian hallmarks – motifs of the Egyptian hawk god Horus or the goddess Isis. One grave dating from the 7th century BC contained a variety of Greek imports, including a cosmetic casket and vases depicting Trojan War scenes.

**Pirate lagoon:** From Utica, the road northeast follows the course of the Medjerda River to a secluded corner of Tunisia where, barely 40 miles (65 km)

from Tunis, women are under wraps from the age of puberty, not just in the Islamic *chador* but full-blown *sifsaris*. Girls of 10 or 11, apparently delighted by their new status, can be seen struggling to master the art of wearing one.

A black gauze veil, covering the whole face, compounded by a voluminous black *sifsari*, is *de rigueur* in **Ghar el Melh**. Such utter concealment is unique to this backwater village, and in keeping with its isolated position – all but cut off to the fore by a still lagoon (a vestige of the retreating sea that left Utica high and dry) and by Djebel Nadour behind – and a slumbrous countenance that belies an adventurous history of piracy and smuggling.

Like the Phoenicians, the corsairs of the 16th, 17th and 18th centuries took advantage of the North African coast's natural harbours to rest their fleets and plan their next forays. Ghar el Melh, or Porto Farina as it was once called, though already beginning to silt up, frequently afforded shelter for shallow-draughted vessels. In 1655 the English

House of
Cascades,
Utica's .

captain Admiral Blake and his men stole upon nine of the Bey's vessels lying peacefully in the harbour. They blew them all up, a feat which Lieutentant Colonel Sir Lambert Playfair described as "one of the most brilliant victories in the history of the British navy."

In the 19th century, when corsairs no longer controlled the Mediterranean, the Husaynids had ambitious plans to turn Ghar el Melh into a more legitimate naval base, but by then silt had made the harbour useless. In addition, it became obvious that Tunisia's navy could not compete with those of Europe, so the beys turned their attentions to expanding their army. Ghar el Melh became the headquarters of one of many new military regiments. Its three forts, later converted into prisons, are now used for housing and educational purposes.

**Best beaches:** Only the smallest fishing boats shelter under the old harbour's crumbling walls. A new harbour has been built at the end of the spit of land that curls round the side of the lagoon, accessible by a palm- and gorse-fringed road. A 3-mile (5-km) track off to its left leads past a succession of small holdings to **Rass Sidi Ali el Mekhi** – a swathe of white beach backed by green hills. Threats of a "tourist complex" have yet to be proved; so far it is colonised by nothing more than two palm trees half prostrate on its sands, a few derelict grass huts and, in summer only, a make-shift shop selling drinks and *casse-croûtes*. To enjoy it at its best, avoid weekends and school holidays.

Alternatively, travel round the headland to the village of **Raf Raf** and its 1-mile (2-km) white beach overlooking Ile Pilau, a sheer rock just offshore. Tourist development is low-key – a few restaurants and the Dalia Hotel (see *Travel Tips*) to catch the busy weekend trade – but to escape even this try the eastern, Cap Farina end. A back road leads to the pine forest behind this corner of the beach; from there it is a short walk through the trees and dunes.

**Cap Zebib**, beyond Rass Djebel (shops and a bank) and beneath the

**Fields near Ain Draham.**

steep village of **Metline** (small market for buying picnic provisions), has well-trodden cliff-top paths and rocky coves. Lanes in these parts are winding, the landscape hilly with a freshwater reservoir in every hollow. Terrain left marshy by the Medjerda river restricted road building until recently, when modern engineering succeeded to drain and conserve water where appropriate.

The **Lake of Bizerte** is really a salt lagoon connected to the sea by a canal first dug by the Phoenicians, who valued the cocoon of mountains around **Bizerte** (then called Hippo Diarrhytus) as an effective barrier against tribal raids. The Romans found this feature less useful, as communication was the key to their empire, but it again proved handy to the corsairs, who would slip quietly into the lake's waters and lie in wait for enemy shipping (200 Knights of Malta were unlucky enough to be captured in one raid launched from Bizerte). In World War II, Axis battleships could undergo repairs while sheltered from attacks by air.

When privateering diminished, so did the fortunes of Bizerte. The beys came here to hunt game, boar and a herd of buffalo (bred from a pair donated by the King of Sicily in 1729) inhabiting the wooded hills hereabouts. Alexandre Dumas, who visited in 1846, had happy memories of the place, calling it a "sportsman's paradise". But in 1869 an event in the eastern Mediterranean revived Bizerte's strategic importance and accelerated French ambitions in Tunisia: the Suez Canal was opened.

**Prized port:** Following the discovery of America, the Mediterranean became something of a backwater regarding international trade. Emphasis shifted to resources in the New World. With the opening of the Suez Canal and an easy trade route to India, it was thrust back into the mainstream of international commerce. France became anxious to establish strong naval bases that could outweigh the strength of the British in Gibraltar and Malta.

One of the first actions of the protectorate was to reinforce Bizerte and build

**Bizerte at twilight.**

an arsenal on the far side of the lake at Menzel Bourguiba, then named Ferryville after the French prime minister Jules Ferry, father of French colonialism. He openly said: "If I have taken Tunisia, it is to have Bizerte!" The Italians were furious; their foreign minister described the town as "a pistol levelled at the heart of Italy".

After their departure in 1956, the French held on to their military base at Bizerte, in spite of promises to evacuate it. This lead to resentment among Tunisians, who felt they were prevented from developing the port for large-scale commercial use, and ultimately to trouble. Bizerte became not only the most contentious issue of independence but, because his tactics backfired, the one most threatening to Bourguiba's early leadership.

Until then the most serious friction during the transfer of power had been caused by a team of Tunisian workmen who had bulldozed a French Embassy wall in order to carry out road improvements. But with Bizerte, Bourguiba de-liberately precipitated a crisis, in part to consolidate his position as leader and divert attention from internal wranglings. He wrote to President de Gaulle complaining that French forces had extended their airfield.

Bourguiba planned to back his protest with political demonstrations, but fighting was triggered when Tunisian forces fired at a French helicopter above the town. French troops retaliated vigorously. There was an unequal four-day battle which ended in 1,365 Tunisians being killed. The Tunisians aroused world-wide sympathy, but it did not budge the French.

Bourguiba faced an alienated French government, at a time when he needed their economic support, and criticism in Tunisia. His political future, jeopardised on all fronts, was saved only by the fact that his Neo-Destour party united behind him and did not break ranks. Gradually relations with France were resumed and in October 1963 French troops evacuated Bizerte.

Nowadays the town is where most of

**Dilapidation is part of its charm.**

those working in the heavy industries of Menzel Bourguiba live. It is also almost a resort. Hotels in town are basic and the handful of concrete hotels on Sidi Salam beach depressing, but along the corniche to the north of town are a number of establishments overlooking a gin-clear Mediterranean and shell-strewn beaches. A small hotel called Le Petit Mousse, with a bar open to non-residents, is well patronised by motoring French (see *Travel Tips*).

Bizerte's **Old Port** is as melancholic as a watercolour. Its quayside houses – some Moorish with tiny grille-covered windows, others with shutters and balconies typically French – and battlemented 17th-century **kasbah** at its neck are exceedingly picturesque. It seems reasonable to assume the port is safe from being tarted up; a *province* so blind as to allow the electric-blue block of flats sitting like a cuckoo in the port's midst is in no danger of realising the cracking potential for a marina and purpose-built tourist village like Sousse's Port el Kantaoui – only real.

**The old port isn't dead yet.**

Other than the Old Port and the kasbah, sights in Bizerte are modest. **Place Slahedine Bouchoucha**, which before the late 19th century was the beginning of a waterway linked to the main shipping canal (and probably the original channel dug by the Phoenicians) boasts a 17th-century fountain; Bordj Sidi el Hanni on the southern quay has been turned into a less than riveting **Oceanographic Museum**; while on a hill behind the Old Port rises the heavily-restored 16th-century **Bordj Sidi Salem**, open to visitors and, in July and August, venue for Bizerte festival events.

**Rare birds:** For the fit, bicycles are best in Bizerte. In a day, cyclists can explore the beaches leading to **Cap Blanc**, Africa's northernmost point, or the lanes to the beach at **Remel** between Bizerte and Cap Zebib, or the shores of **Lake Ichkeul**, twin of Lake Bizerte and a national nature reserve. The lake, designated by UNESCO as one of only two Wetland World Heritage sites (the other being the Everglades in Florida) is a

vital stopping point for birds migrating between Europe and Africa. They feed on the insect and plant life inhabiting its reed beds.

Widgeon, pochard and shovellers are regular guests, and rafts of 200,000 coots can darken its surface; 4 percent of the world population of the rare white-headed duck are residents. In the early 1980s the site was threatened by government plans to dam two of the rivers feeding the lake, but pressure from international wildlife organisations achieved a compromise: the rivers were dammed but sufficient supplies to the lake were maintained.

As most traffic heading west from Tunis takes the fast Medjez el Bab/Béja route, the C51 and the P7 roads from Bizerte across the northern foothills of the Khroumir Mountains to Tabarka are lonely stretches – the former piste in places and the latter corrugated by potholes that could virtually swallow smaller cars. That said, they pass through a veritable rural idyll, green and hillocky and overrun by flocks of fat-tailed sheep and goats in the charge of solitary shepherds. Routes to the coast are few, but there is piste access to Sidi Mechrig and Cap Negre, where families come to camp *au sauvage* for periods of weeks in high summer.

**Sedjenane** is the only village of any size before Tabarka. It does not run to a hotel, but there are shops for provisions, cafés and restaurants, and a bank (if you miss this one, there is another at **Nefza** 9 miles/15 km further on).

**Tabarka**, just 6 miles (10 km) from the Algerian border, is well situated. Mountains press close and, stretching into the distance to the east, there is a magnificent beach dissected by the Oued Kebir. It is backed by dunes and washed by waves almost strong enough to crash. Slumbering offshore to the west of the harbour is an island topped by a lighthouse and the shell of a **Genoese fort**, connected to the mainland by a causeway.

Tabarka's inhabitants make a comfortable living from coral-fishing, independent tourism and the export of cork;

**The Genoese fort of Tabarka.**

the town centre, though just a few streets which degenerate into rough tracks a few blocks either side of **Avenue Habib Bourguiba**, is animated in summer but never packed to the gills. A statue of old man Bourguiba, sitting like a much loved grandfather with his dog at his feet, occupying the roundabout on the way into town, sets the pace. The suggestion is that Tabarka is a place in which to wind down, a place to relax.

For the best accommodation, aim for Hotel Mimosas, whose whereabouts is emblazoned in large letters on the hillside; but, as everybody else does the same, unless you have booked you will probably end up in one of the lesser hotels along Avenue Bourguiba. The pecking order is Hotel Mimosas, Hotel de France, then Hotel Corail. Every evening a mad circus of hired cars rushes from one hotel to another in pursuit of a vacancy; invariably some of the classiest vehicles end up parked outside Corail (no hot water, hirsute bed coverings, sporadic electric lighting, but redeemed by a pleasant owner).

**Father of the Nation, plus dog.**

The atmospherically gloomy **Hotel de France** claims a special distinction. As a young revolutionary making waves in 1952, Bourguiba was kept under house arrest here before being transferred to France. The waiters in its dining-room, a tribute to the skills of taxidermy and described by the travel writer Eric Newby as a "hectacomb of dead game", commemorate this honour by refusing to allow anyone to sit at the table where he liked to eat.

**Christian enclave:** Source books differ on the history of the Genoese occupation of the island, but most claim it was acquired by the Genoese families of Lomellini and Grimaldi in 1542 when they bought it from Charles V of Spain, the Holy Roman Emperor. Apparently, he had captured the pirate Draghut, known as "the drawn sword of Islam", and after a lot of haggling with the Turks, swapped him for the island.

The Genoese wanted it in order to exploit the coast's coral reefs. Incredibly, in spite of the stone's throw proximity of the Muslim mainland, the island's 1,200 Christian inhabitants did exactly this for two centuries (supplementing their income by acting as go-betweens for the Christian and Turkish privateers) before being defeated and enslaved by Ali Pasha in 1741.

Tabarka's associations with Christianity reach back to Roman times, when it served as a port for the export of Simitthus (Chemtou) marble to Rome. *Thabraca*, to use the name the Romans inherited from the Phoenicians, was one of the early strongholds of Christianity. Its position on the border of what was formerly Numidian territory meant that it was developed relatively late, when Augustus settled some of his war veterans in the town; but it quickly flourished and during the latter centuries of the Roman Empire it became a prosperous settlement. Several of the late Roman and Byzantine Christian mosaics in the Bardo museum are from here. The fact that nothing other than a basilica – used as a concert hall during the annual summer festival – remains is because the French administration razed the ruins to erect their town centre.

The coral reefs that attracted the Genoese are still a major earner. Supplies are somewhat depleted and divers must swim ever deeper to cull the red twigs. Avenue Bourguiba has several shops crammed with coral jewellery. Sales assistants exert surprisingly slight pressure on browsers, unlike the mobs of children armed with wooden bowls, ornaments and hatstands (and, depending on season, pine kernels, walnuts or strawberries) stationed on the road between Tabarka and Ain Draham. They defy drivers to knock them down or stop. The bowls are worth a look.

Many drivers first attempt the road to Ain Draham late at night, when no more beds are to be had in Tabarka. Then its character, though hinted at by frequent redoubling and the need for quick gear manoeuvres, is shrouded in mist and darkness. The true perils and beauty of the road – plunging vistas and hairpin bends – are revealed the following day.

**Winter snow:** A handsome stand of eucalyptus trees flank the first innocuous stretch out of Tabarka, then for 7 miles

(12 km) the road climbs 3,000 ft (1,000 metres) into the wooded hills of the **Kroumerie**. The lower slopes, dotted with red-roofed farmhouses, are cultivated; the upper reaches are densely covered with cork, evergreen oak, pine, bracken and ferns. In winter there is snow. Boar, civets, foxes and deer live in the thickets; the last lion was shot in the forest in the early 1800s and the last panther as late as 1932.

It was the unlawful doings of the Khroumir Berbers that finally gave the French a pretext for invading Tunisia. In 1881 tribesmen made a raid over the border into Algeria (under French domination since 1830). There was nothing unusual in this, as Algerian and Tunisian tribesmen frequently snaffled each other's herds, but the French, who had been teetering on the Tunisian frontier for years, did not hesitate to seize their chance.

French troops met with no resistance from the Bey. In May 1881 their right to a military occupation and control over foreign affairs was sealed by the Treaty

**Lazy Sunday afternoon in Hôtel Beau Séjour.**

of Bardo; two years later a further treaty ratified the French Protectorate, which lasted over 70 years.

The Khroumir tribes have now relinquished their wild reputation and adapted to a steady life of farming and catering to the stream of hunters, hikers and summer tourists who stay in the village of **Ain Draham** at the heart of the Khroumir, only a few kilometres from the border. There are two hotels in the village: the wonderfully eerie Beau Séjour, covered by a vice-like creeper and furnished by a herd of stuffed bore, and the dull but beautifully-pitched Rayani. Brushing the border in the forests to the west (best approached on the signposted road from Babouch) is Hotel Hammam Bourguiba, a modern hotel cum clinic exploiting hot springs, which the ageing Bourguiba occasionally liked to visit.

Ain Draham's main street has a scattering of cafés, simple restaurants and shops selling carved wooden furniture and knick-knacks. The newsagent at the northern end of town offers an extensive range of international publications, including London's *Daily Telegraph* and *Sun*, rarely found outside Hammamet or Sousse.

This is one of the few areas in Tunisia where you find Tunisians hiking for pleasure. Whole families take to the hills. Well-trodden routes lead to the **Col des Ruines**, off to the left as the main road descends to Tabarka, and to the summit of **Djebel Bir**. From both, Algeria looks very tempting, but to proceed across the border is virtually impossible for the unprepared. Most Westerners require visas for Algeria, and strict currency regulations operate (see *Travel Tips*).

The countryside south of Ain Draham is also rewarding. The road winds through forests and past the **Beni M'Tir dam** (off to the left) before descending to the bald, elephant-hide landscapes around Fernana. Temperatures climb as the altitude drops. The low hills encompassing the Roman site of Bulla Regia (*see pages 194–96*) refract the hot blast of the Djendouba plain.

**Harvesting near Bulla Regia.**

# THE TELL

Do not let the description "Tell" raise expectations too high. It is an Arabic word for "mountain", but these uplands lying to the south of the Medjerda river are more in the league of the undulating plains of central Europe or the border regions of Scotland than anything Alpine. The area has abundant winter rains and many broad rivers to make it fertile and, as the numerous and extensive remains show, it was settled widely in Roman times and for several centuries afterwards.

Now the Tell is becoming depopulated with a drift away to the bigger towns for the greater regularity of work these are believed to offer. It is an area not much visited by tourists and, because of this, hotel accommodation is often fairly basic, badly maintained and not at all plentiful.

There are, however, two former Roman settlements on the eastern edge of the region that can be quickly reached from Tunis or Hammamet: Thuburbo Maius and Zaghouan. Those not planning to travel to the more splendid Roman sites (or to explore the rolling terrain of Tunisia's interior) can see both sites and sample the scenery comfortably in a day, and be back in their hotels well before dinner.

To reach Zaghouan take the Fouchana road out of Tunis (Route 3) and at Djebel el Oust, after about 19 miles (30 km), fork left. The road is a busy one and devoid of interesting villages save for **Mohammedia** (9 miles/15 km south of Tunis), and that is notable only for some bizarre 19th-century remains which are the result of Ahmed Bey's visit to Versailles and his attempts to emulate Le Roi Soleil.

More impressive is the 2nd-century Roman aqueduct that runs alongside the road after Mohammedia. This aqueduct brought fresh water from the springs of Zaghouan north to Carthage, a distance of some 45 miles (70 km); where hills impeded the route conduits were driven through them. Following destruction during the Vandals' incursion, it was restored by the Byzantines and, later on, maintained by successive Fatimid and Hafsid dynasties. Today, Zaghouan's waters are conducted to Tunis by modern pipeline.

The Roman site of Oudna is also just off this road, but its remains are scanty, its mosaics are now in the Bardo and the sole reward for the visitor is a none-too-imposing Byzantine wall.

**Ancient source:** It's not for nothing that **Zaghouan** is known as the most refreshing town in the whole of Tunisia. Its lofty setting rises from the fertile plain in a confident challenge to the crags and cliffs beyond; the many tinkling fountains encountered at every turn still do their best to give it the atmosphere of a spa – although, it must be said, the frenzy of new building, and the inevitable half-finished look of most of them, does not contribute to restful ambience. Indeed, Zaghouan is now administrative capital of its province and wants the world to know.

In comparison with what the rest of

**Preceding pages** dawn over the Tell. **Left,** the Capitol at Dougga. **Right,** nesting storks.

Tunisia has to offer in the way of Roman remains, those of Zaghouan (ancient Ziqua) are not impressive. There is a 2nd-century arch on the road out to the east and its location commands a fine view, witnessed in antiquity by two statues, and there is the so-called **Roman Temple of the Waters** in the town. In reality, this is a typical Roman fountain built around a spring as it emerges from the rock, common to Roman towns of any size almost anywhere. Dating from the time of Hadrian (AD 117–138), its 12 niches for statues are now vacant and much of the rest is heavily restored.

Of more recent date are the **Old Great Mosque** and a **Marabout of Sidi Ali Azouz** from the early 19th century; and the **New Great Mosque** from 1982. Mount Zaghouan, which dominates the town, looks a tempting climb but it is not as easy as it appears; out of season mists can descend abruptly.

The road from Zaghouan to El Fahs, a distance of 17 miles (28 km), is of secondary class for about half its length,

as far as Bir Halima; it is a pleasant drive, offering many good glimpses of rural Tunisia. The road twists and turns, uphill and down, presenting fine views of mountains to the south that succeed in being impressive without being spectacularly high.

The town of **El Fahs**, which was itself a very minor Roman town (though there is little left to show), is bustling, noisy and dirty – a mixture of North African and French provincial. For better or worse its like is to be encountered all over the Tell and a description of El Fahs is a description of many another. It is strung out along either side of the main through road. With some aspiration towards grandeur, the town makes this a dual carriageway; it has tall lampposts down the centre reservation and, on high days and holy days, strings of coloured lights and the national flag criss-cross from one side to the other.

There are the inevitable cafés opening out on to the passing scene; they are well patronised, for enforced idleness, the unwelcome consequence of lack of

**The Temple of the Waters, Zaghouan.**

work, is rife. Pastry shops and bakers, cluttered with crates of international soft drinks, are further social gathering points, as are the motor car repair shops. Behind the main streets are densely-packed single-storey houses separated by the tiniest of alleyways.

Any open and unoccupied spaces come into their own on Saturdays when El Fahs holds its market and traders of every sort flock in to lay out their wares and do business. In its honest-to-goodness, energetic fashion, El Fahs conducts its affairs without heeding too much the steady flow of foreign visitors who arrive looking for the way to Thuburbo Maius.

**Military town:** The Roman site of Thuburbo Maius is attained from El Fahs by taking the Tunis road north across the railway line and, after a few miles, branching left by means of an acute hairpin bend. Rather further from here than the 1 km indicated, the ruins of Thuburbo Maius come into view on the right-hand side; a none-too-obvious signpost on the right points the way to the car-park and the entrance to the site.

A vast and sprawling site located partly in a hollow and extending up a gentle hillside, it boasts a truly magnificent setting. To the north a ridge of conical hills with stubbly terraced cultivation shows the influence of settlers from the Eastern Mediterranean. Indeed, Thuburbo Maius was occupied before the Romans came: first by Berbers and then by Phoenicians with their characteristic farming methods; all took advantage of the fertile soil and good water.

Although taken over by Rome in 27 BC as one of many North African garrisons established for the veterans of Octavius's army, it was not until the Imperial 2nd and 3rd centuries AD that Thuburbo Maius assumed any importance and, even then, it had its ups and downs. Like many Roman cities in Tunisia, Thuburbo Maius suffered conquest by the Vandals and then a certain amount of reorganisation by the Byzantines, who abandoned the place after the Arab incursions of the 7th

**Mount Zaghouan, a tough climb.**

century. It was rediscovered only in 1875 when a programme of clearing and restoring produced the site as it is today; a great deal of the hyperstylosis (putting one stone back on top of another to re-erect fallen columns) was carried out in 1912.

The remains date from Imperial times and are typical of a Roman city of North Africa. Nearest the entrance is the towering **Capitol** (built AD 168) whose 30-ft (9-metre) high columns dominate the entire site; from this vantage point the extent of Thuburbo Maius can best be appreciated.

Below lies the **Forum**, built between AD 161 and 192 and restored, with some alterations in layout, in AD 376. The Forum, some 165 ft (50 metres) square, once had a colonnade around three sides while the fourth led by means of the surviving broad flight of steps to the **Temple**, sacred to the cults of Jupiter, Juno and Minerva.

To the rear of the pediment of the Temple it is possible to note the massive foundations necessary to support a structure of this size and weight, particularly against the effects of earthquakes – although Thuburbo Maius seems to have been fortunate in escaping tremors. Here, too, behind the base of the Capitol, were Roman **oil factories**, now marked by the deep basins for pressing and treading and the cisterns for storage.

Opposite the Capitol and off from the southern corner of the Forum is the **Agora**, or paved market place, a place of assembly second in importance to the Forum itself. Behind the Agora, on the southwestern side of the Forum, is the **Temple of Mercury**, built in AD 211, with an unusual layout: a ring of eight column bases now remains of the outer court. Close by are the foundations of a surprisingly haphazard **residential area**, a level of occupation somewhat older than the Forum. An imposing portico is, in fact, an entrance to latrines.

Off another side of the Agora, to the southeast, lie the **Winter Baths** in all their splendour; extending to a score of rooms and the customary sybaritic ap-

The Capitol at Thuburbo Maius.

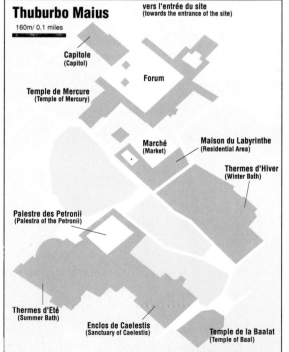

pointments – sunken pools, mosaics and latrines with urinals aplenty. A row of columns to the west marks the **Palaestra of the Petronii**; here the young men sported and exercised with wrestling and boxing as a run-up to the baths. A mosaic depicting boxers (now in the Bardo) helped archaeologists to discover the building's purpose.

Seek out the southern corner and look for alphabetic signs carved in the paving: these are part of the Roman game called Thirty-six Letters, an exercise in literacy. Keen eyes may detect a shrine to the god Aesculapius, once the Greek god of healing (and derived from the Egyptian Imhotep), but adopted by the Romans and here amalgamated with Eshmoun, possibly a local deity. Just to make sure they were finding universal favour, the Romans also set up (just below the hillside) a shrine to Baal and a sanctuary for the worship of Tanit, gods of the long-disgraced Carthage.

Adjoining the Palaestra are the **Summer Baths**, with three sunken cisterns and a great amount of mosaic,

restored in AD 361. On top of the hill there are a monumental storage tank, with a gallery running around the rim, and barely discernible remains of an **amphitheatre**. Ruins of outlying settlements can be seen to the east and, with a bit of luck, the Roman road that leads back to the Forum can be picked up too.

**The Northern Tell:** The road from Tunis to Medjez el Bab (35 miles/57 km) is undergoing widening and other improvements – resulting in the loss of the tall, mature trees that once bordered it in the French provincial style. It is flat, straight and dull; because of this and judging by the number of wrecked vehicles and the profusion of mobile police patrols along its length it must be reckoned dangerous and negotiated with care. The villages of Ghedir el Goula and Bori el Amri are passed almost without notice.

Those cutting across country from El Fahs and Thuburbo Maius to Medjez el Bab by Route 28, a distance of some 27 miles (45 km), will find a goodish road

**Palaestra of the Petronii.**

that is virtually deserted; the country is rather flat until beyond the halfway point; it has a peaceful rural ambience, with lush green crops behind forbidding hedges of cactus, and the by now familiar flocks of woolly brown sheep grazing at the verges.

From Goubellat, a poor one-mosque village with a woebegone air, the landscape becomes progressively more hilly and the cultivation fights a losing battle against the steady encroachment of rocky outcrops and scrub. The approach to Medjez el Bab, by means of a lofty cliff, shows why it was a place of such strategic importance.

**Medjez el Bab** is a middling-sized town strung out on either side of the main road; in addition to the usual cafés and garages it displays its sophistication with a video-club. It is a place of some age, founded by the Romans and, in the 17th century, settled by the Spanish; its strategic value led to long and bloody battles during World War II. A Commonwealth War Grave is laid out in imitation of English parkland a little way out of town in the direction of Testour and is a reminder that the British Army's tradition of burying soldiers where they fall is an economical one, for it is cheaper to do that than transport their bodies home.

Towards Testour (a further 47 miles/ 75 km) the road becomes progressively more interesting as traffic falls away. Each of the tiny settlements has its coffee house, its untidy, oily garage and its kebab stall with a plume of blue smoke billowing overhead and bloody fleece and carcase of a newly-slaughtered sheep hanging from a nearby tree. Presented as explicitly as this, the temptation of a roadside snack of kebabs loses a lot of its appeal.

**Testour** is as attractive a town as any on the Tell; its layout, enclosed by a loop in the main road that runs round a low hill above the Medjerda, comes as a welcome change after the customary one-street villages. That Testour is different comes from the fact that it was built during the 17th century by refugees from Andalusia and has managed

**The Theatre at Dougga.**

to keep a distinctive Southern Spanish character. Historically, the people of Testour were industrious and wealthy and, like all such people, took pride in displaying altruism with public works such as mosques and *medersa* and accompanying bath houses.

Testour has more than its share of finely-decorated mosques and a factory to produce countless thousands of glazed tiles is in business to this day – and not dependent on the tourist trade either, for its products went into restoring the **Great Mosque** quite recently. The mosque, in its traditional place at one end of the main thoroughfare, is a splendid affair with its roof an abiding tribute to local skills. Blocks from the ancient Tichilla, the previous occupation at Testour, can be looked for in its imposing walls.

Balancing the Great Mosque, at the opposite end of the main street, is the **Zaouia of Sidi Nasir el Barouchi**, constructed around the tomb of this holy man in 1733 and, as the attendant groups of women go to show, still a place for those seeking divine favour or a long overdue pregnancy. Another building of note is a mansion, now the **Maison du Culture**, built by a wealthy Jew for his mistress and remarkable for the scandalous story attached to it. Obsessed by the woman, he lost not only his heart and his fortune but also his head. He ended up committing suicide.

During June Testour holds an annual Festival of *mahlouf* music, an Hispano-Arabic music introduced by the Andalusians in the 15th century.

Just off the road from Testour in the direction of Teboursouk, at about 6 miles (10 km) and at a spot signposted **Ain Tounga**, are some remarkably complete Byzantine remains. Predominantly to the south of the road, these comprise fortifications with towers, gateways and walls, some bearing inscriptions in Latin (curious, because the Byzantines usually used Greek). Byzantine workmanship was inferior to Roman and much here looks in danger of imminent collapse. Above, on the hill, is the site of Roman Thignica, hardly worth the climb.

For 25 miles (40 km) between Testour and Teboursouk the road twists and turns and falls and rises as the country becomes seriously hilly. **Teboursouk**, which is worth a visit, lies off to the northwest of the main road, clinging to the hillside and winding around its contours. Although the town is in no way prepossessing in itself, the enviable location and resolutely rural air give Teboursouk an agreeable ambience. The visitor is, of course, here purely for the nearby Roman site of Dougga and a recommendable routine for taking it in is to spend the night at the 2-star Hotel Thugga down by the main road. It offers modest accommodation in rooms around a courtyard and has a restaurant that is more than adequate.

An evening drive back through Teboursouk and 4 miles (6 km) on across the Khalled valley to climb its far wall to Dougga is the approach to perhaps the most impressive site in the whole of Tunisia and, in Roman terms, a singular setting indeed. Park on the esplanade, watch the sun go down, and

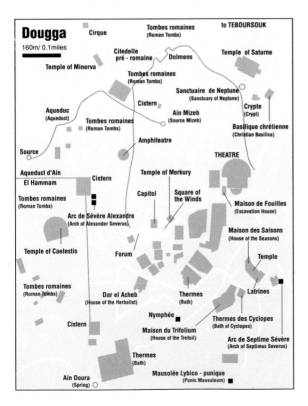

make plans to return early next day, for Dougga is seen best in the morning.

**City of temples:** Perched at a height of some 2,000 ft (600 metres) above the plain and laid out on a steep slope, Dougga is very different from the typical Roman city (which tends to be flat with wide, level approaches). Both its location and the non-Latin name indicate Dougga was already established when the Romans arrived in the 2nd century AD. In fact, Dougga's existence is recorded as early as the 4th century BC and, by the 2nd century BC, it was the base of Massinissa, a local chieftain who, to his enduring advantage, supported Rome against Carthage. After the departure of the Romans, the Byzantines built up and added to the fortifications, though thereafter it was commandeered by local Berbers. Only with the recent arrival of archaeologists has Dougga been cleared of its irregular inhabitants, who are now housed below in New Dougga.

The first of Dougga's monuments to be encountered is the rather oppressive

**Theatre** to the right of the main entrance; it was built between AD 166 and 169 and was funded on the fruits of the surrounding farmlands. Now heavily restored, it is used for the Dougga Drama festival in June, when it accommodates some 3,500 people (the painted numbers guide ticket-holders to their seats). A stiff climb to the top level offers a panorama of the site; it serves also to shake off any unwanted "guides" (if that fails, proclaiming *"archaeologue"* with conviction may suffice).

Above the theatre, to the north, are the remains of the **Temple of Saturn**, its few standing columns clearly visible from afar. The Temple dates from AD 195 and was constructed on the North African plan of courtyard, facade and triple inner sanctuaries; in the foundations was evidence of a pre-Roman sanctuary dedicated to the Carthaginian god Baal. Look out for the curious footprints carved in the paving and, like all who see them, speculate as to their function, if any.

Getting to grips with Dougga proper

**Once the breadbasket of the Roman Empire, Tunisia now struggles to supply its growing population.**

involves descending from the Theatre level, passing by the custodian's lodge and taking the steps down into the unusually tortuous street which leads through the living and trading quarters of the town. Note the grooves worn in the paving by the passage of wheeled traffic, the rows of striations cut in the slabs to give grip to the horses' hooves and the drainage channels. Just before the street opens out on to the square a small semi-circular structure on the left side is the **Temple of Augustan Piety** and, on the age-old example of one religious foundation being taken over by another, close by the remains of a mosque lie over a **Temple of Fortune**.

The **Square of the Winds** takes its name from the "compass of winds", a 26-ft (8-metre) wide inscription in the paving which names all 12 winds. It dates from the end of the 2nd century AD and is claimed to be the gift of the Pacuvi family, who funded other works in this sector – a **Temple of Mercury** to the north and a **market** to the south. But by far the most imposing structure is the lofty **Capitol**, instantly familiar from many a tourist office poster as an inviting symbol of Roman Africa.

The elegant (and therefore not typically Roman) proportions and its imperious position conceal the immense size of the Capitol, although some scale is given by the flight of steps that leads up to it – 32 ft (10 metres) wide and roughly the height of the facade. The building is dedicated to the gods Jupiter, Juno and Minerva and to the glory of co-emperors Marcus Aurelius and Lucus Verus. It was paid for by the Marci family (who also stood the cost of Dougga's Theatre) and erected during the 2nd century AD. All that remains of a statue of Jupiter that stood 20 ft (6 metres) high are fragments, now in the Bardo museum in Tunis, but the pediment carries a relief showing Antoninus Pius, the previous emperor, in difficulties with a giant eagle – doubtless a message of political significance.

Reluctant as the visitor may be to leave the glorious views from the Capitol, especially if blessed solitude pre-

**Women do much of the harvesting work – by hand.**

vails, the rest of Dougga beckons. To the west of the Capitol is the **Forum** and, as with so much of this unique site, it too is out of the ordinary: want of an expanse of level ground limited its size to the merely cosy. The enclosing wall is Byzantine.

West of the Forum and up on the hillside there is the **Triumphal Arch of Alexander Severus**, the great-nephew of the first African emperor Septimus Severus (who is commemorated by a Triumphal Arch on the eastern side of the site). Well worth seeking out on the western extremity is the **Temple of Juno Caelestis**; its semi-circular colonnade adds to Dougga's deviations from the Roman norm.

For a glimpse of demotic Dougga, head back along the way that leads to the Forum and the centre of the residential quarter; there, try to imagine how this looked in its heyday. Even if you picture houses at their original height and know these are dwellings of some substance, their close proximity to one another means it must have been as crowded, bustling and noisy as anything in today's teeming Third World. Continuing around the hillside there are lanes off to the left and the **Temple of Tellus** (the earth god) and, below the mosque and past more domestic remains (some with mosaics that are worth a peek) to the colonnaded **Baths of Licinis**, constructed in the 3rd century AD and designed for use in the winter time.

Further down the hillside is another bath house, called (after a mosaic floor discovered there) **Thermae of the Cyclops**. Most celebrated feature of this area is the 12-seat lavatory with its holes arranged in a horseshoe shape only 16 inches (40 cm) apart. Observers note that the users must have been very short in the leg or did not mind discharging their bodily functions in knee-contact with their fellows; but no one has allowed a simpler explanation: that each of the latrines was used in turn as the last one filled up, in the fashion of country middens in rural England until quite recently. A wall-mounted hand basin (it fills with winter rains) is an- **Near Bulla Regia.**

other tribute to the Romans' concern for scrupulous hygiene.

Adjoining the Thermae is the intriguing **House of the Trefoil**. Down the 21 steps is a central courtyard with rooms leading off, one shaped to give the building its name. Prudery (Muslim as well as Christian) avoids declaring that this was a brothel which, moreover, was a place of some social importance in ancient Dougga and an establishment of style and elegance. Just as any other trade displayed its sign to attract the public so this house of sexual encounters advertised by means of a stone phallus, now sadly gone.

Those wishing to take their leave of Dougga with loftier impressions can seek out the **Arch of Septimus Severus**, some way down the hill past the whorehouse, or the **Punic Mausoleum**, a rare relic of pre-Roman architecture dating from the 3rd century BC, despoiled in the 19th century by an ambitious British consul who filched its inscription for the British Museum and now, after a fashion, restored.

**Roman wheatbelt:** Southwest from Teboursouk the main road leads, after a distance of 42 miles (68 km), to Le Kef (more later); on the way the Roman sites of **Agbia** and **Mustim** can be visited but neither offers much to the visitor with a head full of the splendours of Dougga. Alternatively, striking north from Teboursouk to Bou Salem you attain the northern limits of the Tell and the towns along the western reaches of the Medjerda Valley: Béja, Djendouba and the Roman site of Bulla Regia.

This route is pleasantly scenic, with lush green valleys and rocky hills as far as Thibar. Then the hills fall away in favour of a flat, dull plain. Population here is low and traffic scant, just the men in French or Japanese pick-ups with the women and cattle in open back. Otherwise the means of conveyance is the big brown donkey, of a shade to match the sheep, the cattle and the soil.

The approach to **Béja** from Tunis offers the most dramatic view of the town. It clings to the hillside in a manner that suggests defence, an impression

**Workers dancing in the House of the Trefoil.**

that Béja's colourful history confirms.

Situated at the heart of fertile country, Béja has been a centre for the collection and distribution of agricultural produce since Roman times and, like all trading centres, it has traditionally been a place of wealth and substance. This, in turn, led to sacking and pillage: first, by the native Numidians, who rose against the occupying Romans in 109 BC, and then by the Vandals during the 5th century. But, by the Middle Ages, Béja was being described as one of the jewels of North Africa.

Nowadays, Béja is remarkable for being laid out on a grid pattern, a welcome change from the one main street and ribbon development. There is, however, not a great deal to see. A church on the central square owes much to Islamic architecture and the market that lies behind it is rewarding in that it caters for no tourist; there are a surprising number of mosques here too. The Byzantine fortifications on the hill are now the site of a military base.

A notable example of Roman civil engineering, **Trajan's Bridge**, can be found some 10 miles (16 km) south of Béja by taking route 76, a rough road in poor repair. It is wise to return by the better stretch that runs to Mastouta on Route 6.

**Djendouba**, to the southwest of Bou Salem, is a place of some pretensions; its pleasant tree-lined streets are disposed on the grid pattern and on the whole it has a well-kept, prosperous air. The Hotel Atlas is claimed to be the best in the region. Again the town has a war cemetery, but most visitors will be heading for the Roman city of Bulla Regia, just above the plain.

The route to Bulla Regia leaves Djendouba by the road to Ain Draham through a busy informal market, past the fine new hospital and the family planning clinic and along route 17 for 4 miles (6 km) to the crossroads. Taking the right-hand road for 2 miles (3 km) leads to the site of **Bulla Regia**, strung out over a gentle rocky slope on the left. Compared with Dougga, and even Thuburbo Maius, the location of Bulla

House of the Hunt in Bulla Regia at sunset.

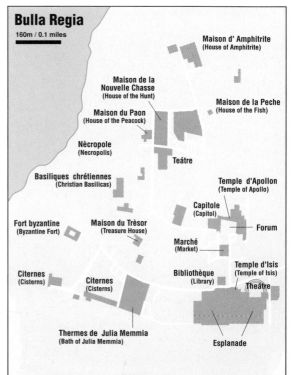

## Bulla Regia

160m / 0.1 miles

Maison d' Amphitrite
(House of Amphitrite)

Maison de la Nouvelle Chasse
(House of the Hunt)

Maison de la Peche
(House of the Fish)

Maison du Paon
(House of the Peacock)

Nècropole
(Necropolis)

Teátre

Basiliques chrétiennes
(Christian Basilicas)

Temple d'Apollon
(Temple of Apollo)

Capitole
(Capitol)

Fort byzantine
(Byzantine Fort)

Maison du Trèsor
(Treasure House)

Forum

Marché
(Market)

Temple d'Isis
(Temple of Isis)

Citernes
(Cisterns)

Citernes
(Cisterns)

Bibliothèque
(Library)

Theâtre

Thermes de Julia Memmia
(Bath of Julia Memmia)

Esplanade

Regia is really quite ordinary; but it does possess some unique features not immediately apparent. A small museum, rest house and parking place are on the right of the road.

The visitor enters the site close by the impressive structures of the **Baths of Julia Memmia** just off the roadside verge. These baths were erected during the 2nd century AD and excavated 1,700 years later at the turn of the 20th century, when restoration was also carried out. Besides the large halls and vaults around the central frigidarium, take note of the exposed clay piping that was used to form the vaults; this will be seen again elsewhere and given attributes not in keeping with its simple structural function.

Allowing Bulla Regia to retain its secrets until last, head up the incline to the north: a couple of **Basilicas** stand to the left of the track while on the right a mound affords a useful view over the entire site. The **Forum** and the **Market** are easily discerned, with the **Theatre** beyond and yet more **Baths** adjacent

**The Baths of Julia Memmia.**

(which suggests they were used by the players). Hard by the Forum is the **Temple of Apollo**, patron god of Bulla Regia, while back down the road is the **Temple of Isis**, a benign and beautiful mother goddess imported from Egypt, propagated by the Romans and the basis of Marian cults to this day.

Bulla Regia's treasures lie underground. In a curious and almost unparalleled fashion the dignitaries of this substantial city appear to have built their houses below ground level: a large hole was dug and, just as in normal construction, a dwelling put up within it, the roof at approximately the level of the surface.

Just why this was done, and why it was done here at Bulla Regia, is a matter for conjecture. One thriving hypothesis has it that, because this is an unduly hot locality, the Romans adopted underground living to keep cool. But it is not unbearably hot in all seasons and Roman skill and ingenuity would surely have contrived something more appealing in the form of, say, cooling foun-

tains to challenge the heat. As it is, the question remains unanswered.

To visit these subterranean villas involves an amount of back-tracking to find the man with the keys (tip expected for opening three houses). These form a triangle towards the upper level of the site; each is named after its most celebrated mosaic.

The **House of the Hunt** is at the west corner of the base and identified by the reddish colour of its columns; it is the finest of Bulla Regia's underground dwellings with its colonnaded atrium (a court open to the sky), its baths and latrines and its spacious chambers lavishly decorated with mosaics. That this bizarre style of building was taken seriously can be seen from the careful construction: note the relieving cavities in the superstructure and, again, the clay pipes used to form arches – not, as the locals claim, fresh air ducts to provide ventilation (they go nowhere and are mostly closed).

In the eastern corner is the **House of Fishing** and some strange marine mosa-

ics; it is of less elaborate and less elegant construction. At ground level are openings for ventilation shafts, while below a semi-circular fountain is installed. The third of these dwellings, at the apex of the triangle to the north, is called the **House of Amphitrite**, although it is Venus who is the star of the splendid mosaics; note too the Romans' love of the flamboyant in the figure of Amor astride a dolphin.

Part of the charm of Bulla Regia is seeing these mosaics in their proper setting; the small theatre contains a mosaic of a bear. It is hoped that pressures of tourism and its concomitant destruction will not force the authorities to move the mosaics to a museum – if the one at Bulla Regia is anything to go by they are closed more often than they are open.

**Border Country:** By returning to the junction with Route 17 (resisting the temptation to head north to Ain Draham and the coast: *see page 179*), and continuing west towards the Algerian border, some lesser but still interesting Roman sites may be visited. It is a minor road: virtually all the way to Chemtou it has a good surface but both the left fork to the site itself and the further stretches to Thuburnic are loosely-metalled tracks that need careful negotiating in the dry and must be impassable in an ordinary car when wet. But this is a peaceful, rural valley with a pleasing ambience to it.

The sites of **Chemtou** (originally called Simitthus) and **Thuburnic** have neither strategic nor agrarian importance. They are here because of deposits of a particular red-and-yellow marble, greatly treasured by the Romans and exported all over the empire. This garish material, known as "Numidian marble", was regarded by Romans as the very peak of luxury and extravagance and no palace of the Imperial city could be without it. It was first quarried during the 2nd century BC and by 80 BC a thriving export trade led to the foundation of the pair of townships; the quarries, deserted now, are represented by gaps in the hills. Access, no less than transportation, caused problems of

**Mosaic *in situ* in Bulla Regia.**

every sort but merely added to the marble's desirability. Hadrian, it is said, was especially enamoured.

Scattered around the hillside is evidence of workshops where preliminary roughing-out was done (to avoid moving a greater bulk than was necessary) and guardhouses for the overseers. Thuburnic, at the foot of the hills, is the more remote site, with a well-preserved Roman bridge but not much else, while Chemtou (also accessible from Oued Meliz) is only a few miles from the main road. The very ruinous remains of Chemtou, its broken-down **Theatre** and the piers of a **bridge** in the dry riverbed, are nevertheless on a scale to show this was, in its day, a place of quite considerable grandeur.

A wide range of smaller objects from these sites – reliefs, mosaics, carved heads and commemorative stelae – is displayed around the yard of the excavation house of the joint Tunisian-German archaeological team. There is no regular admission but, as long as no photographs are taken of unpublished material, it can usually be visited informally (a modest tip to the custodian ensures a welcome).

Regaining Route 6 at Oued Meliz means negotiating just about the worst track in the region; it is only 3 miles (5 km) from Chemtou but it seems a lot more. **Ghardimaou**, the frontier town, is 7 miles (12 km) west along the main road (Souk Ahras, the destination signposted, is 37 miles/60 km across the border in Algeria). The mountain scenery is some mild compensation for the disappointment of Ghardimaou itself; like many another town stuck on a frontier it hardly knows which side of the border to belong to and thus ends up with no character at all.

Ghardimaou is a busy crossing and is full of officials, which may account for its dreary look. **Ain Soltane**, up in the mountains and not easy to get to, is a wild hunting resort; it is close to an unguarded border region and should be explored with due caution.

**Commanding heights:** Travelling south to the major centre of this area, El Kef

*Mosaic in the House of Amphitrite, Bulla Regia.*

(exchanging the Arabic article for the French makes *Le Kef*, an acceptable variant), there is a choice between the rough but rewarding route from Oued Meliz by way of the Mellegue hydro-electric scheme, and the better Route 17 which involves returning to Djendouba. This road south has attractive views to both sides but, after joining the main road from Tunis, the final run in to El Kef crosses a flat plain. It undoubtedly helps to make the setting of El Kef more dramatic; there are many towns in the interior of Tunisia that cling to hillsides, but none has quite the appeal of El Kef winding its way around Djebel Dyr.

**El Kef** considers itself the capital of the western border region although its status is belied by the fact that the international railway line runs elsewhere; the surrounding area suffers severe problems due to lack of employment and there is a resentment that the central government appears better disposed to other parts of Tunisia. Not that this in any way inhibits the bustling populace of El Kef from doing what business it does in the most animated manner; its streets and alleyways teem with life as the most minor of enterprises is conducted with great ado. Whether it is due to this or the commanding location, even the weariest traveller finds new spirit on arriving in El Kef.

The town has a long history: it was settled in prehistoric times, the Numidians left evidence of their burials and it entered the records as Sicca when, after the Second Punic War, the Carthaginians sent their disaffected soldiers here. Under the Romans, who added the suffix Veneria because of the scandalous rites of Venus practised in its temples, it assumed great importance as a trading centre, accumulated wealth and displayed cultural and intellectual attributes. Following the Islamic conquest, El Kef was once again at the centre of strife over territorial claims; nowadays, it feels as if the wider world is passing El Kef by. Until it builds a decent hotel El Kef will have no tourist trade; perhaps the little-used Presidential Palace, advantageously sited up on

**Berber woman in La Kesra.**

the hill, could be given over to this.

The visitor exploring El Kef soon learns why the name means "The Rock". The main street, Avenue Bourguiba, may follow the contour of the hill and be reasonably level, but side streets are so steep as to be stepped. The town is in two parts: the lower one that has grown up around the ancient spring and offers local colour; and the upper, or Kasbah, only recently relinquished by the military.

Taking the main street to its northern end and climbing past the Presidential Palace brings one first of all to the splendid **Zaouia of Sidi Abdelkader**, with its multiple domes and distinctive minaret, once a library. Further along the Rue Ali ben Trad, after forking left, is the modest **Mosque of Sidi Bou Makhlouf** and the so-called **Basilique**, at one time El Kef's principal mosque of assembly, but now a museum.

**Sidi Bou Makhlouf Mosque, El Kef.**

Taking the right fork leads to the regional **Museum of Folk Arts and Culture** which contains some worthwhile examples of nomad artefacts and culture, with an entire nomad tent of the sort to be seen on the wilder parts of the desert plains of Tunisia. Just below it is the **Zaouia of Sidi Mizouni**, built in the 19th century and with inviting gardens in which to pause.

At the other corner above the Palace is the **Bab Ghedive** (Gate of Treachery); through it a ladder descends to a vast Roman cistern with 12 chambers; nearby are remains said to be the **Temple of Venus**, site of the erotic mysteries practised in Sicca Veneria. According to the Roman moralist Valerius Maximus, Carthaginian women visited the temple to sacrifice their virginity in the hope of encouraging good harvests.

Vernacular focal point of El Kef must be **Ras el Ain**, the spring that has served its populace since Roman times. Now it's just a hole in the ground, but the diligent may discern Roman channels for the water and, pressing through the maze of alleys, evidence of cisterns and baths. The nearby Hotel de la Source, recommendable at one time, is now

only for the avidly adventurous and backpackers on a budget. In all, El Kef is a place to be enjoyed less for a sense of style than for its vital self.

The visitor who does not savour its energy in the face of adversity and its unselfconscious determination to do what it has always done and do it in its own eternal fashion – noisy, dirty and often irritatingly sly – had best keep away. But those in search of the heart of an endearing country will find it beating in El Kef.

**The minor outposts:** The principal highway southwest from El Kef runs virtually parallel with the Tunisia-Algeria border but keeps resolutely a 12-mile (20-km) distance from it. To begin with it is purposeful rather than picturesque. The first place of any size is Tajerouine, 19 miles (30 km) from El Kef, and a sort of staging post for north-south traffic to meet that going east and west. Going to the west along Route 18, then south on Route 79 to Kalaat es-Senan, makes a roundabout approach to the curious, flat-topped mountain (4,170 ft/1,271 metres) called "Table de Jugurtha" after the Numidian chieftain who fought the Romans in this region during the 2nd century BC. The ascent is rocky; the view magnificent.

East in the direction of Dahmani (El Ksour), after about 19 miles (30 km) of decent road and a further 4 miles (7 km) of poor tracks, is **Medina**, site of Roman Althiburos. These ruins, which are not considerable and which have not yet been fully cleared, are so remote as to be only rarely visited. They are distributed above and around a river bed and comprise a **Triumphal Arch** with, near the centre, the customary **Forum**, **Capitol** and **Temple**, plus various outlying structures once graced by fine mosaics now safely removed to the Bardo Museum in Tunis.

South along the main route 17, a turning just south of Kalaat Khasba (a phosphate-mining town) leads to the Roman site at **Haidra**, known in ancient times as Ammaedara. As now, it was a frontier town and even when the Romans subdued the territories to the west it

Carpet selling, not unduly strenuous.

200

retained its importance as a trading centre; it was fortified by the Byzantines but then, following the Islamic conquest, it reverted to its original role of border outpost. It became associated with outlaws and cautious travellers avoided it.

As with Althiburos, the site at Haidra has not yet been systematically excavated, nor much visited. In many ways this adds to its historical value, for today's visitor can see how old Roman ruins looked to centuries of indifferent passers-by and the less curious generations of the past 2,000 years. Most impressive of the remains is the **Triumphal Arch of Septimus Severus**, completed in AD 195 and later included in the Byzantines' fortifications. Elsewhere there are traces of a **Capitol** and **Market Place** and, on the approaches, the piers of what was once a substantial bridge. Emperor Justinian, no less, is said to have commissioned the Byzantine fortress here; it is of suitably imposing size.

From Kalaat Khasba to Kasserine is 37 miles (60 km). The landscape is varied but barren. Cultivation is patchy and the farmsteads poor. There looks to be as much rock as there is soil: cattle are few and the sheep and goats are the hardiest varieties. The road climbs up to the bleak village of **Thala**, at over 3,300 ft (1,000 metres) a chilly spot, even in spring, where people wrap up against the cold. Some quarrying and industrial works scar the hillsides but activity appears to be limited to rather despairing agriculture and husbandry. Traffic is light even on market day (Thursday); just a few broken old cars taking a motley assortment of beasts away.

Over the crest of the ridge above Thala the road drops to the plain and snakes off to the horizon; the hills recede and there is more than a hint of the desert. The railway, and Route 13, join the road near Chambi. Some distance to the west and forming part of a natural amphitheatre is **Djebel Chambi**, at 5,065 ft (1,544 metres) the highest point in the whole of Tunisia – and singularly imposing to hold such a distinction. The

**Armed for anything in El Kef.**

run into Kasserine is remarkable for the sudden appearance of heavy traffic, mostly trucks laden with ballast and shedding dust as they go.

Tall green trees make **Kasserine** look like an oasis from afar but, while its streets are indeed lined with lofty palms, the town itself is a loud and uninviting administrative centre well stocked with military personnel.

**Splendid Sbeitla:** Northwest of Kasserine on the broad, tree-lined and much upgraded Route 13, through the dense olive plantations, and a little short of 25 miles (40 km) on, is the Roman site of Sufetula, now called **Sbeitla**, strung out among the scrubland on the left of the road. The dull modern town lies past the Triumphal Arch that once spanned the way east. At the other extremity of the site, beyond the Amphitheatre to the northwest, there is an ugly tourist hotel which offers views of the standing monuments. It is just one of several concrete buildings set on eminences surrounding the site, but at least their particular nuisance is silent. Not so the hordes of importuning locals on their motorcycles who invade the Forum with blaring radios.

Roman Sufetula appears in no records; all that is known about it comes from its walls and stones. An inscription of Vespasian (AD 69–79) is the earliest but it was doubtless settled prior to this. That the Byzantines were established here is shown by the churches they made out of temples and the fact that Gregory gave the area its independence as the tide of Islam was sweeping over North Africa; Sufetula fell to the Arabs in AD 647.

Most impressive of Sufetula's remains are those of the **Forum** and its three **Temples**, enclosed by a later wall. For want of inscriptions it can only be guessed these were put up during the 2nd century AD and, using the example of other Roman cities, that they were dedicated to Jupiter, Juno and Minerva. North of this area is the **Church of Vitalis** (his name in mosaic), remarkable on account of its sunken baptismal font; close by is the **Church of Bellator**

The stones listen in Sbeitla.

with similar lustral amenities; while the Church of **Servus**, converted from a pagan temple by the Vandals, is over by the theatre on the bank of the Oued Sbeitla. Look out for the **tomb of Saint Jucundus** (it is between the two central churches), who was martyred by his fellows, and for the complex of **Baths** with paved pools and hypocaust and a latrine with rows of seats. Most of these have fine, if fragmentary, mosaics; the honey-coloured stone used at Sufetula seems unduly friable and few carvings have any detail left.

The main highway that runs by Sbeitla continues east and north to the Sahel centre of Kairouan and from there north to El Fahs and Tunis; east from Kairouan it goes to the coastal city of Sousse. Serving as the arterial communication for this region of the Tell, the road is fast, boring and with a fair loading of traffic.

From Sbeitla to the Roman site at Makthar is a distance of about 62 miles (100 km). North along Route 71, across desolate landscape, the town of Sbiba is reached at 25 miles (40 km). Sbiba has a desert air to it and, although the site of ancient Sufes, the remains here are not going to detain the visitor long, if at all. **Jedelienne**, next name on the map, hardly exists on the ground and, further on, the self-important dual carriageway of **Rouhia**'s main street appears to be town planning that either went wrong or ran out of steam.

Some 12 miles (20 km) after Rouhia there is a crossroads. Turning right (northeast) leads after 15 miles (25 km) to the considerable town of **Makthar**. This is a run through dramatic changes of scenery: the road climbs between great rocky outcrops to lush upland pastures with cattle grazing, then passes through a ravine and on to rolling moors, and all in the space of a few kilometres. The northern approach from El Kef via Sers is blessed with delightful scenic stretches as well.

**Ancient and modern:** Makthar soon shows what an agreeable place it is. At an elevation of a bit under 3,280 ft/ 1,000 metres, the air is stimulating and

the town green, peaceful and really quite charming. The people are more than helpful, especially when it comes to giving directions: thanks to useless, and often misleading, road signs they certainly get plenty of practice.

Makthar is a place of gentle slopes; the new town, founded by the French in the late 19th century, and the old Roman site face one another through a Triumphal Arch. Numidians established Makthar as a base to repel the Berbers in the 2nd century BC and, in AD 202, it was the headquarters of the great Roman general Scipio before the Battle of Zama, the decisive battle of the Second Punic War.

Roman Makthar is entered by way of the custodian's lodge and museum. Best of the museum's exhibits is the splendid fish-and-fowl mosaic, but the collection of stelae, pediments and carved heads is noteworthy too, and there are smaller items such as lamps and jewellery (one necklace is particularly fetching) in dim display cases. The iconography of the representative objects is interesting in that it shows how "African" elements persisted against the influence of "Romanising" elements. There are other notable fragments stacked around the outer walls of the museum.

The site spreads out over a hill. The track up from the museum leads by a modest **Amphitheatre** on the left; beyond is the **Temple of Hathor Miskar**, an Egyptian goddess of love and beauty adopted by the Carthaginians. The track is crossed by a paved Roman street, running east–west. The spacious **Forum** on the east side is dominated by the **Triumphal Arch** dedicated to Trajan in AD 116. The Byzantines incorporated it in their fortifications, which extended as far south as the **Baths**, preserving the Roman parts in the process; the so-called **Basilica of Hildeguns**, a Vandal structure of the 5th century AD, was used by the Byzantines for tombs.

Taking the Roman street westwards, on the right-hand side there is the **Temple of Bacchus** and, opposite it on the left, the **Old Forum**, an irregularly-

**The Schola of Juvenes in Makthar.**

shaped market place from before the Roman occupation of Makthar. Beyond it, and on another paved Roman street, running north and south, is the **Schola** and its associated buildings. The Schola was a sort of club for the sons of nobles and the well-off Roman middle classes; it was part social club, part school, and part government training centre, where contacts were made and future careers advanced. One of the duties of its pupils was to supervise the collection of the Annona, the grain levied on farmers in the area. The **Quadrilobe**, with windows on all four sides, was where the grain was stored.

Close by the Schola is a cemetery with a very long history: megalithic tombs discovered here pre-date Rome by centuries. From the Roman period there are informal burials with reliefs and inscriptions containing homilies for the living. The more remote monuments of the site include the **Northern Baths** and the **Suffete Baths**, both much modified under the Byzantines, the latter becoming a church. A visit to

Makthar should conclude with another look around the museum; it must be the only site museum in Tunisia that keeps regular hours all year round.

**Hill village:** There are several worthwhile destinations from Makthar, but the one of choice must be that on Route 12 to Kairouan. The reason is the little village of **Kesra**, 10 miles (17 km) from Makthar. The road climbs and winds to an extensive mountain forest of Aleppo pine, with Kesra clinging to the side of a rocky cliff face at a height of 3,526 ft (1,075 metres).

A side road leads off and up to Kesra whose densely-packed houses leave only a narrow, vertiginous ledge for traffic. The houses are built into the side of the mountain and, by the side of the road, a waist-high conduit on posts carries clear, bright water down to green fields below. The view is spectacular. Kesra has that special ambience felt in the scruffier El Kef and the smarter Sidi Bou Said; they instil a feeling of well-being as well as a reluctance to leave.

So rewarding is this stretch of road it

**Kesra, worth a small detour.**

is worth continuing: in spring splashes of purple from fields of clover brighten the landscape as far as the road tunnel at El Garia and, some 6 miles (10 km) further on, a left turn leads to Ouesslatia, another 6 miles north. This too is an intriguing run: there are pale, whale-like mounds of rock by the roadside and an impressive range of scrub-covered hills not too far in the distance. Cultivation here is low-grade, the population sparse; only a few rural vehicles creep along the road. The bird-song has to be heard.

**Ouesslatia**, a neat and tidy place quite at odds with the usual Tunisian township, seems rather sleepy with not much business to conduct. Its streets are lined with clipped trees and the mosque has an attractively-decorated minaret.

The road to Siliana, Route 73, doubles back to round the range of hills and to negotiate the pass at their southern end. Here again are the pastoral scenes of sheep grazing and being watered by the roadside that make travel in the Tell so full of ancient resonances. And more:

suddenly, a few paces from the road as it prepares to turn up a hillside, is what looks to be a Roman tower. It stands some 26 ft (8 metres) high and appears to be on the verge of collapse. A few carved blocks lie at its foot but they have no legible inscriptions; the honey-coloured stone has weathered beautifully and lost its detail in so doing.

A tumbledown wall to the south, a ruined bridge just over the hill and a number of likely-looking mounds of earth suggest that this was a site of some significance. Yet nothing is indicated by a sign, no legend on a map, nor entry in a book. Thus does the country still have the capacity to surprise.

The scenery on the way to Siliana is picturesque in a rugged sort of way. There is a glimpse of the waters of the Barrage Lakhmes on the right-hand side, its flash of deep azure blue contrasting with the dun-coloured hills around. The entrance to this hydro-electric works is imposing enough – not least the notice warning "Entry Forbidden". **Siliana**, however, is situated on a

**Mother and daughter share the cooking and a joke.**

dead flat plain; it keeps its mundane affairs off its broad main avenue which, together with the well-kept hotel and the freshly-painted apartment blocks, aspires to some elegance.

The continuation northwards to Gaafour is hilly and bleak. The Barrage Siliana is impressive even though it will not be fully operational until 1992. This is virtually a desert area, as occasional sightings of nomadic families in black tents show. It is farmed only in small patches, but olive plantations thrive. Then, with one of the dramatic changes that make travel through the Tell so rewardingly varied, the approach to Gaafour is fertile country once again, the crops vivid green, the soil rich and red. **Gaafour** has a pretty location with hills to one side, the rolling fields to the other. It boasts a "Centre Ville" sign, and keeps its business quarter down by the railway.

This is as good an area as any in which to meander the country byways. There are several minor roads not marked on the map. Most have good surfaces and

appear to be newly constructed, but there is a lot of engineering work taking place related to the dams and, it must be borne in mind, some of the roads are being torn up in the process. Detours across fields are sometimes to be encountered. But if irrigation can transform the desert and turn marginal land into fertile then let there be irrigation.

The experience of going through this rural landscape is one of peace and quiet solitude. It is possible to go for an hour along a valley and see no other road vehicle nor habitation (fuel stations are no less scarce on the ground).

**El Aroussa** is typical of the neat backwaters of this region. It also has a railway: these smart, blue-and-white, narrow-gauge (and in this area single-track) SNCFT trains provide an alternative mode of transport. And, as this little enclave proves, they also provide a glimpse of some of the best scenery in the country.

It is, of course, no distance to the main Route 5 at Teboursouk, Testour and Medjez el Bab for the journey to Tunis.

**Left**, weaving in La Kesra.
**Right**, woman of the Tell.

# THE SAHEL

The belly of land that swells from the Gulf of Hammamet to the Gulf of Gabes and includes the cities of Sousse in the north, Sfax in the south and Kairouan like a mole on its back, is the most prosperous part of Tunisia. It is known as the Sahel. The region is well-endowed with natural resources – olive oil inland, crude oil off shore. Two million tourists a year are drawn to sand the colour of gold.

It was equally rich when the Carthaginians and Romans were here. The museum in the kasbah at Sousse displays evidence of sumptuous settlements, and the coliseum at El Djem is the last vestige of what was probably Roman Africa's wealthiest city, founded on profits from 36,000 acres (14,600 hectares) of olive groves.

The early Arabs placed even greater value on the region: Kairouan, the first Arab city in North Africa, developed into the fourth most revered city in the Islamic world, and Mahdia was the seat of the Fatimids, a dynasty that conquered Egypt.

Modern Saheli are renowned for their hard work and success in politics. Many beyical officers came from here, and so did half the students of Tunis's radical Sadiki College prior to independence. They were the early successes of a burgeoning middle class, which again prospered on investment in olives.

Bourguiba's right-hand men were Sahelian, and he was born in Monastir. New blood also rises here: President Ben Ali hails from Hammam Sousse.

But the Sahel is not immune to the natural disasters that plague less fortunate areas. Drought, followed by flooding, always threatens, and vital irrigation is affected by the massive drain on water by the big hotels. In 1988 weather conditions encouraged an age-old enemy to rise, and the Tunisian Army was mobilised. Locusts in swarms of more than 5 million took off from the Western Sahara and made straight for Tunisia's Sahel.

# SOUSSE

Few cities can boast a history as eventful as that of Sousse, renamed and resettled at least five times in the 2,800 years since its foundation. The Phoenicians were the first to appreciate the potential of this natural harbour on Tunisia's fertile eastern coast. It was a thriving trading centre more than a century before the founding of Carthage.

Hannibal used the port, then called Hadrumetum, as a base for his campaign against the Roman general Scipio during the Second Punic War. After Scipio defeated him at the battle of Zama, between Makthar and Siliana in central Tunisia, he returned to the city before fleeing to Asia Minor at the end of the 3rd century BC.

The city briefly became known as Hunericopolis when the Vandals invaded, but after a hundred years it was rechristened Justinianopolis by the Byzantines who, under the command of Belisarius, routed the Germanic settlers in 533. After the Arab invasion led by Oqba Ibn Nafaa in the 7th century, the town was largely destroyed (the Arabs, at that point a desert people, not seeing any virtues in a sea-based town); but, in calling the place Susa, Oqba gave it a name that was to last. Today, its former identities are commemorated by the names of the town's numerous hotels.

Notwithstanding their initial lack of enthusiasm, the Arabs quickly realised the value of Sousse's location and the town revived as a major port. It was from Sousse that the Aghlabids launched their successful invasion of Sicily which led to the sacking of the Basilica of St Peter in Rome in 846. Sousse survived the attentions of the Normans, Spanish, French and Venetians, and now the harbour, light manufacturing and tourism have consolidated Sousse's position as Tunisia's third city.

**Battle scars:** Access to the medina was improved in dramatic fashion in 1943 when Allied bombing destroyed part of the walls near the Place des Martyrs. Although much of the new town was flattened, the two great 9th-century monuments which dominate the northeastern corner of the medina – the Ribat and the Great Mosque – survived relatively intact.

The **Ribat** is one of a series of fortified monasteries erected along the north African coast by the Aghlabids and, later, the Almoravids (a Moroccan dynasty whose influence spanned the whole of the Maghreb). From Ceuta in Morocco to Alexandria in Egypt, they were intended to forestall attacks from marauding Christians and were manned by religious soldiers called *murabatin*. The exceptional thickness of this *ribat's* walls, and those of the Kasbah, is because Sousse has no natural defence against land attack.

Simplicity enhances the grandeur of the Ribat's design. Unlike many of the great monuments in Arab medinas it is not crowded by later buildings. A broad paved area surrounds the fort, allowing the visitor an unimpeded view. Seen from here the Ribat looks like an over-

**Preceding pages:** shady dealings in Kairouan's carpet souk; land of the olive tree. **Left,** Sousse, crowned by the Kasbah.

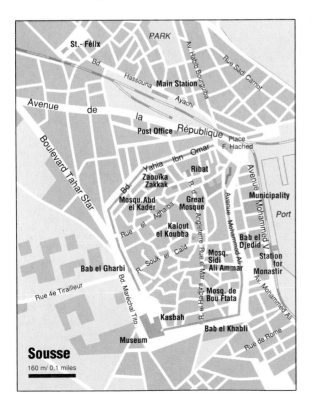

Sousse
160 m/ 0,1 miles

the-top set design for a Verdi opera.

The tall narrow entrance is framed by two columns, one of which has almost eroded away. This leads into an open rectangular courtyard, which slopes downward to a central drain. The courtyard is surrounded by an arcade leading to a series of small cells, home to the warrior monks who studied here in time of peace. They are about 10 ft (3 metres) square with high arched ceilings. Each has a small niche in one wall. Although their construction is virtually identical, it is worth having a peak in each cell because some are used to store fragments of carved or painted stonework.

Stairs by the main gate lead up to a broad concreted walkway which forms the roof of the ground floor arcade. Cells, slightly larger than those below, lead off it. There is also a prayer hall on this level, near the stairs; look out for the dome above the *mihrab*. At this height the walls are a solid 6 ft (2 metres) thick.

A further set of stairs takes you up to the ramparts, where there is a room above the main gate with a set of four slits in its floor. These might have been used to channel boiling oil (the olive variety) on to enemies or to raise a portcullis. (They are not roped off, so be careful not to allow small children to wander around unsupervised).

The circular tower (or *nador*) was used by the Germans to spot enemy aircraft during the war. The reward for climbing the 75 dark steps is a view across the medina, the new town and the port, and down into the courtyard of the Great Mosque, at its most animated on Friday afternoons after prayer.

The **Great Mosque** is a little way southeast of the Ribat. Tickets cost 300 millimes and are sold by a guardian who sits in the shade on the far side of the square in front of the entrance. The mosque was commissioned by Abou el Abbas Mohammed, an Aghlabid Emir, in 850. Like the Great Mosque in Kairouan, it has the appearance of a fortress, but the "improvements" of succeeding generations have been carried out less obtrusively, making it aesthetically more pleasing.

**A colourful market.**

214

The courtyard is paved in a pattern of concentric rectangles. Normal slabs alternate with fragments set in purple mortar. As in the Ribat, the floor slopes down to a central drain which carries water to an underground cistern. A colonnade runs around the courtyard, above which a single line of stylised Koranic inscription is carved. The arches of the colonnade are supported by short square columns, a style continued inside the prayer hall (through the series of large varnished wooden doors, but only Muslims are allowed inside). In one corner of the courtyard a broad roped-off staircase leads up to the ramparts, an octagonal sundial and a squat domed minaret added sometime in the 11th century.

Many of the traditional industries of Sousse's medina died when the city found its niche as a tourist resort; but between the Ribat and the medina wall, just to the north, there still exist several streets dominated by woolworkers' houses. Piles of wool waiting to be spun can be seen in small workshops; freshly-washed and dyed threads hang outside to dry.

On the other side of the Ribat, opposite the main gate to the Ribat, is the **Rue de Sicile**. At one end is the succinctly named Café Ribat Drink and at the other, neatly framed by the buildings of the narrow street, is the minaret of the **Zaouia Zakkak**. Its octagonal shape is evidence of Turkish origin; the third of its four storeys is largely open, with loudspeakers peeking out between the painted tiling. Its small proportions make this one of the most attractive minarets in the town.

The **Rue de Paris** leads into the centre of the medina from the southern corner of the Great Mosque. It is the main tourist route and the first few times you walk along it you will be plagued by eager salesmen suddenly emerging from their shops.

**Markers and mosaics:** The **Rue d'Angleterre**, running parallel to the Rue de Paris, leads into a vaulted brick **souk**. Clothes and trinkets give way to food. Cows' heads hang on spikes –

*Avenue Habib Bourguiba at night.*

their eyes shut and mouths artistically stuffed with herbs; young boys look after open carts of snails, periodically retrieving their slow-moving charges. The fish market is on the **Rue de France**, which runs along the section of the medina wall nearest the port – to get there follow your nose.

Rue de France leads past the Place Djabanet el Gourba, where the children of the Medina Club play football. Just afterwards, a right turn heads up a long hill to the kasbah in the southwestern corner of the medina.

The kasbah was constructed around the 9th-century **Khalef el Fela Watchtower**, which stands at Sousse's highest point. It now houses the town museum.

Sousse's museum is well worth visiting. Even those who have seen the Bardo in Tunis will be delighted and impressed. It contains many fine mosaics excavated in the area, some from the 3rd and 4th-century catacombs which were discovered near Sousse at the beginning of the 20th century. They are all well laid out around small cloisters, and are supported by explanations in Arabic and French.

The museum entrance leads into an open courtyard full of shrubs and statues. This leads to a large hall containing, as one might expect, several mosaics on the theme of the sea, including one of Neptune being pulled through the water by seahorses and followed by a dolphin, and another well-known mosaic depicting varieties of fish.

Just before you get to the museum's garden there is a badly-signposted corridor to the right which leads to another three rooms. These contain oil lamps, statuettes and Carthaginian tombs from Sousse and other parts of the Sahel, some of which were discovered under the Kasbah itself.

On the far side of the garden, three galleries contain some of the largest and most impressive mosaics in the museum. Look out for the calendar depicting the seasons and note how often the swastika (a primitive religious symbol) was used as a decorative device. One hall has a small set of steps to allow a

**Tunisians like to be well equipped.**

better view of a vast deerhunt mosaic covering one wall. In a small alcove sits a sad statue of Priapus – painfully mutilated in a later age.

**Downtown:** The focal point of Sousse is the **Place Farhat Hached**, where the port, the new town and the medina meet. The port is to the east. A large basin allows cargo ships to dock very close to the centre of the town. The roads between the port and the medina walls contain a plentiful supply of good but cheap fish restaurants.

The new town is north of the square. On the other side of a perilous road and railway junction is **Avenue Habib Bourguiba**, the main street of the new town, lined with hotels, cafés and tourist shops. There is a good department store at the southern end (with a food hall upstairs) and, on the other side of the road, a small newsagent which sells foreign newspapers and some English-language books.

Avenue Habib Bourguiba and Route de la Corniche have the best selection of places to eat in Sousse, especially when

Restaurant Les Sportifs (Habib Bourguiba) reopens after renovation. Cheaper rotisseries can be found along nearby side-streets. Most of the cafés have tables on the pavement and, during summer, are crowded with tourists coming in from the hotels along the coast. The *Topkapi* nightclub has been around for years. If you have yearnings to dust off that old medallion, this is the place; you won't feel inhibited by Ibiza-style fashionableness. Many of the hotels have discos, pumping out staple Italian pop and charging sky-high prices for drinks.

The northern end of the Avenue Habib Bourguiba joins the **Boulevard Hedi Chaker** which runs next to a long sandy **beach** stretching all the way to Port el Kantaoui. The water here is warm but reputedly polluted. Back from the beach are the hotel complexes. Their swimming pools are excellent. If you are not staying in a hotel with a pool, a confident demeanour should allow you to enjoy one of these without too many questions being asked.

*Sousse beach, not for the solitary.*

SCANDIC
SNACKBAR

The stretch of coast north of Sousse has been the front line in the conflict between Tunisia's traditional lifestyles and the homogenised demands of international tourism. Ancient villages bravely stand their ground against the relentless advance of whiter-than-white holiday monoliths, which reach their zenith at Port el Kantaoui, and the plush Western-style villas of Tunisia's elite. The coast road stays a respectful distance inland. Glimpses of President Ben Ali's luxurious, well-guarded residence are routinely pointed out by the taxi-drivers who make their living from the coast-road run.

It is easy to sneer at **Port el Kantaoui**, to recoil in horror at the thought of a "traditional, Andalusian-style" harbour whose ancient origins can be traced back to the 1970s. But, by the standards of most holiday developments, it has a lot going for it. Based on Sidi Bou Said, the fashionable village north of Tunis, the development centres on a large artificial harbour providing moorings for yachts from all over Europe.

**Model village:** A broad paved promenade, at night attractively spotlit, runs around the marina, with shops, restaurants, terraced cafés and apartment blocks leading off. Although the Andalusian style is consistent – whitewashed walls, flat roofs, arches and shaded balconies overlooking the water – the architects have avoided relentless uniformity. The white architecture is offset by colourful splashes of palm, jasmin and bougainvillaea.

Side streets are authentically winding, but unauthentically clean. Their shops sell mostly holiday essentials – food, medicines, stamps, postcards, books, newspapers and nylon camels which would be a conversation piece on any suburban sideboard.

Watersports and riding are available from the long sandy beach to the north of the harbour. Behind the beach are the hotels, dominated by the vast Marhaba complex, a grotesque and expensive cross between Sleeping Beauty's castle and a sheik's palace.

Pleasure boats, some floating restaurants, leave the promenade regularly. The food in most of Port el Kantaoui is bland international cuisine, although the Restaurant Ezzarda's menu is a little more adventurous. For those of more modest means, however, there are worse ways to spend an evening than sipping freshly squeezed orange juice in a waterside café as you listen to the badly amplified strains of Phil Collins's last album but one.

If you accept the fact that Port el Kantaoui has little to do with life as a normal Tunisian lives it, then it is still worth a visit to see how a tailor-made holiday resort should be done. If you find yourself lulled into a belief that this *is* the real Tunisia, just keep an eye open for the notices nailed to every wall: "Cleanliness is the collective responsibility" and "Green areas are created for you. Save them." Tunisia? More like Disneyland.

Several picturesque villages lie just to the northwest of Sousse, notably Akouda, Hergla and Takrouna. Akouda, 4 miles (6 km) away, is the easiest to reach because it is not far off the coast road that heads up to Nabeul. Local buses go there from the north wall of Sousse's medina.

**In contrast:** Like most hill villages, **Akouda** is dominated by its mosque. Its narrow, bustling streets have an unthreatening shabbiness. Akouda has been economically depressed since the mid-19th century, when the bey doubled the area's taxes. The villagers, together with tribes from the interior, staged a successful revolt, but lost their victory when internal schisms allowed the bey's forces to regain the upper hand. Heavy fines were imposed, property was seized and villagers were tortured and killed.

**Hergla** is a delightful village, clinging precariously to a cliff top 12 miles (20 km) north of Port el Kantaoui. Just after the Kantaoui junction, the bus from Sousse heads sharply inland through the **golf course** (see *Travel*

Preceding pages: Port el Kantaoui's immaculate marina; paragliding, one way to escape. Below, all aboard for Toy Town.

*Tips*) and the half-finished backlots of more hotels. After winding through olive groves and joining the Tunis road for a few miles, it darts back to the coast and climbs up to the clifftop village. If you drive yourself you can stay on the coast route.

The village mosque in Hergla overlooks the sea from one side of the main square. Thick whitewashed walls surround the open courtyard and the prayer hall is topped by a low dome. The mosque was built in the 18th century and is dedicated to Sidi Bou Mendel, a Hergla man who, according to local legend, sailed home from Mecca on his handkerchief.

The courtyard looks across a set of rickety blue metal gates to a graveyard, the tombstones topped with white tiles, turquoise paint and sometimes sleeping goats. The steep slope gives an unnerving impression that the graves are about to tip up and slide into the sea.

At the bottom of the cliff large boulders have been used to create an artificial harbour and boatyard, principally for small fishing boats. The sickly smell is of drying fibreglass. If you walk to the end of the spit there is a fine view across the graveyard to the village.

On the inland side of the main square there are a couple of half-hearted basketwork stalls. There is also a spartan but mercifully cool café next to the mosque. It is a good spot to wait for the buses back to Sousse, which wheeze their way up to the cliff-top every three hours or so.

Slightly further from Sousse (about 25 miles/40 km) and 9 miles (15 km) inland is **Takrouna**, pitched like an eagle's eyrie on a rocky outcrop on the Enfidaville plain. The area was the Germans' last line of defence in the Tunisian Campaign, and site of much bloodshed – the fallen are buried in cemeteries round about – but now it is a popular tourist spot. Takrouna's villagers, including the women, impeccably dressed in all their Berber finery and touting souvenirs, lie in ambush for the coaches that arrive regularly from Sousse and Hammamet.

**Takrouna, lying in wait above the Enfidaville plain.**

**Monastir** has several high-rise hotels, yet succeeding to dominate the town is the family mausoleum of its most famous son, Habib Bourguiba, born here in 1903. The multi-million-dinar edifice topped by gold and green domes and gold-tipped minarets looms over a cemetery of modest white tombstones and *koubbas*. At night it is illuminated like Brighton Pavilion.

The town did well out of Bourguiba's long presidency, receiving a succession of expensive favours. Within three years of his coming to power $12 million had been spent on his home town, one-eighth of Tunisia's annual budget at the time. It quickly gained all the modern city trappings, such as an international airport, municipal gardens, imposing new mosque and public buildings, and was developed as a tourist resort with a marina for 400 moorings. In 1975 it acquired a university.

Despite such efforts, the former textile and fishing community never quite carried off the role of showcase city assigned to it. Although Monastir has a long history – an 8th-century *ribat*, a great mosque dating from the 9th century – it feels like a new town. Compared to its neighbour Sousse, with which it has much in common historically, it lacks heart. Out of season everyone retreats into the medina and its down-town area is deserted.

Nonetheless, the people of Monastir are proud of their new city. In the wake of Habib Bourguiba's downfall and his replacement by Ben Ali in November 1987 they were crestfallen and disbelieving. One of the first public relations stunts of the new regime was to stage a carefully organised celebration in Monastir's town centre. A cheering rent-a-crowd carrying placards praising the new president was ferried in and as soon as the clapper-board operator signalled action the television cameras rolled. Locals could have been forgiven for thinking they were witnessing the latest shenanigans of IMF (International Monastir Films), a film location agency based in the town.

Posters of Monastir usually feature views of the **Ribat of Harthema**, either from the sea or from an angle which includes the Great Mosque next door (great in name rather than size and dwarfed by the Habib Bourguiba Mosque opposite). Like the one in Sousse, the Monastir Ribat was a defensive monastery. It was built in 796 by Harthema ibn Ayun, who served in the army of Harun el Rashid, Caliph of Baghdad and hero of *The One Thousand and One Nights*. As one of a series of *ribats* built along the North African coast, its purpose was to protect the new territories of Islam from attack by Christians. The *murabatin*, its holy inhabitants, were expected to defend *besiff*, "by the sword", if necessary.

The building has been heavily restored over the centuries and is always undergoing repointing and other works, partly because it often doubles as a film set (the studios of IMF are in front). On the right-hand side as you enter there is a museum containing old but not very impressive exhibits: a few gold and silver coins, Fatimid and Abbassid ceramics, oil lamps, papyrus parchment dating from the 8th and 9th centuries and some Persian miniatures.

The museum is situated just below the *nador*, the look-out tower (a good position for making out the fragmentary layout of the town). On the southern side of the tower is an area known as the women's *ribat*, the purpose of which remains a mystery. Although there is a story that three days spent in the garrison opened the gates of paradise, this is supposed to refer to the extreme spirituality of the *murabatin*, not to the fact that they had a harem.

The **Mosque of Habib Bourguiba**, directly opposite the Ribat, was built between 1963 and 1966. Alas, non-Muslims are not able to judge its multi-vaulted and pillared pink marble prayer hall hung with glass chandeliers, or its *mihrab* inlaid with elaborate gold mosaic and flanked by onyx columns – not even from the courtyard.

Preceding pages the Bourguiba mausoleum in Monastir; looking for a buyer. Below, sheep, no respecters of the dead.

228

**Resting places:** Begun at the same time as the mosque, the **Bourguiba family mausoleum** was expanded several times after its initial completion. The older President Bourguiba got, the more he embellished his tomb. In 1978 the shrine was considerably enlarged and in 1980 the minarets were added. Finally came the domes: the smaller green ones to mark the tombs of his parents and second wife, the 18-carat gold-plated one for himself.

A wide palm-lined esplanade, dissecting the cemetery, leads up to the gates of the mausoleum. At its foot are two octagonal open kiosks; one of them honours those who died fighting for independence, the second awaits a new cause to commemorate.

**Route de la Falaise**, behind the cemetery, leads to most of the large hotels, strung all the way past the airport and on to Sousse. A Toy Town train operates between the city centre and the hotels, delivering guests at the right door. They are nearly all three or four-star establishments booked up by tour operators. Monastir's cheapest decent hotel is the one-star Hotel Yasmine on Route de la Falaise, but it is likely to be full in summer (see *Travel Tips*).

Exit roads on the other side of town plunge into the Sahel conurbation of Ksar Hellal, Moknine and Djemmel. These villages were once quite separate, and committed rivals. Their feuds over land were an obstacle which the Neo-Destour party encountered in 1947 when it was trying to organise itself in the region. Ksar Hellal and Moknine, barely more than a mile apart, each insisted on having its own branch.

Not until Mahdia, a still unspoiled town 30 miles (50 km) down the coast does the road begin to shake off new urban development.

**Mahdia** was the original home of the Fatimid dynasty, which for a while conquered all the Muslim lands from Morocco to Egypt. It takes its name from *El Mahdi*, meaning saviour, the title adopted by the town's founder, Ubaydalla, a leading promulgator of the Shi'ite branch of Islam which emerged

*Jasmine to wear behind the ear or lace a pot of tea.*

to challenge the mainstream Sunni movement after the Prophet Mohammed's death.

The Shi'ites believed that the caliph should be descended from the Prophet rather than elected, and that a descendant of Ali (the last caliph related to the Prophet) would emerge as Mahdi and save mankind. Ubaydalla, who claimed descent from Ali and the Prophet's daughter Fatima, decided to seize the Mahdi title and set about establishing a Fatimid dynasty which would conquer the Islamic world.

He set up base in Tunisia's Sahel. First he overthrew the Aghlabids in Kairouan, then he moved to the coastal village he called Mahdia, where he was better placed to further his ambitions in the Muslim East. One of his ways of financing his plans was to make all pilgrims to Mecca pass through Mahdia and tax them for the privilege. By 969 his descendants had conquered Egypt.

The Fatimids' rise in Tunisia didn't go unchallenged, but Mahdia's location on the needle-sharp peninsula of Cap Afrique was their best defence. Kharidjite opposition, fomented in Kairouan and supported by the Berber tribes, could not penetrate Mahdia. Abou Yazid, a Kharidjite revolutionary, succeeded in capturing Tunis and occupying Kairouan, but he stormed Mahdia for 10 months without success, and in 947 he died from his battle wounds. According to the historian Ibn Khaldoun, he was given a suitably humiliating send-off by his victors: he was flayed, stuffed with straw and dumped in a cage with two monkeys.

When the Fatimids moved their headquarters to Cairo, Mahdia remained a valuable strategic prize for those seeking to dominate Tunisia's seas, religion or land, including Roger II of Sicily in 1149, the Turkish corsair Draghut in 1547 and the Knights of Malta in the 17th century.

Due to the Spanish, who blew up the town's 35-ft (10-metre) thick walls in the 16th century in their attempts to ferret out Draghut, the deep gate known as the **Skifa el Kahla** (black passage) is

**Refreshment in Mahdia's Place du Caire.**

the only evidence of Mahdia's famous defences. It too was damaged, but the Spanish rebuilt it for their own purposes – to take cannon.

The gate leads into the main street of the medina, **Rue Oubad Attah el Methi** (Tourist Office just on the right), which eventually runs to one of the most atmospheric squares in Tunisia, the tiny **Place du Caire**, sleepy in the afternoons, an animated social club at night. After eight in the evening the square is packed with people playing cards and dominoes and enjoying a smoke. It is a firmly male party; though occasionally white-veiled figures creep out of the Moustafa el Menzah Mosque and vanish like shy apparitions.

**Fortress mosque:** A short walk beyond the square leads to the **Great Mosque** and the rear of the town. The mosque is a replica of the original Fatimid mosque Ubaydalla built on this spot in 916. Bourguiba commissioned its reconstruction in the 1960s, when the original was deemed beyond repair, as part of a public works programme that also included restoration of the Great Mosques of Sousse and Kairouan. Its austere appearance is typically Fatimid: fortress-like walls, no minarets, an imposing main entrance that was reserved for the Mahdi and his cohorts (in stark contrast to the Sunnis, the Shi'ites are elitist). When the Spanish occupied the mosque in the 16th century they had no compunction about turning it into a church and using its courtyard as a cemetery, though when they evacuated the town they were careful to exhume their dead and take them too.

The Muslim cemetery on the peninsula's tip, lapped by the sea on all sides, makes a pleasant walk, especially in spring when flowers are thick. A broad path picks its way through the white graves, each carefully oriented so that the dead (who are buried on their sides) can face Mecca. The ruined arch on the rocks below is the last remnant of the **Bab el Bahr**, old sea gate of the Fatimid port; and the **fort** (admission 800 millimes) at the cemetery's summit was built by the Turks in 1595 and later used

**Weaving a marriage wrap in Mahdia.**

# THE OLIVE

Even – indeed, especially – in Roman times, one of Tunisia's most valuable assets was its oil, the fuel which turned the wheels of empire, burning in lamps and providing heating. It was not oil of the petroleum variety, but olive oil, used in cooking as well but never as, say, a salad dressing. It was considered unfit for human consumption.

The olive tree was not indigenous. The Phoenicians first imported it, and there are groves still to be seen around their old coastal settlements of trees so gnarled as to appear old enough to have been part of the original consignment.

It was the Romans, however, who put the cultivation of olives on an industrial footing. One of the anomalies of modern Tunisia, as mentioned elsewhere in this book, is how an unprepossessing town like El Djem could once have required or justified not only its own massive amphitheatre, with seating for 30,000, but also a second one only slightly smaller a few miles away.

The missing factor is the immense Roman irrigation system which transformed the Sahel into rich agricultural land. The olive trees alone survived the destruction of the irrigation system by the Vandals, although many of these were lost in the scorched earth tactics later used by the legendary guerrilla queen El Kahina against the Arab invaders. Nevertheless, trees re-established in endless groves, constituting practically the only scenery on long stretches of the GPI motor route, are as much as survives to prod the imagination into a vision of how the Sahel must once have looked. The area around El Djem was rich enough not only to support a population inconceivable today but one which felt able to challenge Rome itself for control of the empire.

Olive oil was second only to Tunisian grain in the convoys which plied across the Mediterranean and whose arrival brought crowds running down to the Italian ports, but with the drop in grain production it eventually became one of Tunisia's largest exports and remained so until modern times. In Islam, the olive tree is associated with light and virility, and with the Prophet.

Olive oil is ubiquitous in Tunisian cooking but not quite as obtrusively as in, for example, Greek. That is not to say, however, that Tunisians do not consume it in heroic quantities – nearly five gallons (about 20 litres a year), man, woman and child. Putting the stuff away at this rate, it is hardly surprising that the Tunisian, like the Greek, would be mystified by degrees of virginity and other esoteric considerations which, under the influence of Italian cognoscenti, have made the superior grades of olive oil as expensive as vintage wines.

For the inhabitants of the Sahel, the olive is a staple and a livelihood. While to the untutored eye an olive on a plate is either green or black, whole or de-stoned, there are in reality some 50 varieties and as many ways of preserving them. Straight from the tree they are intensely bitter, whether they are green (picked while young) or black (allowed to mature on the tree). From there, they are soaked in water for six to 10 days, then in salt brine. Afterwards they are often flavoured with an aromatic marinade containing bitter oranges, preserved lemons, herbs or *harysa*.

Trees represent a family's principal and perhaps only assets. They take seven years to mature, not requiring an inordinate amount of care in their lifetime but, come September, the picking must be done with almost the urgency of a grape harvest. The job requires many hands at the best of times; the problems are compounded if a family's trees are not in one place but have been dispersed by the vagaries of inheritance and dowry over a wide area.

There is very little waste. One of the products is soap made from the pulp of crushed stones. Although the trees famously live to a great age, they do become barren or die, at which point the easily-worked wood is carved into the objects hawked about by an army of small boys.

A drought does not kill a tree, but in conserving moisture the tree produces no fruit. So dependent are the families of the Sahel still on the fruit of versatile tree that the economic consequences to them are no less grave than they are to world industry when the producers of the other kind of oil threaten to turn off the tap.

as a prison by the French. According to legend rather than history the fort marks the egress of a tunnel leading all the way to El Djem. It was by this subterranean passage that the 7th-century Berber virago El Kahina is reputed to have made her escape to Mahdia after her ammunition of wet fish, supplied via the tunnels, failed to defend El Djem from the Arab invaders (*see page 42*).

Mahdia is a major port, fishing having replaced silk manufacture as its main industry (even the museum of silk just inside the Skifa el Kahla no longer functions). A rocky shelf off the coast is rich in plankton – suggesting the world's most polluted sea (the Med) is a little less so here – which is perfect feed for smaller fish such as sardines, anchovies and mackerel. The method for catching them dates from Carthaginian and Roman times (witness mosaics depicting fishing themes). Each night boats strung with lanterns head out to the feeding grounds. The fish, attracted by the light, are drawn to the surface and their fate – the town canneries, conven-

*see page 42*

iently close to raw materials such as Sahel olive oil and salt from Sfax.

The route to Sfax divides at Ksour Essaf. By taking the road via El Djem, the spectacular Roman amphitheatre (*see page 251*), you won't miss much on the coast road, just some meagre Roman remains at Salakta. It too turns inland past Chebba, and there are no undiscovered beaches on the way, just larger and larger olive groves.

**Veils of smoke:** Industrial chimneys rather than minarets herald **Sfax**, the country's second city. Mounds of phosphate transported here by rail from Metlaoui near Gafsa are more noticeable than sand dunes along its shore; and on its outskirts the skies suddenly turn cloudy – pollution, not warning of a downpour. But the pleasant city centre is like an oasis in this industrial landscape, and it is appreciated most by those arriving from the real desert further south.

In spite of the medina's vast enceinte walls, parts of which date from the Aghlabids, Sfax's old and new quarters

*see page 251*

**Left**, the olive tree, associated with virility. **Below**, wide variety.

have tight links, possibly because the medina is still a warren of manufacturing workshops as industrious as the refineries and factories on Sfax's shores.

**Bab Diwan**, the main entrance to the medina is clearly visible north along **Rue de la République**, past the Café de la Paix, whose former status as a brasserie is mourned by dusty advertisements for Pernod and Cognac on shelves now occupied by Boga and Coca-Cola bottles. The gate is always an animated spot, packed with people buying bread straight from the oven.

Immediately inside the medina walls, the left-hand thoroughfare leads to the **Great Mosque**, which though of Aghlabid origin owes more to the Fatimids, who altered it in the 10th century, and eventually emerges at the market just outside the northern gate of the medina. The other route, **Rue Mongi Slim**, wriggles past a succession of cheap restaurants and hotels and then wends north. About half way along its length there is a signpost to the **Museum of Popular Arts and Traditions**, housed in the 17th-century Dar Djellouli. It is the best museum of this kind in Tunisia and the house itself – three storeys around a tiled courtyard – is an Andalusian masterpiece.

The ground floor is devoted to domestic life during the time of the beys; each room off the courtyard pertaining to a particular household activity, such as cooking, bathing, dressing, or receiving guests. For once, exhibits are well supported by explanatory text and diagrams. Some of the simplest but most interesting exhibits illustrate various culinary arts still practised, such as distilling flower water and making *harysa*, the fiery red pepper sauce with a kick like Semtex.

On the top storey there are fine examples of calligraphy, including scripts so highly decorated that they approach the pictorial, and several paintings on glass, a speciality of the Sfax region and popular interior decoration in the early 20th century. Common themes were Koranic verses and illustrations of the lives of holy men – the Islamic edict

**Sfax, industrious as well as industrial.**

forbidding animate subject matter not being upheld as rigorously then as in previous centuries.

The new town lies between the medina and the port. A statue of Bourguiba on his horse still stands its ground on the square at the foot of Rue de la République, though it is probably about to be dismantled (under Ben Ali's government, towns are gradually erasing Bourguiba's memory), and behind it the extravagant civic building sporting a clock as well as neo-Mauresque embellishments is the **Town Hall**, which contains a small **archaeological museum**. To the east, Avenue Habib Bourguiba leads to the luxury Sfax Centre Hotel, full of suited businessmen. Opposite which a bulb-shaped kiosk disguises the **Tourist Office**.

Sfax was a key supply port for the Germans during the war, and consequently it suffered heavy bombing by the Allies in January 1943. Most of the buildings in the new town are therefore post World War II. There are even some attempts at architectural innovation.

**Café du Tunis, Sfax.**

The modern office cum apartment complex facing the medina on Avenue de la République incorporates a mosque with minaret. It is a reminder that a modern industrial society does not necessarily mean secular, something Bourguiba failed to appreciate when he prohibited the veil in Sfax classrooms shortly after coming to power.

Many of tourists visiting Sfax are staying in Kerkennah, a string of islands barely breaking sea level offshore. All provisions for its sparse villages and few hotels are transported by ferries which travel to and fro throughout the day (see *Travel Tips*).

Although Kerkennah is sufficiently distant from the mainland (16 miles/ 25 km) to avoid its pollution, descriptions of a desert island paradise are exaggerations. Don't let tour operators talk you into a two-week package holiday on Kerkennah unless you have an inexhaustible interest in watching fishermen or see paradise in palm trees that look as though they are suffering from arboreal alopecia.

# KAIROUAN

Divine revelations are not without their drawbacks. When, in the year 670, a barren, inhospitable plain was miraculously suggested to Oqba Ibn Nafaa as a site for the holy city of Kairouan, he might well have wished to renegotiate. Kairouan stands isolated in Tunisia's arid steppe interior. During the summer it bakes like a piece of pottery left to harden in the sun. In the spring and autumn, when it does rain, it floods.

But Oqba Ibn Nafaa, a disciple of the Prophet Mohammed, found the hint rather too heavy to ignore. According to the legend, his horse lost its footing and a spring suddenly appeared in the ground. Beneath the water shone a golden goblet that had vanished in Mecca some years before. Oqba, who at the time was leading 150,000 troops on the third Arab invasion in 25 years, wasted no time; he banished "noxious beasts and reptiles" from the area and set about establishing the first Arab capital in North Africa.

It seemed unpromising, but Kairouan's location was not without some secular logic. It lay on caravan routes (Kairouan means caravan) midway between the two greatest threats to the Muslim invaders – the native Berbers in the mountains and the Byzantines on the coast. What's more, the terrain was what they were used to, and therefore easiest for them to defend.

Similar advantages apply today. Kairouan has survived relatively unscathed by the invasion of organised package tourism which is now entrenched along Tunisia's eastern coast, being too hot and dusty for most people's taste. And yet, at less than three hours' drive from the airport of Tunis (and just an hour from Monastir), it is not as inaccessible as the mountain settlements to the west or the oasis towns of the Saharan fringe.

Kairouan has a lively, compact old quarter and several notable examples of early Islamic architecture. It lacks the romantic reputation of Fez and Marra-kesh, the ancient Arab cities of Morocco, but is more relaxed. Fez, although undeniably exciting, confronts its visitors with a gruelling test of endurance. Kairouan, much smaller, never overwhelms. The people and their city are approachable and unintimidating.

The 9th-century Aghlabid dynasty turned Kairouan into a capital of monumental splendour and intellectual renown financed by thriving agriculture and trade. But when the Fatimids overthrew the Aghlabids in 909 they ruled from Mahdia on the coast, and Kairouan went into decline. The process accelerated in 1057 when the city was sacked by the nomadic Banu Hilal and Banu Sulaym tribes.

Nowadays Kairouan is a successful but unexceptional base for farming and industry, with a population a little over 100,000. Carpet and cigarette manufacturing are important, as is the trading of local agricultural goods. It remains, however, Tunisia's most important religious centre.

The original city, the medina, is en-

circled by vast crenellated sandstone walls. On summer evenings these walls radiate a red glow, the heat absorbed during the day giving a warm undercurrent to the first cool breezes of dusk. Successive occupants have dismantled or restored sections of these walls – first built in the 8th century – according to their needs. Most recently the Germans used the flat, broad bricks to build a wartime runway.

**Sweets and carpets:** Their main gate, **Bab Ech Chouhada**, takes you from the relatively bland suburbs of the French *nouvelle ville* into the heart of the medina, a thriving community that has been buying and selling, eating and drinking, sitting and talking in much the same way since Oqba Ibn Nafaa first set up camp.

**Rue Ali bel Houane** is the main artery, tapped at every yard by shops, stalls, cafés or rotisseries. At the less chaotic southern end are the bank, bookshop and a general store piled high with dusty tins, and the double doors of Meilleur Makrouth, inside which the

owner, elegant and correct in his spotless white coat, stands surrounded by geometrically-perfect piles of sweets, pastries and glistening *makrouth* – lozenge-shaped sweetmeats filled with date paste. He, together with the mirrored walls and the smart, light blue woodwork, looks as if he might have been spirited here from the most bourgeois town in France.

Further north, commerce takes a more energetic turn. Sellers of carpets, toy camels, engraved brasswork and patterned leather goods spring from their ludicrously overstocked shops like greyhounds from traps, and anyone who gives more than a glance is tugged by the arm to have a "closer look". But once you have wandered up and down the avenue a couple of times stallholders will come to recognise your face and the futility of their charm. It's then possible to examine what is on offer to the local shopper: for the most part, multi-coloured piles of spices, bags of dry doughnuts, brightly-dyed yarns and battered kitchen utensils

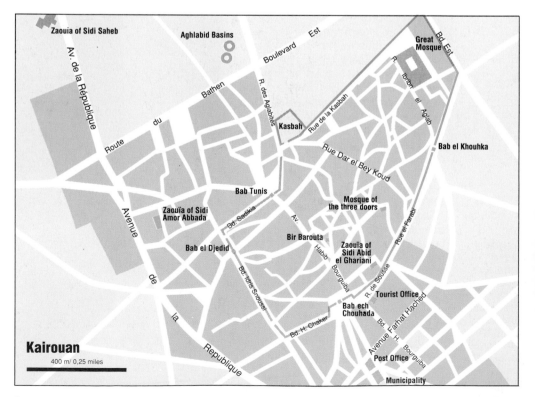

heaped on shaded stalls or open carts.

In the centre of the medina the avenue forks to either side of the Café Halfouine's triangular terrace, a favoured place to sit and watch the daily life of the old city. A less carcinogenic spot for coffee is tucked in the souk, a warren of brick tunnels running at right angles to each other to the east of Avenue Habib Bourguiba. Café Pâtisserie Errachid – its alcoves covered with matting, cushioned benches lining its walls – is a cool, quiet refuge in which to unwind over some fresh fruit or pastries and a tiny cup of *café turc* – a delicious mixture of coffee and chocolate with the texture of warm silt.

Kairouan is well known for its carpets and rugs, as the salesmen of the souk eagerly explain. If you do want to buy, however, the souk is not the cheapest place to do it. It is better to head out of the medina at Bab Tunis, at the northern end of Rue Ali bel Houane. If you cross the road and turn left, there are some quieter markets to your right, with good selections of woven *mergoum* rugs. If you want a general idea of the price and quality of carpets or *mergoums* before you start to bargain, look round the official Organisation National d'Artisanat Tunisien (ONAT) shop on the Avenue Ali Zouaoui.

Behind the souk is the main residential area of the medina, scattered with workshops and mosques. Hidden among the whitewashed, blank-walled houses, on the south side of the Rue des Tapis, is the well of **Bir Barouta** – reputedly Oqba Ibn Nafaa's original spring and, even less likely, supposed to be connected to the well of Zem Zem in Mecca. If you climb some stairs you find a blinkered camel drawing water by walking in never-ending circles, no doubt hoping to meet the desert. Legend has it that a taste of the water (distributed by the camel's owner) will ensure the imbiber's return to Kairouan.

The **Mosque of the Three Doors** lies east of the Bir Barouta, near the end of the Rue de la Mosque de Trois Portes, beyond Rue des Cuirs. This 9th-century mosque is closed to visitors but it is

**The Aghlabid Pools, robbed of all signs of age.**

worth locating for its impressive carved facade with three pointed horseshoe arches. Several bands of inscription are topped by a cornice on 25 supports.

**Islamic heritage:** Kairouan has always been an important religious centre and not only for Tunisians. It was in Kairouan that the Malikite school of Sunni Muslims developed, and it is the fourth holiest city in the Muslim world, after Mecca, Medina and Jerusalem. According to some, seven pilgrimages to Kairouan confer the same blessing as a pilgrimage to Mecca, which all Muslims are urged to undertake.

Kairouan was the focus of resistance to ex-President Bourguiba's efforts to secularise Tunisia in the 1960s. When he attempted to abolish the Ramadan fast, Kairouan observed it a day later than the rest of the country in a gesture of international Islamic solidarity. This independent spirit is not simply confined to religion. Kairouan is also the base of an underground theatre group which tours the country spreading controversial messages about women's rights and social justice to the young.

*Mouloud*, a celebration of the Prophet's birthday (a moveable feast governed by the lunar calendar) is a major festival which attracts Sunni Muslims from throughout the Islamic world. During the festivities the town is decked out with lights and flags.

**Ticket first:** There are numerous buildings in Kairouan which reflect the veneration in which the city is held. To get into the most important ones you need a ticket from the Tourist Office just across the Place du Commandant Mohammed el Bejaoui from Bab Ech Chouhada. This costs 1D and is divided into sections, one for each monument.

Closest is the 14th-century **Zaouia of Sidi Abd el Ghariani**, down a side street to the right just after you enter the medina through Bab Ech Chouhada. A small antechamber leads into the main atrium. This is surrounded by a colonnade, through which a series of rooms lead off each side. The lower parts of the walls are covered with tiles painted in intricate geometrical patterns of green,

**A medina with plenty of spice.**

orange and blue. The *mihrab*, in the centre of the eastern wall, is topped with a horseshoe arch in black and white marble. This surrounds stuccoed plaster in the shape of a peacock's fan.

Restoration has been underway at the *zaouia* for some years. The various antechambers are only now being opened to the public, and the guardians are still wary about people wandering around the upper floor unaccompanied.

Kairouan's most impressive monument is undoubtedly the **Great Mosque**, which stands in the northeastern corner of the medina. The best way to find it without getting lost is to follow the city wall by turning left at the back of the Zaouia of Sidi Abd el Ghariani. As this is one of the few spots in Kairouan where the modern equivalent of the Byzantine invaders accumulate in large numbers – convoys of coaches ferry holidaymakers from the coastal resorts daily – it is worth getting here early in the morning if you want the Great Mosque to yourself. It is not difficult to recognise.

With its enormous buttressed walls, sturdy ornamental gates and three-tiered minaret, the mosque looks more like a military stronghold than a place of devotion. It is grand in a dignified and unfussy way. Like the city walls, the mosque has been dismantled and rebuilt and renovated several times since Oqba Ibn Nafaa founded it in the 7th century. The present mosque was built by the Aghlabids in the 9th century; its defensive character is typical of early Arab religious architecture.

The prayer hall stands behind riveted wooden doors at one end of a huge courtyard. It is topped by a grooved brickwork dome and filled with an extraordinary assortment of columns. Marble, porphyry, onyx and granite – the materials are as varied as the styles. Most were lifted from Roman sites, notably Carthage.

Until 1972 non-Muslims could explore the prayer hall for themselves, but insensitive tourists changed all that. Now one has to be content with gazing into the large, dimly-lit chamber and

**Baskets and henna.**

watching the swallows as they swoop between the columns. The floor of the prayer hall is covered with blue and white rugs, some of which are wrapped around the bottoms of the columns. Far above are the massive mosque lamps, generally extinguished during the day. Even without their aid, the *mirhab*, the arched niche indicating the direction of Mecca, with its exquisite faïence surround crafted in 9th-century Baghdad, and the *minbar*, the fabulously carved 9th-century cedar staircase from which the *imam* leads prayer, are visible from the prayer-hall's doors.

The courtyard can, reputedly, accommodate 200,000 people. It also acts as a vast funnel for rainwater, which comes rarely but suddenly in Kairouan and needs to be controlled and conserved. The paving stones slope down to a circular drain where dust is decanted before the water flows to cisterns beneath the ground. A large sundial stands near the drain, with steps leading to a platform scored with lines and Kufic script. Nowadays it serves more as a plinth for posed photographs than a means of telling the time.

The **Aghlabid Pools** are the next monuments to which your ticket provides access. To get to them you have to follow the north wall of the medina from the Great Mosque to Bab Tunis, and then head north along Rue des Aglabites to Avenue de la République.

The Aghlabids built these pools to hold water carried more than 20 miles (32 km) by aqueduct from Djebel Cherichera. They are unique among the monuments of Kairouan in being entirely missable, though the fact that the two that have been restored could be mistaken for part of a modern industrial plant must be a credit to the 9th-century engineers who designed them. If they did not lie between the Great Mosque and the last of the outstanding monuments there would be no good reason to walk out this far.

The **Mosque of the Barber** is one of the most beautiful in North Africa. Its ornate and intricate decoration could not be in greater contrast to the austere

**Below, Mosque of the Barber, place of pilgrimage. Right, Pillar of Islam.**

# RAMADAN

The most important time of the year in any Islamic country is Ramadan, the month of fasting when, the Koran stipulates, not even a drop of water should pass a Muslim's lips during daylight hours. A few are exempt: pregnant or menstruating women, travellers on a long journey, the very old or sick and children under the age of about 11. But almost everyone else, whether they practise their religion or not, upholds this "pillar of the faith", if only out of tradition or because it would be obvious to others if they did not.

To Christians, a month of contemplation might seem a poor way to celebrate the revelation of the Koran. More like Lent than Christmas. Not just food and drink, but sex and tobacco too are off the agenda until the hour when a "black thread cannot be distinguished from a white one". If the moveable fast (controlled by the Hegira calendar) falls in the summer when the sun rises early and sets late the mood is particularly subdued. Irrational behaviour, bad driving, short tempers and all errors are all blamed on lack of sustenance.

Banking and office hours have to be reduced, and cafés (with the exception of those serving tourist resorts) are firmly closed, though their patrons, governed by habit rather than wishful thinking, still tend to congregate on their cheerless terraces.

But as each afternoon lengthens and dusk approaches restlessness in the towns and listlessness in the villages, where there are fewer diversions from gnawing hunger, metamorphose into a swelling sense of expectation. Just before sundown the streets empty, as everyone who is not at home reserves their place in the opening restaurants. When the mosque lamps signal nightfall and the *muezzin* calls "*Allah Akbar*" for the sunset prayer, Tunisians everywhere fall upon a thick soup, the traditional break to the fast, as though synchronised by the unseen hand of Allah. (Tourists be warned: within half an hour all but the best restaurants have run out of food; dither too long over a menu and you may be waiting another day to get a hot meal.) In private homes supper is followed by *shebbakia*, deep-fried wheel-shaped pastries dipped in boiling honey, either home-made or bought from the special *shebbakia* stalls that spring up on every street during this special time of year.

With everyone replete, the atmosphere relaxes, and in Sidi Bou Said, Tunis and Sousse it is positively festive. Cafés catch up on the business they have missed in the day, families parade the main boulevards, and the clothes shops do their best business of the year – the purchase of new clothes in preparation for the end of Ramadan, Aid es Seghir, being as essential as gifts are to Christmas. Eventually everyone drifts home to bed, where the suburban bourgeoisie, mindful of their work commitments, sleep soundly until dawn; but in the medinas and villages, the bastions of traditional Tunisia, the night's rituals are not yet over. Just before daybreak drummers patrol the streets and alleyways rousing households for the *assohour*, traditionally pancakes spread with honey, a sleepy feast which children particularly love.

Each evening is a little celebration, but the 26th day of Ramadan, which directly commemorates the first revelation to the Prophet, is marked by a more elaborate feast and a night spent reciting the Koran in the mosque, at least for the devout. A few days later, on the 29th or 30th evening, depending on the appearance of the new moon, the fast ends. The following day is Aid es Seghir, "little feast", a public holiday when new clothes are worn and the country's poor knock on doors to claim alms.

A month of late nights and disturbed sleep on top of the daily fast takes its toll on the nation's energies; but there is no sign of Ramadan declining in importance. It is Tunisia's one manifestation of Islamic solidarity.

Habib Bourguiba, in his attempts to secularise the country in the 1960s, repeatedly tried to dissuade people from observing the fast. "If it becomes incompatible with the necessary struggles of this life, religion must be amended," he said. But he could not legislate to make people eat. Defiantly drinking an orange juice at a public rally during Ramadan in 1964 was his last-ditch attempt to influence public opinion on the matter.

grandeur of the Great Mosque. The Zaouia of Sidi Sahab, to give the mosque its proper name, is 10 minutes' walk to the west of the Aghlabid pools along the Avenue de la République.

A 17th-century minaret stands at one corner of the main courtyard. Beneath it a tiled archway leads into a series of antechambers, each of which is tiled with complex coloured designs based on stylised plant, urn and arch motifs. Green benches (for the constant stream of pilgrims) line walls topped by restrained stucco plasterwork. In the last of the antechambers the ceiling is a dome of spectacular lace stuccowork and coloured glass, slightly spoiled by the string of fairylights which has been run behind it.

The antechambers lead into an inner courtyard. Columns support a tiled facade above the entrance to the shrine of Sidi Sahab. Non-Muslims are not admitted, but through the doorway, always guarded by an attendant, you can just make out the bright green cloth over the tomb. Sidi Sahab (which means "the

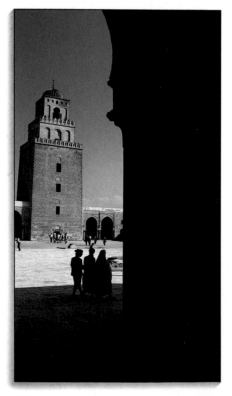

companion") was a disciple of the Prophet, called Abu Zama el Balaoui. The mosque gets its popular name from his habit of carrying three hairs of the Prophet's beard wherever he went. The whiskers are reputed to be entombed with him: one placed under his tongue, one next to his heart and one over his right arm.

The inner courtyard, which has matting spread around its perimeter, is a delightfully cool resting spot. Other than the birds the only sound is the slapping of women's sandals as they cross the marble courtyard to the shrine.

**The New Town:**As is so often the case in Tunisia, the development outside the medina walls comes as something of an anticlimax. The area just to the south of the Place du Commandant Mohammed El Bejaoui contains the main supermarket, the bus station (now much better signposted than it used to be) and a number of cafés, bars and Western-style shops.

Kairouan's outskirts have even less to recommend them. The ancient *koubbas* that painter Paul Klee claimed altered the rest of his life as an artist and led him to announce "Colour and I are one" nestle in a copse of tin cans and building rubble. But the untidy suburbs fall back quickly, and the roads out of town are shaded by gum trees.

At Rekada (6 miles/10 km on Route 2, marked Sfax), where the Aghlabid rulers established their palaces (partly to distance themselves from powerful and critical religious elements in Kairouan), a former presidential palace has been turned into the **National Museum of Islamic Art**.

Although established back in 1986, the museum is still only sparsely furnished; the not overworked custodians greet visitors eagerly in the hope of a coach party. So far, it contains 10th-century Korans from the Great Mosque in Kairouan, a large collection of coins, examples of pottery and tiling and an ancient lamp also from Kairouan's Great Mosque. There are many closed doors in the museum but it's difficult to establish what they conceal. The museum only just merits a stop.

**Left**, the Minaret of the Great Mosque, appropriate to a fortress. **Right**, the ubiquitous kaftan shop.

# EL DJEM

The road and railway route between Sousse and Sfax leaves the coast to pass through a monotonous landscape of olive groves. Motorists may be inclined to press on, but not to make the detour through **El Djem** would be to waste one of the most extraordinary spectacles Tunisia has to offer. Modern El Djem is a grubby little town, but as the road straightens for the final approach to the centre it reveals, memorably, something it has been holding up its sleeve. The El Djem **amphitheatre** (AD 230) may not be as well preserved as its counterpart in Rome – a fallacy that has been doing the rounds in guidebooks since the 19th century – but because of the incongruous setting its impact is every bit as awesome.

It is enough at first to indulge in a phantasmagoria of gladiators, wild animals and Christians being led up to the arena from dungeons below, the emperor and his coterie taking their places in one or other of the imperial boxes depending on the position of the sun, and 30,000 spectators buzzing with anticipation in three steeply-raked tiers of seats. The imagery, is of course, padded out with details like the up or down gesture of the imperial thumb which determined a gladiator's fate.

**The sport:** In El Djem, as well as in other Tunisian amphitheatres, a bizarre Christian sect known as the Donatists could lend an unusual touch to the proceedings. They happened to believe not only that the Second Coming was imminent but that it was better to be dead when it came. They found "a sensation of joy and pleasure in the midst of the most exquisite tortures", so much so that they are reputed to have goaded the lions and other wild beasts into attacking them with maximum ferocity. The same Donatists, incidentally, were subject to fits of frenzied piety which would make them go up to total strangers and demand to be murdered there and then. Anyone who demurred was threatened with murder himself.

Chariot races could be quite as brutal as gladiatorial contests. It was customary to write the names of particularly desirable victims on the scything blades attached to the wheels. The charioteer's prayer did not waste time with notions of fair play. A typical example began with the incantation of the names of drivers and horses likely to offer the stiffest competition and continued: "Stop them, chain them down, drain them of their strength so that they may not leave the stable, may not pass the gate, may not advance an inch on the track. As for the drivers, may they be paralysed so that their hands cannot hold the reins, so that their eyes cannot see, so that they cannot stand upon their legs. Hurl them from their chariots so that they may be trampled under the horses' feet. Without delay, without delay; at once, at once!"

The chariots were owned and entered by wealthy Romans but, contrary to the impression given by Charlton Heston, the drivers were locals who hired out their services to the highest bidder and

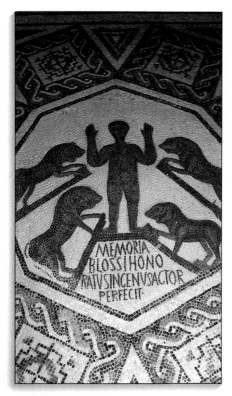

could become immensely rich on the proceeds. North African drivers were so highly regarded that they monopolised racing in Rome as well. One of them, a certain Crescens, earned enough in 10 years to qualify as a millionaire – in the currency of the time, true, but even so it put him into the same exalted category that the term denotes today.

The upper tiers of the amphitheatre, which must have seen hundreds of such races, provide a commanding view of the town and surrounding countryside, an unimpressive panorama which gives no clue to the need or rationale for such a massive stadium. The present population of the area is no more than a few thousand, and if they all crowded into the amphitheatre at once it would still look rather empty. Moreover, the ruins of **Bir-ez-Zit** only a few miles away reveal that it, too, had an amphitheatre, albeit a smaller one with a capacity of about 10,000. Why?

A glimpse of El Djem in Roman times (then known as Thysdrus) is provided by one of the magistrates who had his achievements recorded in stone. He boasted of having built a water supply which fed fountains in a chain of public squares across the city and provided, luxury of luxuries, running water in many private houses. From other contemporary sources, it appears that El Djem also had a colossal temple. The population was probably 100,000, in which case it was second to Carthage.

The key to El Djem's prosperity, and to its subsequent decline, was water. To begin with, the Romans simply took over and enlarged on Phoenician settlements and these, as we have seen in the history section of this book, were established at intervals along the coast in the interest of maritime trade. The Romans were not too concerned about the interior, it was too dry: "*Caelo terraque penuria aquarum*", which translates loosely as "Not a drop of water, in heaven or on earth".

An expanding empire and with it a growing number of mouths to feed redoubled the demand for cereal crops, and it did not escape Roman notice that the soil of North Africa could be, in the

**Preceding pages**: the amphitheatre of El Djem, sole survivor of an extensive Roman town. **Left**, mosaic depicting Daniel in the Lions' Den, inspiration to the Donatists.

right circumstances, enormously fertile. Travellers in Tunisia today are treated to the bizarre sight of traffic jams on the fringes of the Sahara at certain times of the year. Vehicles are suddenly cut off when even a moderate amount of rain transforms bone-dry and unbridged wadis into roaring torrents. Before the Romans and, as we shall see, after them, these floodwaters drained uselessly into the desert sand. The Romans set about conserving them with a vast complex of reservoirs and underground cisterns, some of the latter capable of holding several million gallons. By these means, El Djem developed as the heart of "the granary of the Roman Empire". The harvest was shipped out mostly through Mahdia, the closest port, and excited crowds gathered at Italian ports like Naples when word was received of the arrival of a fleet of grain-laden galleys.

The importance of El Djem was such that in AD 238, eight years after the construction of the amphitheatre, it was capable of fomenting and very nearly pulling off a revolt against Rome itself. The local population had the confidence to challenge the gross misrule of one of Rome's more deplorable emperors and went to the dangerous lengths of acclaiming their own emperor or, as it happened, dual emperors, the unlikely combination of a geriatric father and a libidinous, though well-read, son.

Many centuries later El Djem was the last Berber bastion against the Arab invasion. (Both the election of the Gordians and El Kahina's defiance are recounted more fully in the history chapters.) The walls of the amphitheatre stood intact until 1695 when the Ottoman ruler of Tunisia, Mohammed Bey, blew a large part of them away in the pursuit of rebels who had holed up inside. By then the amphitheatre had long been an empty symbol of its glorious Roman past. The Vandals who overthrew Rome destroyed the aqueducts, the reservoirs and cisterns, and slowly but inexorably the desert reclaimed the land. The town of El Djem was never the same again.

**In the round.**

# DJERBA

Like Kerkennah, **Djerba** barely noses above sea level. Arriving over the causeway at El Kantara, newcomers are struck by the same disorientating flatness. There is not the slightest hill to act as landmark or offer clues to the island's topography. The only perpendicular is provided by the palm trees, uniformly high and regularly spaced except where they have been felled to make way for Djerba's three arterial roads.

**Lotus land:** Little by little along the inland road to the capital Houmt Souk, the advantages of Djerba unfold. Kerkennah's strip of land is parched, like a bone bleached by the sun. Djerba, in contrast, is lush, bushy-topped; and the sandy lanes that criss-cross its interior lead to farms, olive orchards, fields of melons, even vines and crops. The beach on the eastern side of the island is long, sinuous and blonde.

Djerba is one of three sites claimed for the Land of the Lotus Eaters that detained Odysseus (known to the Romans as Ulysses) and his men on their return from Troy – Menorca and Majorca being the other two. But precious little water meant that life on the island was never one of "indolent forgetfulness". When new age Lotus seekers, early devotees of Club Med, turned up on Djerba in 1954, the deprivations of life on a desert island were too much for the bead-trading hedonists to bear and the complex closed down until services could be improved.

Since then, Djerba has steadily acquired all the facilities of a modern resort, including a new pipeline that brings water from the mainland. More and more Europeans are discovering the island and there is an international airport to receive them. Hotels run the length of the beach, the Plage de Sidi Mehrez – though they are well-spaced and, apart from Club Med, do not annex it with proprietorial fences. Also, Djerban has its enclave of Aladdin's Caves and Sinbad's Bazaars.

An unattractive west coast curbs fur-ther expansive plans. In summer it may be better to avoid Djerba's over-loaded beach and over-syphoned wells, but just out of season the island is a find.

Djerbans react in two ways to the annual influx of foreigners. Renowned throughout Tunisia as shrewd shop-keepers, Djerban grocers have diversified. Houmt Souk restaurants and souvenir shops are locally-owned.

At the same time, Djerbans are among the most conservative Tunisians and make great efforts to keep their particular identity intact. Their resolve is fortified by a religious separatism. When the Kharidjite revolt of the 7th and 8th centuries waned and the rest of Tunisia returned to Sunni ranks, a pocket of this puritanical schism of Islam was preserved on the Berber stronghold of Djerba. In spite of its small size (approximately 25 sq. miles/ 40 sq. km), the island has 246 mosques. Nearly all its women are traditionally dressed in white or sombre colours with a veil like a nun's wimple and a pointed straw hat on top. They are very photo-

Preceding pages: pistols, daggers and powder boxes. Left, one of Djerba's 246 mosques. Right, water, a precious commodity in spite of modern pipelines.

genic – but dislike being photographed.

Architecture, too, reflects private lives. Even modest homes are surrounded by a *tabia*, a formidable hedge of cactus. The larger residences, known as *menzels*, are protective structures of cubes and domes with high, tiny windows and buttressed walls, a design dictated by a vulnerable past.

Djerba was a well-known port of call to the Phoenicians, its sandy shores being gentle on their fragile ships. They called it Meninx and set up a base for harvesting its prodigious beds of murex shellfish (*see page 160*). Later, they constructed the first version of the causeway, which the Romans destroyed and rebuilt when they set up a busy trading port.

It was the Middle Ages, when Europe was divided into independent city states, which put Djerba on the map as a strategic foothold. As the historian Wilfred Knapp noted, Djerba became a barometer of the strength of rival powers in this part of the Mediterranean.

The Aragonese admiral Robert de Loria invaded Djerba in 1284 and seized a "vast amount of booty" after a brief bombardment; but in spite of being pronounced Count of Djerba by the Pope and building the Bordj el Kebir at Houmt Souk, he was unable to hold the island. In 1432 Alphonse V of Aragon and his men made another attempt, and tried to pre-empt a counter-attack by cutting the causeway; but Hafsid ruler Abou Faris took advantage of low tide and quickly sent them packing. Sixty-five years later, in 1497, the Sicilians moved in, but they withdrew by 1500; and in the early 16th century the Barbarossa brothers (*see page 51*) set up base on Djerba. From here they launched their successful campaign to expel the Spanish from Algiers.

Djerba remained in the clutches of the privateers, and Draghut commandeered the island in 1550. He was not welcomed and found it difficult to maintain control; but when, in 1559, the Knights of Malta turned up to seize Draghut and, finding him absent, raided the island instead, the Djerbans were relieved to

**Potter in Guellala.**

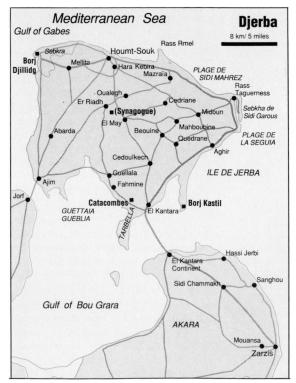

see the privateer unexpectedly return. He destroyed 28 of their 48 galleys, took 5,000 prisoners, and massacred those who had holed up in the Bordj el Kebir. The skulls of the Christians were piled on the beach and stayed there as a sober reminder until 1846.

This history of incursions made the Djerbans determined to find strength in industry and trade. Weaving, olive oil production, agriculture, sponge fishing and pottery flourished, and in the 19th century European merchants found Djerba a safer base than Gabes for conducting trade, a preference that stirred up rivalry on the mainland. When the French arrived they found an unexpected welcome on Djerba, where they were seen as protection against increasingly menacing mainland tribes.

**Jewish enclave:** Throughout this time Djerba's individualism was underlined by two communities of Jews, who date their presence on the island either to 590 BC when, following the fall of Jerusalem to Nebuchadnezzer in 586 BC, those Jews not captured fled, or to the arrival of refugees after the sack of Jerusalem in AD 71 (historians know no better). **Hara Kebira** (big ghetto), **Hara Seghira** (little ghetto) used to be quite large villages of several thousand Jews but after Independence in 1956 most of them left for Israel. This was not because of racism. Anti-Semitism had only been a serious problem during World War II. In 1943, the Germans ordered Djerban Jews to pay a communal fine of 10 million francs within two weeks; when they failed to raise the amount, the Germans confiscated 110 lb (50 kg) of gold.

The number of Jews has considerably dwindled, but Djerba's Jewish heritage is distinguished by the **Ghriba synagogue** at Hara Seghira (now called Er Riadh); it is a place of pilgrimage for Jews worldwide and Djerba's most famous tourist attraction.

The present synagogue was built in the 1920s, but the original was supposed to mark the spot where a holy stone fell from heaven in 600 BC. According to the story, a mysterious girl

turned up to direct the building works.

Its interior is surprisingly brightly tiled and painted; and usually a few Biblical-looking retainers lie reading on the mat-covered benches. On one wall there is a wood and glass cabinet containing one of the oldest Torahs in the world and various silver plaques engraved with messages from pilgrims. A guide shows visitors around, indicates where marriage ceremonies take place – rarely these days – and then produces a lot of postcards for sale.

Other than the synagogue, most of Djerba's "sights" are in **Houmt Souk**, the island's capital on the north coast. Its centre is inland of the shore, and to the east of Avenue Habib Bourguiba. All available maps of the town are inadequate, especially the one provided by the **Syndicat d'Initiative** (set back from Avenue Habib Bourguiba about half-way down) for which they have the nerve to charge 500 millimes. But after initial confusion, based on the fact that the town centre does not follow the line of the shore, as one might expect, but is

at right-angles to it, Houmt Souk is suddenly found to be not much larger than a village.

The **fort** that Roger de Loria built after he arrived in 1237 is right on the shore at the top of **Rue Taieb Mehri**, a street lined by eucalyptus trees and market stalls selling mainly hardware and clothing. Its outer walls have been irrevocably restored and there are plans to start work on its interior (at the moment, potentially perilous for unguarded children). The fort's modest size suggests that the number of Knights of Malta massacred by Draghut is probably an exaggeration; nonetheless the tower of their "5,000 skulls", removed in 1846 to the Christian cemetery, is marked by a small monument visible towards the harbour.

Also on this side of town is the **Museum of Arts and Popular Traditions** attractively housed in the **Zaouia of Sidi Zitouna** on Avenue Abdelhamid el Cadhi. Like such museums in other towns, it displays local costumes, jewellery, furniture and implements. The

**Wells are meeting places.**

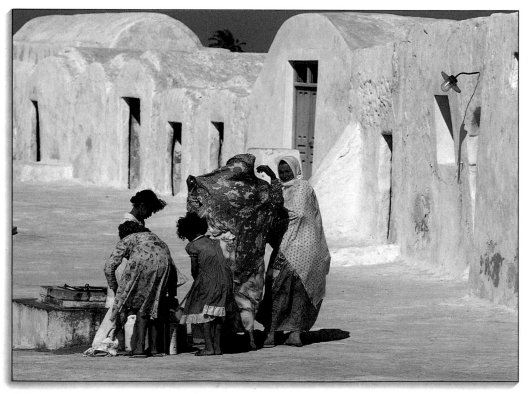

costumes and jewellery are perhaps the most interesting exhibits, reflecting the islanders' skills in jewellery-making and textiles.

A short walk down Avenue Abdelhamid el Cadhi from the museum is a collection of distinctive mosques. They are all prohibited to non-Muslims but worth tracking down for the unusual shapes of their domes and minarets. The multi-domed white building with a minaret shaped like the top of an oasthouse, between Place d'Algérie and Rue Moncef Bey, is the **Mosque of the Turks**; also domed but with a band of Koranic script around a delicate square minaret is the **Mosque of the Strangers**; and the squat, buttressed building with a bell-shaped, tiled dome (a loud speaker perched on top) belongs to the **Zaouia of Sidi Brahim**, a 17th-century saint. Perfectly at home between them is the belfry of a white **Catholic church**, which in the 19th century served the Maltese, Italian and Greek fishermen who settled on Djerba. Its entrance is on **Place L'Eglise**, a picturesque sandy square of peeling colonial architecture where men sit and spin wool.

**Place Hedi Chaker** is the town's focal square, the liveliest spot day or night. Tourists and islanders converge on the café here; but its restaurants (see *Travel Tips*), quite expensive by Tunisian standards, cater almost exclusively to holidaymakers seeking a change from the menus at their hotels. Behind it, the web of alleyways conceals a few hotels more modest and traditional than the ones along the Plage de Sidi Mehrez. **Hotel Marhala** (run by the Touring Club de Tunisie) and the slightly pricier **Hotel Arischa** both occupy converted *fondouks*.

Formerly lodging places for the merchants visiting the town, these resemble *ghorfas* in construction; their entrances lead to colonnaded courtyards flanked by double tiers of barrel-shaped cells. The rectangular courtyards slope towards central cisterns, once vital for collecting rain water (at Hotel Arischa this has been converted into a tiny swimming-pool). To the

**Mosque of the Strangers in Houmt Souk.**

bemusement of guests, guided groups of tourists are regularly trouped through the *fondouks*. Invariably the members of these tours are staying in one of the much more expensive hotels spreading low along **Plage Sidi Mehrez**, the Zone Touristique on the island's east coast.

**On the beach:** The disadvantage of staying in one of these larger hotels (which range from the luxurious four-star Abou Nawas to the merely moderately-appointed Hotel Tanit, is that they are not within walking distance of Houmt Souk. Unless you have a car, you must rely on taxis to ferry you at least 6 miles (10 km) each way or be content to spend evenings locked with renditions of Perry Como's hits in a bar the size a football stadium. Those staying in town, however, can take the number 11 bus to the beach by day.

The beach has everything the Mediterranean hot-spots have – riding ranches, watersports, paragliding, pizza parlours just a pebble's throw away – plus, particular to North Africa, camel rides and a constant passage of snack and souvenir touts. If boredom strikes in spite of all this, take a bus or rent a bicycle or moped and explore the other villages on the island. Most of the hotels hire out bikes, and so do the car rental firms along Avenue Abdelhamid el Cadhi in Houmt Souk. A car is wasted on the island, tending to obscure Djerba's more recondite charms with constant clouds of dust.

Obvious places to make for are the Ghriba synagogue (described earlier) and the **mosque at El May**, both located at the centre of the island. The mosque is like a tiny, whitewashed castle, with enormous buttresses and an acorn-shaped minaret. Alas, **Guellala** in the south, known for its pottery, really only caters for the tourist trade these days, as does the Friday market in **Midoun**.

The western side of the island is bleak, relieved only by the **Bordj Djillidj**, an 18th-century Turkish fort close to the airport. Like the shallow waters off Kerkennah, the sea here is partitioned by a zig-zag of palm-frond fences to trap unsuspecting fish.

**The Mosque at El May.** **Right**, in the **Ghriba synagogue.**

# TUNISIA'S JEWS

The Ghriba synagogue in Djerba is the most important Jewish shrine in Africa and a place of pilgrimage. The present building – on a site which legend lays claim to in 590 BC – is unremarkably 20th-century, but some of the contents are intriguing, either as items of profound historical and religious interest, like the ancient Scrolls of Torah, or as a reflection of the curious position of Jews and Judaism in Tunisia right up to present times. Given the Arab League headquarters in Tunis, the exile given to PLO leaders and guerrillas in Tunisia, and the general rhetoric of Jewish-Islamic relations, it is hard to imagine any other Islamic state where a synagogue would not only receive an official visit from the president, in this case Bourguiba, but then choose to commemorate the event by mounting a portrait of him in a prominent place.

The story of the Jews in Tunisia has very little to do with ghettos, money-lending and other such stereotypes. There actually was once a ghetto in Tunis, and there were Jewish refugees from Christian persecution in Europe who were prominent traders, but a flip through the pages of Tunisian history and travel literature shows Jews in some extraordinary circumstances.

"One is astonished to find how in many respects (Tunisian Jews) so little resemble their co-religionists in other countries," the Danish traveller-cum-anthropologist Daniel Bruun wrote in the 19th century. He discovered that one of the troglodyte communities in the Matmata mountains was Jewish; in another a Jewish man was living in a hole with the Berber family into which he had married. Other early travellers reported that, especially on Djerba, young Jewish women virtually monopolised the unvirtuous position of dancing girls.

The Berber tribes have been notably pragmatic in the matter of religion, seemingly content to bend with the prevailing wind or at least to give a fair hearing to new religions as they came along. In greater or lesser numbers, they have made the transition between paganism, Christianity and Islam. Some, then, chose to become Jews, and it is possible (though debatable) that Tunisia's Joan of Arc, the redoubtable El Kahina who led Berber resistance to the Arab invasion was Jewish. If not, she was probably Christian.

Although many Jewish Berbers accepted Islam under the Almohads, others clung to Judaism, their numbers being added to with successive waves of refugees from Jewish persecution in Europe. Jews suffered under the Visigoths in Spain, Justinian in Byzantium and again during the religious fervour stoked by the Crusades. They found comparative safety in Tunisia under both Arabs and Turks.

The two strains of Jews, native and European, were known respectively as Touensa and Grana. The former were indistinguishable from their Muslim neighbours: the women, for example, wore the hand of Fatima as amulets against evil spirits, and necklaces of coloured stones and fishbones against disease. The generally tolerant Turkish beys, however, did require Jews to wear distinctive garments: sleeveless blue shirts, black pantaloons and slippers and a black skull cap. They were allowed to wear stockings only in winter and were not allowed to ride mules or donkeys with saddles.

Discrimination ended with the French protectorate in 1881, and from 1910 Tunisians were given the option of French citizenship. Most of those who accepted it, and subsequently emigrated, were Grana, which dealt the economy a grievous blow. Those who stayed behind were relatively well-off in Tunisia while Fascism swept through Germany and Italy, but the collapse of France in the early days of World War II and the occupation by Germans put them in a perilous position. The Jews of Djerba survived only on the payment of a large ransom in gold.

The haemorrhage to Israel began immediately after World War II, 46,255 leaving between 1948 and 1967. Nevertheless, in 1959 there were estimated still to be 67,000 Jews left in Tunisia, 55,000 of them in Tunis alone. The Arab-Israeli wars, however, did nothing to staunch the flow. More recent statistics are hard to come by: the present population is probably measured more realistically in hundreds rather than thousands.

# KERKENNAH ISLANDS

In high summer when Sfax swelters under a veil of factory smoke, people cut loose to the islands of **Kerkennah**. Holidaymakers, day-trippers, homeward-bound islanders and trucks laden with foodstuffs or palm branches jockey for position at the port from the time the first ferry of the day departs (7.30 a.m. sharp).

The surprise is that the islands don't snap from the weight of them all. They lie like thin crusts adrift on the sea. Some people call them desert islands, others would say desolate; everyone would agree they are dry. Nothing much grows here apart from a scattering of ill-nourished palms. Practically all food, including fresh fruit, meat and vegetables, is imported.

Such inconveniences entirely suited the Romans, who needed somewhere austere to send troublemakers. They built the first causeway bridging **Ile Gharbi** (where the ferry stops but where no one stays) and **Ile Chergui** (the larger island, with a "capital" called Remla). Exiles who ended their days on Kerkennah included Caius Sempronius Gracchus, guilty of seducing Emperor Tiberius's daughter. Later, the Arabs banished adulturous women here.

The history books also record that the Kerkennah Islands were raided by the Aragonese admiral Roger de Loria in 1237 and by Alphonse V of Aragon in 1424 – though it is hard to see what they were after. By all accounts, unlike their neighbours the Djerbans who were also invaded, the islanders have never been wealthy. When, in more recent years, the opportunity arose, most packed their bags and left.

**Tourist development:** Modern developers were undeterred by lack of amenities and in the 1960s placed further strain on the island's water supplies by building a small number of hotels on the north coast at **Sidi Fredj**, reached by turning left a couple of miles past the causeway. They dubbed this area "Zone Touristique". Now a few holiday clubs

and the hotels Grand and Farhat front a beach of, admittedly, very white sand and turquoise sea.

It isn't an idyllic beach, though, as it is too meagre a scrap, but brochure photographs contrive to make it look that way. A few date palms leaning over the water's edge strike a classic desert island pose. Just add a hammock and a pretty girl.

Swimming is the most strenuous thing you will find to do, mainly because you must walk so far before the sea covers your knees; but all the hotels have swimming pools. They also provide windsurfing boards – the shallow, mill-pond conditions are ideal for children and beginners – and hire out bicycles for those who have to explore. There are two crumbling forts of Turkish origin to see.

Other than that, the main diversion is messing about in boats. Trips with local fishermen are standard excursions from the hotels and they are what make a visit to the islands worthwhile, especially if the one you take is in a splendid lateen

sail vessel. The usual practice of the fishermen is to drop anchor at a suitably quiet spot down the coast – though no-where in Kerkennah can be called bust-ling – and, while the tourists hunt shells or swim, they build a fire and grill lunch: invariably mullet or sardines.

Tourism supplements the islands' economy but the main income still comes from fishing. The deeper seas off Kerkennah secrete sponges (located by means of a sort of sub-aqua telescope, then snatched by a long hooked pole), but most fishing is done close to shore. There are two notable methods: one uses coercion, the other pure bluff. The palm fronds piled on the lorries on the Sfax ferry are used to stake out vast V-shaped fences all around the shore and these channel the fish into waiting nets. The other method employs strings of clay pots, often seen assembled on the quays. Each night during October to May the empty pots are lowered into the water; by mid-morning they are occu-pied by sheltering squid, a high-earning fish popular in the hotels but mainly exported to Japan.

Inland, Kerkennah is dusty. There is one main road stretching the length of the islands (22 miles/35 km) and it is served by a bus; but drivers should ex-pect to give lifts to islanders slogging to and from **Remla** (a few shops, a small hotel, a bank and a restaurant). Even women, bundled up in clothing and laden with packages, are not too shy to wave down vehicles.

Perhaps because tourism is still low-key, Kerkennah people are surprisingly open. An extraordinary but true story concerns a Kerkennah woman who lost her husband and, without family to help her, existed by living like a man. She donned men's clothing, kept a knife in her belt, and each night went fishing. The woman is still alive. She lives alone, and breaks various Muslim ta-boos, but her fortitude is respected and she is accepted by the men as an equal.

Although tourism and the high price of squid have brought a partial revival to Kerkennah, the lives of the islanders have traditionally been hard. Their pri-ority is simply to survive.

# THE SOUTHERN OASES

This is the Djerid region, a land of pink rocks and sandy desert that owes much to the phosphate mines, and it's true Sahara. After leaving the populous and prosperous coast (regular bus service from the bus station on Avenue Farhat Hached in Gabes) the drive inland towards Kebili passes through a lonely but impressive stretch of semi-desert. The crush of palms flanking the road soon bow out to a parched landscape.

To the north the land falls away gradually, down to the eastern extremity of Chott el Djerid, called Chott el Fedjadj. The long, narrow extension of this salt lake, a vestige of a once larger Mediterranean, is the largest chott in North Africa.

**El Hamma**, 25 miles (40 km) from Gabes, is the last settlement of any size before Kebili, and famous for its hot springs since Roman times. Providing it is early in the day and their temperature hasn't risen to an excoriating level, stop and sample the waters – stone seats for the purpose are set into the pungently sulphurous pool.

From El Hamma, the Djebel Tebaga, a majestic range of mountains running parallel to the Kebili road, provides a backdrop of desolate beauty. Its peaks are flattened where the caps of harder rocks have resisted the erosive powers of wind and rain. Beneath the range, the desert scrub of thorn bushes support herds of camel belonging to the semi-nomadic Nefzaoua people, who graze them here before mid-summer heat forces their return to the oases.

Sand may obscure the tarmac road just before the **Kebili** oasis. The town is an administrative centre, a role inherited from the days when its Foreign Legion garrison commanded the region. It gained notoriety by being the main dropping off point for slaves captured further south. Indeed, the flourishing slave markets here closed barely 100 years ago. Walking the dusty roads between the small, white houses you are quite likely to brush shoulders with de-

scendants of black Sudanese, whose displacement is almost certainly owed to the 1,000-year trade. Again, there are hot springs, on the right-hand side as you enter town from the east.

Maps display Kebili almost as a peninsula on the edge of a blue-coloured lake. In fact, much of the chott lake is dried to a white crust even in the middle of winter.

**Desert bound:** Little in Tunisia could equal the drive south to the Douz oasis, particularly just before sunset. Leaving Kebili, the road passes through a gap in the Djebel Tebaga mountains, the gateway to the Grand Erg Oriental. Scrub is gradually replaced by dunes; and palm-frond fences attempt to prevent sand from obliterating the road.

Near Douz, the view from the top of these roadside sand hills is breathtaking: the pink rim of Djebel Tebaga on the horizon and a scattering of palm trees half-buried by dunes. The mineral, desert rose, sold in every bazaar, is very common in the sand hereabouts and young boys may be seen digging for the

rose-shaped sculptures, as if for gold.

The town of **Douz** is a maze of narrow streets and sandy-coloured houses. On Thursdays these thoroughfares are filled with *burnous*-clad nomads coming from the outlying oases to sell their vegetables and cloth. The main square is then transformed into a sea of bobbing white head-cloths as they barter over sacks of beans and piles of precisely ordered carrots.

Few of the roads are of tarmac around here, most are just sandy paths. Travellers can easily become disorientated in the labyrinth of tracks, especially to the south and east. The road west from the main square in Douz passes close to the army garrison, which commands a view across the palmerie and desert. This is the perfect place to watch the sun set over the Sahara against silhouettes of camels (a peace-shattering high whistle means someone is pointing their camera too close to the army base).

The Douz palmerie is a delight. Taking the route beyond the well-sited Hotel Saharien, the traveller can wander through tranquil glades of palm trees. Bulbils and turtle-doves call from the tops of the palms whilst groups of sand-grouse fly in to wet their feathers in the irrigation channels. The only traffic in the palmerie is likely to be donkeys pulling carts of decanted sand. Palmerie workers have a constant battle against sand whipping in from the Grand Erg oriental. Palm fronds, cut each winter, are used to form defences against the encroachment.

Beyond the palms the track enters the desert, first passing under a high arch of red brickwork. For most of the year only goatherds take shade beneath its walls, but towards the end of each December this flat expanse of desert overflows with 50,000 locals, nomads and tourists who come to watch and participate in the annual Festival of the Sahara, 10 days of fantasias, horse-racing and camel charges.

For most travellers the only route out of Douz is back to Kebili. Sandy pistes do radiate out in all directions but only with care and preparation should they **Edge of the Grand Erg Oriental.**

be attempted. Few are signposted. Until the Libyan border, 220 miles (350 km) due south of here, there is nothing but a sea of sand dunes. If your quest is to be rid of the many tourists that come to Douz, there are several delightful and quiet oases close to the Chott el Djerid. The rocky, corrugated piste that leaves Douz square for the west crosses the salty edge of the chott to **Zaafrane**, **Nouil** and **Toulba**. All are isolated oases. Yet more remote is **Sabria**, south of Toulba. The piste is very sandy, and one wonders how the dune-locked oasis can survive the onslaught of the Grand Erg.

**Mirages:** When, thousands of years ago, the Mediterranean flooded much of low-lying North Africa, the hinterland of Tunisia was severely affected, and when the sea retreated into the Gulf of Gabes it left a legacy of salt lakes or chotts. The largest was **Chott el Djerid**, which split Tunisia in half. Until very recently the only guaranteed passage from north to south was therefore via the coast. Even now Route 103 between Kebili and Gafsa has its dangers where it crosses the crust of Chott Fedjadj.

Route P16 is a straight highway that traverses the 34-mile (55-km) stretch of chott between Debabcha and Kriz. It used to be a hazardous trek outside the driest summer months, and a deviation from the piste could result in breaking the surface crust of salt and descending into the abyss. Norman Douglas, who travelled these parts a century ago, heard how 1,000 baggage camels were swallowed up by the chott. "Then," he recounted, "it became like it was before, as if the thousand baggage camels had never existed."

Due to the number of more recent, and credible, fatalities the army has now constructed a raised causeway making a fast crossing to the famous date palms of Nefta and Tozeur. The passage is a lonely one, broken only by an opportunist souvenir seller who has set up stall at its centre. For a "lake", the chott possesses very little water and would be of only limited interest except for the fascinating sight of one mirage after another. Sunlight, reflective salt crystals

**Salt patterns in the Chott el Djerid.**

and the flat surface as far as the eye can see create images of palmeries where the map denotes only desert.

The Roman frontier town of **Tozeur** overlooks Chott el Djerid and from here it is only a short drive to the Algerian border. It is the administrative centre of the Djerid region, with a sizeable airport where tourists arrive several times a week. Ochre-coloured geometrically-laid brickwork, echoed in the designs of carpets, is distinctive to Tozeur and Nefta, and is particularly beautiful on the mosque minarets.

The oldest part of Tozeur, the Ouled el Hadef, has undergone major renovation, to the extent that the 600-year-old buildings look brand-new. In fact, the **Great Mosque** at **Bled el Hader** dates from the 9h century and has foundations of Roman origin.

The relative prosperity of Tozeur owes much to the date harvest. A quarter of a million palm trees make a formidable sight. Over 200 springs bring water up from the water table and carefully constructed irrigation streams,

called *seguias*, guide the water down rows of palm trees. Date palms have separate sexes and only one in a hundred of the trees are male. During the spring the male flowers are removed and used to pollinate the female plants artificially. By November the clusters of dates weigh heavily. Between 220 and 440 lb (100–200 kg) of dates per tree will then be harvested ready for the Christmas period in Europe.

Buying them locally is easy and cheap. Street sellers abound and several rates of charge apply. The semi-translucent variety (called *deglat ennour*) are best, but avoid the very cheapest as normally they are riddled with tiny maggots near the stone.

The **Belvedere rock**, which is signposted off Avenue Abou el Kacem Chebbi, has the best views of the oasis and the chotts. Just beneath it, tucked under the palms, is an idyllic camping site. Men and boys come to bathe in the gushing springs round about, and tourists are welcome to join them. Female bathers should expect close scrutiny; some of Tozeur's women show only one eye to the world. The women's traditional outdoor dress is a generous *haik*, all black except for a single white stripe. Different oases have variations on the stripe colour, and in Nefta, 14 miles (23 km) west the stripe is blue.

**Holy oasis:** The route west from Tozeur towards the Algerian border rides high upon a desert ridge. To the south the barren land falls away to an expanse of chott and a horizon of mirages. Suddenly, a massive swathe of over 2,500 acres (1,000 hectares) of palm trees greets the eye. After passing under a road arch you enter **Nefta**.

Sufi Muslims have come to this holy place of pilgrimage since the 9th century. The presence of many small white-domed *marabouts* bears testament to its religious significance. It was here that many famous Muslim mystics, such as the Moroccan-born Sidi Bou Ali, practised meditation in search of an understanding of God. The shrine in his honour is near to the Nefta arch.

Over 150 springs feed the oasis, many of them hot and sulphurous. They en-

**Drummer boy in Douz.**

couraged the Romans to establish a settlement here. The best place to see the palms and springs is from the high ground overlooking the Corbeille (or "basket"), a huge terraced basin filled with lush vegetation and protected on all sides from the hot sandy winds that blow in from the desert. Early evening is the time to be sitting outside the Café de la Corbeille, looking southwest as the sunset settles on the white domes of mosques and *marabouts* and the steam rising from the hot springs drifts between the palms.

The *jardins* of the palmerie, each tended by a particular family, have been established for many centuries. Their well-worn paths offer quiet walks and the chance to see and hear a wealth of birdlife, such as egrets, storks and, occasionally, the beguiling glossy ibis. The economy of the area is not dependent solely upon the dates. A six-tier farming system operates: 40-year-old date palms shade pomegranate trees which, in turn, protect orange groves. Beneath these, broad beans, barley and onions are grown. An elaborate system of concrete irrigation channels brings water from the springs.

Nefta is a relatively affluent oasis. Those that are not active within the *jardins* are busy extracting dinars from the tourists. Persuasive to the extreme, the horse and carriage drivers trawl the hotel areas offering tours around the oasis and to the rather elusive dunes near the Algerian border.

**Mining towns:** The northern oases can be somewhat of a disappointment after the charm and beauty of Nefta and Tozeur. **Gafsa** is the busy heart of the phosphate industry and not particularly picturesque. Norman Douglas agreed with the words of an old Arab song about the town: "Gafsa is miserable; its water is blood; its air is poison; you may live there a hundred years without making a friend." The Romans liked it though, especially its hot springs, and most visitors come to see the **Piscines Romaines**, the only Roman remains.

Although well-signposted, finding these two pools through the maze of

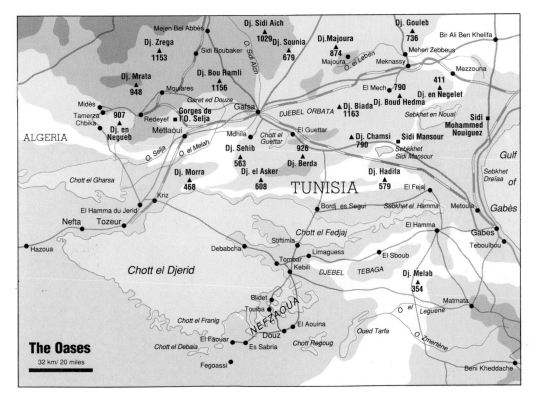

The Oases
32 km/ 20 miles

streets can take a while. There is no shortage of local children prepared to show you the way and then, for a dinar or two, terrify you by launching themselves into the water from the tops of palm trees, regardless of other children walking down the stone stairway to collect water for home.

A rail and road link provides good communications between Gafsa and Tozeur. Centred, almost equidistant, amongst the pink mountains, is the phosphate town of **Metlaoui**. Mining spoil heaps abound. A Frenchman, Phillipe Thomas, discovered the rich deposits of phosphate here at the turn of the century. To begin with, the local French administrator wasn't keen to be bothered by "scientists". Thomas recorded his reception in Metlaoui as "several degrees below zero". Today, phosphates provide one of Tunisia's most important revenues.

For the traveller Metlaoui is an important staging post for a trip into the beautiful **Seldja Gorge** and mountain oases of **Chebika** and **Tamerza**. The road out of Metlaoui to Moulares passes through the heart of the phosphate hills.

Alternatively, a train, known as *Le Lezard Rouge* and a gift to the Bey of Tunis from the French in 1940, can be used during the summer months (1 July–30 September) to escape to the cooler climate of the mountains. The train stops in the middle of a rocky desert, a short walk from the spectacular gorge carved out by the River Seldja, a famed local beauty spot.

The mountain oases were, like their desert counterparts, determined by the force of water. Most are located in ravines and narrow gorges. The oasis of Chebika is based around a stream that cascades out of the rock near the old settlement. The palmerie is especially picturesque. Tamerza is Chebika's twin, with a similarly attractive waterfall and stream. Both remain unspoilt, though Tamerza does run to a modest hotel. Known in Roman times as, respectively, Ad Turres and Ad Speculum, they were, as today, among the final outposts.

**Left**, selling sheep in Douz. **Right**, properly equipped.

# EXPEDITIONS

The ultimate experience of Tunisia must surely be an expedition into the desert. Unfortunately, there is only so far a small Fiat, Peugeot or Renault can venture; going for a careful crawl round the *ksour* south of Medenine is certainly as intrepid as the car-hire firms like their customers to get. Desert safari companies run four-wheel drive trips from most of the coastal resorts, particularly Gabes and Sousse, which may be either a one-day sortie or could take up to a week crossing every type of Tunisian landscape. Drivers and camping equipment are supplied.

But package trips such as these tend to be restrictive and can be costly. There is nothing quite like the independence of your own four-wheel drive vehicle. As they are expensive to hire, the best solution is to bring a vehicle properly prepared in advance.

When choosing a vehicle, a number of factors must be considered, such as the price, availability of spares, load-carrying capacity and which engine/fuel is preferable. Diesel's advantages over petrol include cheapness, better mileage to the gallon and easy maintenance, as there are no electrics and a low fire risk. Petrol has the advantage of being better understood than diesel, producing faster cruising speeds and being quieter and cleaner. The latest diesel engines are very sophisticated, with turbo and intercooling bringing their performance close to the smoothness expected from petrol, but again this could be a disadvantage in a Third World country if they were to break down.

The Land-Rover Series Three was manufactured between 1972 and 1982. Tried and tested, it is still the king of the Sahara. Spares (especially secondhand) are widely available in Tunisia and any bush mechanic could repair one. Ex-Ministry of Defence Land-Rovers can be good buys, and Japanese vehicles, Toyota especially, are a common sight everywhere in North Africa.

Whatever vehicle is considered, load carrying capacity is important. Most four-wheel drive vehicles are built in short or long wheelbase forms.

The latter is the more suitable, making overloading less likely. The long wheelbase Land-Rover can take five people comfortably, with a large space in the rear which could seat a further six. Another plus for the Land-Rover is the huge number of accessories available to equip the vehicle for the desert.

When preparing a vehicle, fitting new or nearly new tyres is the starting point. Keep them in good order by checking the pressures daily. The type of tread required depends on the terrain. An aggressive tread, normally used for mud, is not suitable for sand. The latter demands little or no tread but a wide surface area to help float the vehicle over the sand rather than cut into it. Michelin XS tyres are specifically for sand but are no good on rocky ground, so unless sand is the most likely ground condition keep to a general tread such as Michelin XZY.

Spare wheels can be very heavy. Rather than taking several, consider a set of tyre levers and a repair kit. Also fit a heavy-duty suspension, not so that more luggage can be loaded but so that the weight that does have to be carried can be done so with more safety. Roof racks are a temptation to carry too much, and off-road a heavily-laden one will upset a vehicle's stability. Treated with care, they are ideal for carrying self-recovery equipment, such as a high-lift jack, rope, shovel, sand ladders, and jerrycans.

Spares are vital. Consider the age of the vehicle and the duration of travel when deciding what to take. Even if no one in a party can fit, say, a clutch, it is worth taking. It will be much easier to find a bush mechanic than spare parts in a remote spot. Spares need to be well packed so that they do not rub together. An ideal place to put them is in padlocked steel boxes bolted to a roofrack.

Careful route planning is essential, so that fuel and oil consumption can be estimated. Off-road driving increases these considerably. Plugging through sand in low-range gears may drop a normal 18 mpg fuel consumption to only 8 mpg (7.6 to 3.4 km/litre). Inevitable navigation mistakes will also use valuable fuel reserves.

Before venturing into Africa, practise off-road techniques, including self-recovery. Better still, learn by enrolling at an off-road driving school.

# THE KSOUR

André Gide found paradise in the coast oasis of **Gabes**: "Gardens profuse with blooms, alive with bees, from which fragrance arose so insistently that they well-nigh replaced both food and intoxicating liquor." Not surprising, then, that his fellow writer and countryman George Bernanos breathed his last here.

The extensive palmerie stretching for nearly 4 sq. miles (7 sq. km) around Gabes, was Gide's inspiration for such hyperbole and it is still the town's main attraction; though don't expect an oasis such as Nefta or even Tozeur. It contains a zoo and a so-called "crocodile farm", a few desultory villages such as Chenini (not to be confused with the spectacular hill-top Chenini south of Tataouine) and some *zaouias*; but the drivers of *calèches* waiting to take visitors on a guided tour find it hard to drum up trade now that Gabes is so plainly committed to industrial development.

Gabes deals in phosphates, sulphuric acid and fertilisers. Off its coast lie valuable sources of oil – the most recently exploited deposits being the 7 Novembre oilfield discovered in 1988.

The town commands the **Gabes Gap**, an important corridor between the sea and the natural obstacles of the chotts and the Tabaga and Matmata mountain ranges. It was through here that the early Arabs made incursions and the trans-Saharan caravans carrying gold, ivory and slaves came. For centuries the passage was known for its warring tribes and perils for travellers. It was plagued by Berber highwaymen, who after seizing a caravan would force the merchants to drink large quantities of hot water in order to extract any gold they might have swallowed – quite kindly treatment compared to their earlier custom of slitting gullets.

In 1939 the French, fearing that Mussolini's troops in Libya would attempt to expand into Tunisia via the Gap, established the Mareth Line; it was a 20-mile (32-km) defence system composed of concrete pillboxes, wire, anti-tank ditches and Oued Zigzaou, a formidable anti-tank barrier dry or wet. Ironically, the only time it was tested was in 1943 when Germany and Italy used it as a defence against the Allies. The Line was so difficult to penetrate that Field-Marshal Montgomery was forced to support his advance on Gabes by a flanking assault via a tricky defile through the Matmata mountains. Montgomery's curses were held responsible for the five years of drought that followed his campaign.

Gabes may not be worth much attention, but it is an obvious springboard for travelling into the Djerid and the Ksour regions. The road west heads through the chotts, parting successive veils of mirages all the way to Kebili, Douz and eventually Tozeur; the main road south via the Gap leads to Medenine, the island of Djerba and the Libyan border; and a southwesterly direction climbs up to Matmata, famous for its troglodyte dwellings, in the Djebel Dahar.

Four-wheel drive jeeps monopolise these roads. If you want to be in one,

**Preceding pages:** Ksar Ouled Soltane; carpet seller in Tataouine. **Left,** wedding procession in Toudjane. **Right,** spinning yarn.

expedients can be arranged in Gabes or even Sousse (see *Travel Tips*), though many of the vehicles you see will be travelling terrain perfectly accessible in small hired cars.

**Lunar landscape:** The **Matmata** road is at its most atmospheric approaching sundown, when the landscape, flat and tussocky surrounding Gabes then gradually contorting into hills spiked by isolated palms, is full of pink tints and shadows. Alas, from the point of view of finding overnight accommodation, this is the most inadvisable time to reach **Matmata**, so if you want to spend the night in a hole, and most people do, book ahead.

New Matmata, 9 miles (15 km) before the troglodyte village, was built in 1961. Bourguiba, misinformed on the matter (*see page 95*), thought that caves were unfit habitation for dignified humans, and Matmata's population should be rehoused. In a speech in 1960 he said: "The task that will be accomplished with state control in the next three years is destined to efface the mud huts, which mar our countryside, and rid our local population and tourists from this depressing sight."

Bourguiba may not have understood tourists, but some enterprising locals did. Not only are there now five or six troglodyte hotels, ranging from the two-star Matmata Hotel, with air conditioning and swimming pool, to **Les Berbiers**, very basic with no hot water, but rehoused villagers offer guided tours of their old homes – tip expected on departure. At night they return to their new abodes to count the day's takings, and old Matmata is deserted except for roaming packs of tourists wondering where the action has gone.

There are other, smaller troglodyte communities around Matmata, sometimes just a few pits grouped together and often simple caves in a vertical stretch of hillside. Camouflaged by the sandy, pockmarked landscape, they are not obvious at first sight.

Easily accessible to the west of Matmata (in the right weather, i.e. not wet nor too hot, an invigorating hike of

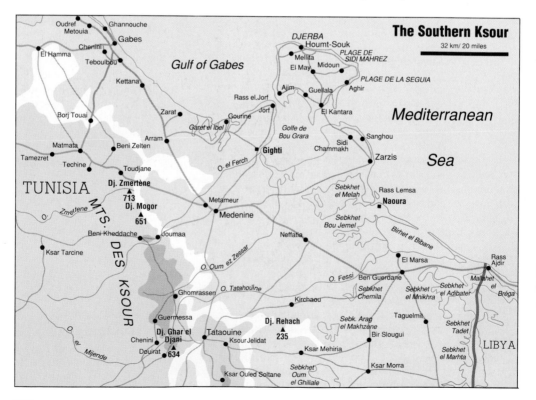

6 miles/10 km each way) is the tiny Berber village of **Tamezret** perched on a hill. Although the road there is tarmacked, not many tourists venture along it. The scenery is full of unexpected vistas: the pink and blue Djebel Tabaga in the distance, pockets of cultivation in steep ravines, and white *koubbas* in relief against the dun-coloured hills. The village is walled and tiny; a handful of men congregate around a café; occasionally a woman in a blazing red *mellia* caught emerging from her home will stare hard before bolting inside.

Only four-wheel drive vehicles should attempt to continue west of Tamezret, and the same proviso might be applied to the route southeast of Matmata, a track which crawls along the backbone of the Matmata hills before descending into Metameur (39 miles/63 km altogether). It is accessible by ordinary cars, but with great difficulty. Although it is newly surfaced as far as the turning for Techine (first 8 miles/12 km), further on vehicles must

**Matmata, mainly subterranean.**

crawl up sheer rock. Should you breakdown on the piste, you may wait hours before anyone comes along. Local traffic is scarce, but there are occasional bands of soldiers engaged in a sort of aimless shovelling.

That said, the scenery is stunning, with views unfolding as far as the coast. And just as your vehicle attacks the most impossible point of the track, there are shouts of encouragement. A pair of Berbers have set up a primus stove at a spectacular site above the village of Toudjane. They provide sweet tea, warm Coca-Cola and welcome human contact. Although they say a small hotel is planned, this seems a bit ambitious in view of the modest nature of their improvised café and it would be premature to say watch this space.

**Toudjane** (which may be more easily gained from Ain Tounine) is visited by a small number of tourists but it succeeds in remaining unspoilt. Like the caves in the naturally-cratered landscape around Matmata, the flat-roofed stone village is camouflaged against the

rock strata. From a distance it is hard even to distinguish the quite large village; drying washing or the bright clothes of the women are discerned before the outline of a building.

After Toudjane, the road descends to Metameur. It is still piste (hopes raised by intermittent stretches of tarmac are soon dashed), though as the landscape subsides into a flat plain it becomes much more tame. Those with the time and the nerve for further tricky piste might take the more scenic route via El Hallouf and Beni Kheddache (turn right after about 12 miles/20 km), though both are more easily attained direct from Medenine.

**Distinctive architecture:** Twenty dusty miles (32 km) from Toudjane the village of **Metameur** appears on a knoll just to the right of the road. It provides the first glimpse of *ghorfas*, the loaf-shaped mud cells that, piled one on top of the other and set side by side, comprise the *ksour*. They are a defensive form of architecture, generally crowning hills but occasionally built on the valley floor, that were used by nomads to store grain (*see page 95*). As a result of the more rigid law and order imposed by the French the tribes abandoned the *ksour* and began to store their grain near the fields. Sometimes these *ksour* were converted into homes.

The *ghorfa* cell was, and still is, a basic architectural template in Tunisia. It was adapted in the building of elaborate mountain villages, such as Chenini and Douiret. Some *ksour* are supposed to be 600 years old, but such ages are based on the dates of their founding rather than on the ruins that are left as, being vulnerable to winter rain, they were constantly patched up, repaired and replaced.

Many that were inhabited have been abandoned, sometimes for the new villages that have been built close by but often for very different pastures. The decline of the nomadic lifestyle of the tribes has meant steady urban migration. In Tunis colonies of immigrants from southern Tunisia are still organised along ethnic lines: migrants from

**Toudjane, at the end of a perilous piste.**

Chenini have a long tradition of becoming newspaper vendors; Douiret emigrants tend to work in the central market; many people from Ghoumrassen earned their first crust in the big city by making and selling doughnuts, a speciality of their village.

Metameur's location on the plain means that it is not one of the more dramatic *ksour*; but it is worth a closer look and there is a ghorfa hotel for those who want to stay. Although this is basic, you will not find much more salubrious accommodation at **Medenine**, 4 miles (6 km) further on, the regional capital of the Medenine Province. Medenine was once full of *ghorfas* belonging to the nomadic Touazine and Khezour tribes, but these have gradually been demolished; the one remaining ksar at the centre of town has been turned into a carpet-draped bazaar.

According to literature issued by the Tourist Office, drivers venturing further south should register with the National Guard at Medenine. It seems a bit over-cautious to people who just want to potter around a few *ksour* and have no intention of straying far from the beaten track, and only those planning to exceed Remada or cut across rough country will be sent back by patrol police if they neglect to do so, but when a disaster happens (as it did in 1988, albeit near Douz) and tourists perish in the desert, it is this kind of warning that the authorities point at. The Tourist Office would like to see everybody exploring the region by coach of course.

With this in mind, the road from Medenine to Djoumaa and Beni Khaddache has been specially improved. A broad, new road snakes up the Djebel Dahar; at intervals there are turn-outs for the coaches to park, so that their occupants can get out and take photographs of the view. Such pandering to package tourism undoubtedly takes the thrill out of *ksour* country, but the road is useful for those with limited time or who, having approached Beni Kheddache by a more difficult route (say from Ghoumrassen or Toudjane), want to take the fast way back to town.

**Traditional oil press.**

Louages and mini-buses also cough their way up the long incline; the latter leave Medenine at 8.15 a.m. and 10 a.m, but check times, as they are quite likely to change.

At the summit of the hill (22 miles/36 km from Medenine), **Ksar Djoumaa**, now deserted in favour of the new village close by, is just visible on a spur to the left (look behind). The outside wall is formed by the blank rears of *ghorfas*, the series of roof arches functioning as crenellated battlements. The entrance, inscribed with the hegira date of 1174 (which, if it refers to the date of the *ksar*'s founding, makes it 18th-century), opens upon the usual courtyards, cisterns and honeycomb of mud cells. Its original three storeys have collapsed to two, but it is still littered with household bit and pieces such as clay pitchers and straw panniers.

The new village of **Beni Kheddache**, on a high plateau (7 miles/11 km) further on, is built around what remained of the old *ksar* after it was demolished by the French. The road forks round it, flanking still-inhabited *ghorfas* on one side and mosque and modern farm buildings on the other. There is very little left of what Lieutenant Reginald Rankin, who came here in the 1890s, described as a "Saharan Windsor in its bold massiveness", but it is a busy rural village, with a market, cafés, modest restaurant and grocery shops.

Not far beyond Beni Khaddache the broad road peters out. Signposts are confusing, but helpful locals will rally round to find a French-speaking villager who can direct. A reasonable track leads north to El Hallouf and Metameur; to the west treacherous piste crosses the stony plain to nowhere in particular (those equipped with 4-wheel drive, proper maps and desert permits only), though after 6 miles/10 km, a lonely piste turns off to the mountain village of Toudjane. Just before Beni Kheddache, a more frequented but still not easy track (not to be attempted late in the day) wends south across the valleys to **Kerachfa** (3 miles/5 km east of the main piste) and **Ksar Haddada**.

**Evening landscape in the Djebel Dahar.**

The formerly impressive ksar Kerachfa is dilapidated, but part of Ksar Haddada has been professionally restored to a hotel. This *ksar* hotel has the edge on the one at Metameur; it boasts a bar.

A tarmac road leads to **Goumrassen**, one of the most visited villages in the region, though it has yet to acknowledge this with a hotel. Its modern quarter – with a market, shops and even a bank – lies in the lap of a steep valley; the old dwellings – cave and *ghorfa* hybrids – line the softer strata of the slopes and dot the upper spurs.

From here it is easy to travel to Guermessa, a similar though less frequented village, or to make for Tataouine (served by buses and louages), the best base for exploring the *ksour*.

The main road to **Tataouine** from Medenine (30 miles/50 km) is a fast drive running parallel with the Djebel Dahar over a plain of esparto grass and thorn. The town, once a Foreign Legion outpost, is very average, but it has a compact centre, plenty of modest restaurants (warning: they all close early)

and a comfortable if unprepossessing two-star hotel, La Gazelle d'Or (there are basic alternatives if this is fully booked). On Monday and Thursday a market draws merchants and farmers from miles around.

**Heart of the *ksour*.** Tataouine affords easy access (no pistes) to the most spectacular villages of the region: Chenini, Douiret and Ouled Soltane. The roads to all of them are overlooked by minor *ksour*, which cap the flat-topped hills. One of them, **Ksar Magabla**, slightly out of town on the Remada road, is just a short walk; a signposted road leads up to a mosque and collection of new houses, and beyond them a track twists up to the *ksar*.

**Chenini** is the highlight of the *ksour* and prominent on the tourist circuit; but it is still possible to arrive here and be the only foreigner around. An early morning visit assures this, but as the road from Tataouine is sound, and returning late in the day is no problem, another good time to arrive is an hour or two before sundown. During summer

there is a basic *relais* restaurant where it is possible to stay. The village is some way past the sign.

The extensive cave and *ghorfa* community grips a V-shaped ridge; the oldest quarters, crowned by a *kalaa* (fort) built to defend the village from attack, cling to one leg; the newer and still inhabited settlement curls round the other. Sitting on the saddle between them is the mosque.

Villagers quite rightly want to make a few dinars out of all the tourists who crawl over their hillsides, and so there is some pressure to visit their homes and the communal olive press. To escape insistent invitations head up to the *kalaa*; the prospect of a long climb in the heat soon puts them off.

A switch-back path leads to its summit. From here views extend across the palm-sprinkled valleys on both sides of the ridge, into the courtyards of the still-inhabited caves behind, and across to the terraces of dwellings on the other side of the spur. The white mosque and the women's red check *sifsaris* – from a

distance pink – are startling against the multi shades of brown.

From here, the common design of the dwellings is clearly visible. As elsewhere in the region, rows of caves are excavated along the rock's softer strata. They are fronted by courtyards and buffered from the public pathways by *ghorfas* (used for animals or storage), the backs of which double as walls. In contrast to the foot of the village, where men lie talking in the shade of the café and women flock round a well in great animation, the top of Chenini is absolutely silent. Occasionally a solitary villager, invariably an old man done up like an Old Testament prophet and on his way to the mosque, is announced by the soft tap of his staff.

**Douiret**, too, commands a magnificent valley. From Tataouine it is approached by a good road after turning right at Ksar Ouled Debbab on the way to Remada (direct from Chenini it can be reached by a short but awkward piste). Those who are determined enough can drive right up to the mosque on the lowest level of the *ksar*, but it is advisable to park down by the complex of modern buildings – the headquarters of the French administrator at the end of the 19th century – and walk up the last rocky stretch.

The design of the *ksar* is similar to Chenini, though with much broader alleyways. Again, each cave is fronted by a courtyard, then a couple of outhouse *ghorfas* in which the animals would have lived. There are a number of olive presses, exuding a pungent scent of olives and camel, apparently still in use; to find them, look for tar-like stains on the paths, indicating where the olive sediment has been tipped over the edge of the hillside.

As is clear from its vast shell, Douiret was extensive. Closer examination of the cemetery below, which at first sight appears to contain just a handful of white-domed tombs, reveals hundreds of insignificant, rough-hewn stones. When the French official was counting, the population numbered over 5,000.

Such evidence gives Douiret a very melancholy air. In spite of its many

**Tattooed lady.**

well-preserved dwellings, they have nearly all been abandoned for New Douiret or urban Tunisia. The handful of families left, who live by cultivating strips of crops on the terraces at the bottom of the *ksar*, have the look of outcasts rather than the stoics that they are. Douiret's mosque (no access to non-Muslims), containing an unusual Berber inscription (Berber not being a written language), is their one focal point. The quietness of the children is deafening.

**Desert madness:** From Douiret or Chenini, four-wheel drive vehicles can get into gear and tackle the 30-mile (48-km) piste heading west for **Ksar Ghilane** on the edge of the Grand Erg. To travel is probably better than to arrive. There is not a lot to see there – just a Roman fort and a well – but there may be plenty of Suzuki jeeps. It is well-patronised by adventure tour groups who sum up the Sahara for their clients by a sing-song round a campfire and a night in a bat-like bedouin tent.

To the southeast of Tataouine (take the tarmacked lane to Beni Barka off the main Remada road) the hilltops are craggy with innumerable minor *ksour*. With the exception of the one at **Maztouriya**, which has an unusually imposing stone gateway, the *ksour* differ only in their varying levels of decay, and are not particularly worth a climb. The real object of the journey is to see **Ouled Soltane**, the most perfect example of a *ghorfa* used for grain storage. To get to it, fork left past the village of Tamelest; the final signpost appears to have disappeared.

The *ksar* comes into view undramatically, just over a small knoll, and to the right of the village of Ouled Soltane (quite lively, with useful grocery store, café and brand-new post office). As usual, from the outside its walls are blank; but through the gatehouse two impeccable rings of *ghorfas*, connected by a passage, rise to four storeys. Access to the upper levels is by means of precarious ledges and steps.

It is worth walking or driving to the very end of the village, where the hill

Nomads enjoy some comforts, including a TV powered by a car battery.

suddenly drops to a plain. In the right weather conditions the view is magnificent: like a pink, blue and lemon-coloured sea. At ground level this gravel plain is less inspiring; the tarmac road continues for a couple of miles before abruptly turning to piste past the village of Mghit (unless properly equipped, it is not advisable to venture too far).

The right-hand route at the fork before Ouled Soltane is tarmacked for a further 5 miles (8 km), until Ramtha, where a track carries on to Remada (four-wheel drive and desert permit holders only). It is a monotonous journey, interrupted by a mere sprinkling of roadside houses, whose inhabitants look astounded to see a stranger on the hot, dusty piste; it has no advantages over the main C112 road to the military town of Remada.

Anyone intending to go beyond **Remada** – and there is no hotel for anyone hoping to stay – is required to secure a military pass, available from the National Guard there. This applies mainly to those on trans-Saharan expeditions through Algeria or Libya and beyond. Tunisia's improved relations with Libya, and the subsequent re-opening of the border in 1988, haven't lessened the amount of security in these parts, so you are unlikely to proceed far without one.

The main C112 continues another 34 miles (55 km) to the Libyan border at **Dehiba**. More minor roads (properly equipped four-wheel drive only) descend into the long tail of Tunisia, culminating at the Tunisian, Libyan and Algerian border point at **Bordj el Khadra** (mosque, a few trees and lots of barbed wire).

It is a beautiful route, in parts skirting the dunes of the Grand Erg and crossed by gazelle. There are no signs of civilian life, but just to the east of Tiaret at **M'Chiguig**, yards from the Libyan border, there is an old Foreign Legion fort, now manned by the Tunisian military. Behind it is a curious obelisk, a memorial to a self-styled French adventurer called the Marquis de Mores who was

Camels, wealth of the Nefzaou.

murdered on this spot by Taureg tribesmen in 1896.

**French adventurer:** By all accounts it was a murder instigated by higher powers. De Mores had been a thorn in the side of the French government since making allegations of incompetence about the Resident General of French Indo-china. He saw himself as a pioneering iconoclast – even wearing Wild West cowboy hats. In North Africa he hatched grandiose plans for a French and Arab alliance that would take over the whole Sahara.

It was all too much for the French government, who wanted to proceed in a much quieter way, so they had him murdered. Edward VII said that if the Marquis de Mores had been English, he would have been made a Viceroy.

The C111 from Tataouine to the busy northern border post with Libya, **Ras Ajdir**, is a fast road over a scree and esparto grass plain. There is nothing much before **Ben Guerdane**, the last town before the border, where as well as farming extensive olive orchards the townspeople make a tidy living meeting the needs of travellers to and from Libya, not least changing their money on the black market. The road to the border is thick with smoke (from restaurant braziers), pottery stalls and men and children waving large wads of banknotes.

Those who need visas for Libya (all Westerners) will not be allowed as far as the border without one. Anyone just wanting to amble up for a curious peak at Colonel Gaddafi's republic will get involved in tedious police checks.

The obvious antidote to a strenuous tour of Tunisia's *ksour* region is a relaxing sojourn on the island of Djerba, which claims to be the Land of the Lotus Eaters that detained Odysseus and his men. From Ben Guerdane a road dogs the edge of the Gulf of Gabes to Zarzis – a town that tries, unsuccessfully, to rival Djerba as a resort – and then to El Kantara where a causeway leads to the island. On the the way is the strange Birhet el Bibane lagoon and the Sebkhet el Melah, site of an enormous salt mine.

**Making bread, the mainstay of all meals.**

# TROGLODYTES

Matmata resembles a ghostly moonscape, particularly at dusk when the dying rays of the sun cast the shadows of dome-shaped hills and smoke curls mysteriously from unseen fissures in the ground like the parting shots of an exhausted volcano. A lonely figure, perhaps leading a mule, may be visible against the skyline one minute and gone the next, apparently spirited from the face of the earth. The surreal mood may not last, however, if the tourist is then accosted by a local fellow who in halting English and as many words says: "Hello, I'm a troglodyte! Wanna come and see where I live?"

"Troglodyte" (sometimes shortened to "trog") carries slang connotations of neanderthal savagery, but strictly speaking the term simply means cave-dweller or, as in the Matmata mountains, someone who lives in a hole. It should not be assumed that a hole in the ground is the last bastion of abject poverty. In fact, Tunisia's troglodytes have a rich tribal culture and before their conversion to Islam (a long time ago) erected impressive altars to their pagan gods.

One of the first Europeans to befriend the troglodytes under the newly imposed French protectorate at the end of the 19th century described them as "lively natives" with "expressive eyes, happy disposition, and a ready smile". The real reason for their underground existence is, as we shall see, practical commonsense, although it has been the subject of colourful conjecture.

In any event, Tunisia's troglodytes are reputed (by the Greek historian Herodotus and others) to have lived through the unsettling experience of being hunted down like animals in the ancient past by neighbours mounted on four-wheeled chariots. Daniel Bruun, a pioneering 19th-century Dane, had a long list of questions which he wished to put to the troglodytes about their history. The excitement of finally catching up with them caused him to fire off all six chambers of his revolver in the air. This gesture went down so well that his host expressed the hope that he would be staying with them for 40 years. It was intimated that a wife could be made ready for him in a day or two. Bruun felt flattered. Normally, he noted, they guarded their women carefully because of "the reputation of being light of morals".

Bruun may have been the first, but he was certainly not the last, to make the troglodytes realise that there was a considerable amount of foreign interest in their style of life – they themselves could not at first understand what all the fuss was about. The amiable stranger who these days strolls up and, having presented his bona fides as a "troglodyte" (possibly one of no more than two or three foreign words in his vocabulary), then extends an invitation to look around the house, has merely turned that continuing curiosity into a full-time business. The modern guest, unlike Bruun, may leave after half an hour without giving any offence. The experience of life underground may comfortably be extended in a number of dwellings which have formally been converted into well-appointed tourist hotels.

Bruun drew a blank when he made enquiries into their ancient history. He learned, though, that when they plundered, a habit which died out only with the arrival of the French at the end of the 19th century, they did so "thoroughly". Not satisfied with carrying off herds, they ordered the owners to strip, leaving them with "only a scrap of shirt which barely covered them". He recorded the custom of a bridegroom holding the scented end of a heavy stick under his bride's nose: "So long as she conducts herself properly, her life will be mild and pleasant like the scent… should she misbehave she may be sure of being well punished."

The holes in which a bridal couple would settle with the rest of the extended family are generally not visible until one is right on top of them, but they are quite large and open to the sky, hence the curling smoke from cooking fires. A single dwelling usually consists of two holes about 30 ft (9 metres) in diamater and as many deep. These serve as courtyards and are linked by underground corridors with bedrooms, animal pens and so on dug out of the walls on either side. The living quarters are often laid out on two levels, the staircase between them hollowed out of the walls. Access to the whole is by a sloping tunnel which surfaces some distance from the dwelling, thus accounting for the apparently precipitous descent of lonely figures, with or without mules, into the bowels of the earth.

The furnishings may be fairly lavish, as they were in Bruun's time. He commented on "household pots and pans prettily arranged on the inner wall" and couches covered with carpets on which inmates slept without undressing. He was disapproving, though, of "frightful framed pictures, apparently supposed to represent the Prophet, and evidently cheap rubbish bought at Gabes, corresponding in all respects to the coloured prints of the Christ which we find in every cottage in our country". The Berbers of Matmata were and are not zealous Muslims; the Prophet lately seems to have surrendered pride of place on the walls to

in the Gabes Gap was so disrupted by repeated waves of invaders that the inhabitants elected to take themselves underground. That way they could plunge out of harm's way, pull down the hatches and pop up again when the coast was clear. It's an attractive theory which fits in with Herodotus's description of a people who had every reason to feel insecure, not to say paranoid, but it fails to stand up when you remember that there were people in contemporary Malta and elsewhere who also chose to lead a troglodyte existence without any great threat to their lives.

The rest of what Herodotus had to say about these "Ethiopian hole-men" in the 6th century BC may not be without interest, and his use of terms like "Ethiopian" have no bearing on later geography. Because they were constantly chased by

posters of pop stars, notably Prince and Madonna.

The Matmata mountain range runs like a low spine along the narrow corridor which links Mediterranean Tunisia with the desert hinterland. The Gabes Gap, as it is known, is 11 miles (18 km) wide; on one side the sea, on the other the Chott el Djerid salt flats. It has always been the overland invasion route from Libya and the African interior. Egyptians of old discovered – and the Allies in World War II remembered – that at the wrong time of year the fragile crust of the salt can cave in and swallow an army whole.

It has been supposed in some quarters that life

whooping charioteers, they became, he said, "exceedingly swift of foot". Another writer claimed they could outrun a horse. Herodotus refers also to their diet – a liking for snakes and lizards – and to their language. "Like no other," it resembled the screeching of bats, he maintained.

The most plausible explanation for living in holes is probably very simple. The terrain is treeless and there is not much else in the way of convenient building materials. The earth, on the other hand, was easily excavated and of a consistency which kept walls and ceilings intact without the need for shoring up. Moreover, underground dwellings were cool in summer and warm in winter. Faced with the perennial problem of a growing family, the head of a troglodyte household could merely call for a spade…

**Left**, troglodyte grandmother. **Above**, pits are about 30 ft (9 metres) in diameter. **Overpage**: on the Lézard Rouge.

299

# GETTING THERE

## BY AIR

The national airline, **Tunis** Air, flies direct to Tunis from London Heathrow twice a week. Flying time is approximately 2 hrs 30 min. Apex tickets (which must be booked at least 14 days in advance and cannot be cancelled) cut costs considerably.

If you wish to travel by schedule flight from London to Monastir, Sfax, Djerba or Tozeur it is necessary to fly via Tunis. However, Frankfurt, Geneva, Lyon and Marseille have direct schedule flights to Tunis, Djerba and Monastir; Paris has direct flights to Tunis, Sfax, Djerba and Monastir; and Rome, Nice and Brussels have direct flights to Monastir and Tunis

The London office of Tunis Air is at 24 Sackville Street, London W1 1DE (tel: 071-734 7644). The Tunis Office is at 48 Avenue 7 Novembre (tel: 01-288 100). There are branches of Tunis Air in all major Tunisian towns.

GB Airways also operates direct flights to Tunis, from London Gatwick. Flying time is slightly longer, at 2 hrs 45 mins. Their prices are the same as those offered by Tunis Air, with similar reductions for Apex flights. They do not offer connections to other destinations in Tunisia. British Airways handles their reservations in London (tel: 081-897 4000). The Tunis office of GB Airways is at 17 Avenue 7 Novembre (tel: 01-244 261).

Charter flights usually arrive at **Monastir**. This is a convenient airport, close to Sousse and within a few hours' drive of Tunis, the north coast, the southern oases and the interior. Depending on the time of year and the pattern of sales, excellent flight-only bargains can be found at British travel agents.

## BY SEA

Ferry and jetfoil services to Tunisia get fully booked by migrant workers in summer; forward planning (of several months) is therefore advisable.

Ferries to Tunis operate from Marseille in France (21 to 24 hours), from Trapani in Sicily (8 hours), and from Naples via Cagliari (in Sardinia) and then Trapani (45 hours). There is also a ferry from Genoa direct to Tunis once a week (24 hours).

**From France**: Ferries from France to Tunis depart from Marseille. To book from London, contact Continental Shipping & Travel, 179 Piccadilly London W1V 9DB (tel: 071-491 4968). To book from France, contact SNCM, 61 Boulevard des Dames, 13002 Marseille (tel: 91 56 3200). The Tunis office handling passages from France is Compagnie de Mixte Agents, Navitours, 8 Rue d'Alger, Tunis (tel: 01-249 500).

**From Italy**: For ferries between Tunis and Cagliari and Trapani contact: Tirrenia Agents, CTN, 126 Rue de Yugoslavie, Tunis (tel: 01-242 775). The British agent dealing with Tirrenia bookings is Serena Holidays, 40–42 Kenway Road, London SW5 (tel: 071-373 6548/9). The Tirrenia agent in Naples is at Stazione Marittima, Molo Angionino (tel: 720 1111/551 2181).

The crossing from Genoa to Tunis is also made by Tirrenia, but there is no agent handling bookings in Britain. The Genoa office is at Stazione Marittima, Ponte Colombo (tel: 26981).

There is also a jetfoil service, operated by Alscafi Bavigazione, between Trapani in Sicily and Kelibia on Cap Bon in Tunisia between the months of July and September. The journey takes little more than three hours. The offices of Alscafi Bavigazione are at the port in Trapani.

## BY RAIL

A railway line runs from Casablanca in **Morocco** right across **Algeria** to Tunis, but as yet there is no through train. It is necessary to change at Oujda (near the Moroccan border), then in Algiers and Constantine. The journey takes about 45 hours and a single second-class ticket costs approximately £40. Reservations are essential. The main obstacle is not the Atlas Mountains but

Algerian bureaucracy. Most European nationals (including the British since 1990) need a visa to enter Algeria and are required to change the equivalent of around £100 at the border, which unless they plan to sojourn in Algeria, will be difficult to spend. It's worth checking that this requirement still applies; L'Union du Grand Maghreb, in theory aspiring to be a North African Common Market, established in its latest form in 1988, may succeed in abolishing such regulations. There is also talk of a Trans-Maghrebian express which will dispense with the need to change.

## BY ROAD

From Europe it is necessary to take a ferry from France or Italy to Tunis (see *By Sea*), Morocco or Algeria, but this is an expensive option. Although car hire is not cheap in Tunisia, it is doubtful that it would be worth bringing your own car unless you are planning to stay more than a month or it is a 4-wheel drive vehicle which you intend to use in the Sahara (see feature on *Desert Driving*). If you do take a vehicle, book your ferry passage well in advance; in summer thousands of migrant workers ply this route.

To enter the country with a vehicle, you must be over 21 years old, possess either an acceptable national licence or international licence (a British driving licence is acceptable), the vehicle's registration book to prove ownership, and Green Card insurance. Suitable insurance can also be obtained on the spot from the Tunisian Customs for periods of 2, 7 or 21 days, and should be paid for in hard currency.

**Importing vehicles**: To the disappointment of migrant workers and some entrepreneurial tourists, it is no longer possible to import and sell cars that are over two years old. Even newer models are not normally eligible for sale by visitors. In exceptional circumstances permission might be given, but only after customs duty has been paid.

**Shared taxis** and **buses** operate to Tunisia from towns in **Algeria**, including Annaba, Constantine and El Oued, and from Tripoli in **Libya**. Typical durations of journeys are: Constantine to Tunis, 9 hours; Annaba to Tunis, 5½ hours; Tripoli to Tunis, 16½ hours.

Once a week a bus travels between Tunis and Cairo (the journey takes a gruelling 54 hours and costs 90D single). It is possible to join the bus at other departure points, e.g. Sousse and Sfax; to find out more, contact the bus station at Bab Alleoua in Tunis. Most nationals need visas to enter Libya and Egypt (the British Embassy in Tunis will supply an Arabic translation of British passports – a Libyan requirement); remember this before setting out. Also remember that there is no consular protection in Libya for the British. Although the Libyans officially claim that they do not take hostages, in 1986 Colonel Gadaffi detained members of a French family cruising between Malta and Libya and they were not released until 1990.

# TRAVEL ESSENTIALS

## VISAS & PASSPORTS

Despite new laws requiring Tunisians visiting Britain to possess visas, the Tunisian government, mindful of the fact that tourism is now their number one industry, has not retaliated and does not require visas from holders of full British passports or British Visitor's passports. Nor do American and Canadian passport holders require visas, but Australian nationals do. Holders of EEC passports do not need visas, with the exception of nationals of the Netherlands, Belgium and Luxembourg. In theory, everyone is expected to have a return ticket and proof of accommodation.

Stays of up to three months are automatically granted on entry to holders of the above passports. Other nationals should check with the Tunisian embassy; sometimes only one month is granted, and renewal in Tunisia can be a frustrating business.

## MONEY MATTERS

The Tunisian *dinar* is divided into 1,000 *millimes*, which, somewhat confusing, can be called *francs*. Recent official rates average at about 1.51D to £1; 0.979D to $1; 1.447D to 10 French francs; 4.918D to 10 Deutschmarks.

Visitors can import as much foreign money (in cash or traveller's cheques) as they wish but cannot import, or export, any Tunisian currency. Because of this, banks at airports are open throughout the night if an international flight is expected. Exchange rates are fixed, whether you are changing money in banks or hotels, and commission is nominal (around 300 millimes).

In remote areas, you may have trouble changing traveller's cheques – especially if they are in sterling and you are somewhere unfamiliar with British tourists. Thomas Cook traveller's cheques seem to be more acceptable than even those of the biggest British banks. To be on the safe side, always make sure you have enough money to see you through a couple of days. Don't forget that banks close after 11 a.m. in summer, for two hours at lunchtime during winter, every afternoon during Ramadan and on Saturdays, Sundays and public holidays (see *Business Hours*). You cannot depend on a hotel to change money for you unless you are staying in it. Even then, its bureau de change may keep to proper banking hours. In an emergency you may have to resort to the bank at the nearest airport.

If you run out of money while on holiday, it is possible to telex your bank at home and have money sent within 24 hours. Do this via any large Tunisian bank. Alternatively, you can use major credit cards to obtain money in main banks. This takes minutes, but you will have to pay interest on the sum from the day it is borrowed.

When you leave, it is possible to reconvert as much as a third of the total money you exchanged into Tunisian dinars. To do this, you will need to produce receipts of all your bank transactions.

## HEALTH

Many people don't bother with any vaccinations when visiting Tunisia and none are required by the Tunisian government unless visitors are coming from a recognised yellow fever or cholera infected zone.

That said, to be absolutely safe, some doctors and holiday companies advise taking precautions against cholera, typhoid, hepatitis, and polio, all of which occasionally break out. If you are worried, seek up-to-date medical advice a month or so before you depart. Rabies is present in Tunisia. If you are bitten or scratched, seek medical advice immediately.

The health problems most commonly contracted are **upset stomachs** and **sunburn/sunstroke**. According to a survey conducted by the British Consumer Association's publication *Which?*, 34 percent of visitors to Tunisia become ill during their stay.

**Cutting the risks**: use bottled water (tap water is safe, but the change of water may cause adverse effects), peel fruit and choose your restaurant carefully. Humble establishments shouldn't be avoided necessarily – they often provide excellent food – but pick those where turnover looks brisk and any food on display fresh. Food that has been standing for a day or two is the greatest threat to health.

Should you suffer any minor health problems, visit one of the excellent pharmacies. Antibiotics are available over the counter, but you may not wish to take these without a doctor's recommendation (see *Emergencies*). For mild stomach upsets, drink plenty of bottled water and eat a few peeled cactus fruits – it's a cheap, tried and tested local remedy. In cases of more serious attacks of diarrhoea or vomiting, replace body salts by using a rehydration solution, and if symptoms persist for more than three days see a doctor. Amoebic dysentery – caused by amoebic parasites rather than bacteria – can be serious if left untreated. Avoid heatstroke/sunstroke by acclimatising your body gradually, keeping to the shade during the hottest part of the day, wearing cool, loose clothing (see *What to Wear*), applying a good suntan lotion and wearing a sunhat. You should drink much more than usual (not alcohol!) and take more salt to replace body salts lost through sweating. Never underestimate heatstroke, it can also be serious.

**AIDS:** There is little information on the

extent of AIDS in Tunisia, but it is not thought to be great. It is not one of the African countries suffering an AIDS epidemic.

Anyone worried about the remote possibility of receiving medical treatment involving infected needles – though clinics and hospitals are usually reliable – should think about taking an Aids kit containing plasma and a collection of sterile needles and syringes, available from large chemists.

## WHAT TO WEAR

If visiting Tunisia out of season, you will certainly need to take some warm clothing for evenings and cooler days. Before May and after September (October is the wettest month of the year) you should take something waterproof; downpours, flash floods or persistent drizzle are likely at some point in your stay. In summer, temperatures can be very hot indeed, so take cool, loose, lightweight clothes. Good sunglasses are recommended. Eye irritations, caused by bright sunlight and dust, are common.

It's polite and advisable to dress with some discretion: i.e. off the beach, don't wear very revealing clothes. In the few mosques and zaouias open to non-Muslims, headscarves or overgowns are usually available to women unsuitably dressed. Shoes must be removed before entering a mosque.

## WHAT TO BRING

Medical insurance (including cover for repatriation), as all healthcare must be paid for.

Most essentials can be bought in Tunisia, but the following deficiencies should be noted:
- high protection suntan lotion is difficult to find
- film costs about the same as it does in the UK, but you may find fewer varieties
- decent maps of Tunisia are difficult to come by. If you're touring, it's best to take a good map with you (see Orientation).

## ON ARRIVAL

You will need to fill in an official form, stating your name, address, profession, length of stay and addresses in Tunisia. Even if you are planning to tour and have no pre-booked hotel, it's worth putting something on the

form: Tunisian immigration officials are happier if you do.

If you are in Tunisia as a professional photographer, and therefore carrying a lot of equipment, you are bound to meet problems on arrival. It's best to secure a letter of introduction in advance from the Tunisian Tourist Office, and also a special licence. This takes a few weeks to organise.

## CUSTOMS

For anyone over the age of 18 the legal tax-free limits on goods are:
400 cigarettes or 100 cigars or 500 grammes of tobacco
1 litre of alcoholic beverage of more than 25 percent proof
2 litres of alcoholic beverage of less than 25 percent proof
0.25 litre of perfume
1 litre of toilet water

The good news is that duty-free shops in Tunisia's international airports are open to arriving and departing passengers. They do not accept Tunisian currency.

If you are taking any particularly valuable items into the country, it is a good idea to register them with Customs. That way you will be able to take them out without difficulty later.

## RESERVATIONS

If you intend to tour in high summer or during school holidays, it's best to book your hotels ahead, especially in places such as Tabarka, Ain Draham, Tozeur, Matmata, Djerba, Sousse and Hammamet. If you don't, try to arrive early in the day. Those without pre-booked accommodation who are arriving on a charter air ticket to Monastir Airport are more likely to find accommodation in Sousse than Monastir. Both towns are accessible by train from the airport, and taxi fares are the same to each.

## EXTENSION OF STAY

To prolong your stay for more than the three months granted on arrival, you must apply to the police station in the district where you are living before the three months expire. You must explain why you wish to stay and provide evidence of sufficient funds.

## ON DEPARTURE

In theory, visitors leaving Tunisia, should have documentary evidence of all their bank transactions and receipts for any expensive purchases (e.g. a carpet, leather jacket, *objet d'art*). There is no duty to pay on items costing less than £900. You will need to fill out a simple departure form at the airport.

# GETTING ACQUAINTED

## GOVERNMENT

Post-independence, Tunisia's traditional ruler, the bey, was deposed and the country became a republic with a democratically-elected president, Habib Bourguiba. But within only a few years the extent of that democracy was contracting: opposition parties were steadily quashed by Bourguiba, the government controlled the press, and after two elections Bourguiba was made president for life (which was why eventually he had to be toppled by a coup).

After replacing Bourguiba in 1987, Ben Ali introduced various measures to increase democracy. They included: election of the president by universal suffrage every five years, with a restriction to three consecutive terms of office; the cautious introduction of a multi-party system, providing new political parties work within the constitution; and a relaxation of the press Code, including allowing Islamic Fundamentalists to publish a newspaper. The Conseil Supérieur du pacte National was also set up, a body designed to give fresh impetus to democratisation.

Despite these long overdue changes, critics feel they don't go far enough and that the Conseil Supérieur may be a time-wasting white elephant. Although there are now five parties in addition to the ruling RCD (Rassemblement Constitutionel Democratique) party, the Islamic Fundamentalists were not allowed to stand as a party in the 1989 elections – they had to stand as independents – and the media remains very pro-government, failing to cover the opinions of parties other than the RCD or automatically denigrating them. But it is the electoral system that is considered the most undemocratic aspect of the constitution. Under the present system all the seats in each multi-member constituency go the party that receives most votes. This meant that in the April 1989 election all the seats in the Chamber of Deputies (Tunisian parliament) went to Ben Ali's RCD.

## ECONOMY

Tunisia's biggest exports are petroleum, phosphates and olive oil; its chief imports are foodstuffs. The 1970s were a period of steady economic growth in Tunisia – tourism boomed, oil flowed – and the gross domestic product (GDP) almost doubled. The 1980s, however, heralded problems. Output of petroleum peaked in 1980 and then steadily declined, and agriculture was devastated by droughts. A sudden fall in the price of petrol in 1986 caused a balance of payments crisis and the government had to go cap in hand to the IMF. A recovery in 1987 was thwarted by another severe drought in 1988, exacerbated by plagues of locusts.

Clearly, Tunisia's economy is tempestuous. Tourism has now overtaken petrol as the biggest earner of foreign currency and by the year 2000 it is expected that Tunisia will be a net energy importer – unless important new oilfields are found.

Feeding and employing the rising population does not help. Unemployment (officially at 15 percent) is alleviated by the number of migrants who work abroad and send money home, though France, Tunisia's traditional market for labour, is closing its doors fast.

To counteract problems, the government is trying to promote exports other than petroleum, and has devalued the dinar to make goods more competitive. In addition, it is attempting to boost agriculture and encourage foreign investment.

## GEOGRAPHY

At approximately 63,000 sq. miles (163,000 sq. km), Tunisia is not much bigger than England. The tail of the Atlas Mountains, a range that rises close to the west coast of Morocco, 1,100 miles (1,800 km) away, dominates the north, a region of mixed forests and fertile valleys. Southwest of the River Medjerda, the only perennially flowing river in the country, roll the high plateaux of the Tell – a wheatbelt – which gradually decline to the Steppes, sparsely inhabited plains colonised by nothing more nourishing than tussocks of esparto grass. Further south lie the *chotts*, curious salt lakes lower than sea-level, and then the Sahara. Within a distance of 280 miles (450 km), from the north coast to Douz, the climate and landscapes change from Mediterranean to desert.

The eastern coast is the richest and most densely populated part of the country, comprising both the main commercial, industrial and tourist centres – Tunis, Sfax and Sousse – and substantial agricultural lands. Cap Bon, the hilly peninsula southeast of Tunis, is especially suited to the growing of citrus fruits while the Sahel, the flat coastal region south to Sfax, is carpeted in vast olive groves, making Tunisia the fourth largest producer of olive oil in the world.

## POPULATION

The last census was held in 1984, when the population numbered approximately 7 million. Today, it is estimated at around 8 million. What was recently a predominantly rural population is rapidly becoming an urban one. A rural exodus continues despite government efforts to promote country areas and reduce the stress it places on the towns.

In 1984 the population growth rate was 2.5 percent a year. By following policies to promote birth control, the government hopes to reduce it to 1.1 percent by the year 2021. One of the most serious consequences of a high birth rate is the need to import more and more foodstuffs, something the country can ill-afford.

## TIME ZONE & CLIMATE

Tunisian time is one hour in advance of Greenwich Mean Time. This means that in summer it is equivalent to British Summer Time.

A Mediterranean climate – hot, dry summers and mild, wet winters – prevails in the north; desert conditions, with extremes of temperature, prevail in the south. The table (on the next page) shows average maximum daily temperatures for a number of cities. It should be remembered that these are average. Maximum temperatures often reach over 50° C (122° F) around Medenine and Remada during summer (June–September) and temperatures of over 40° C (104° F) sometimes hit northern and coastal regions in July and August.

Spring and early autumn are the most comfortable times to travel, though they can be wet (October is the wettest month in the year) and are usually cold during evenings. Spring offers spectacular displays of wild flowers and blossom, particularly inland, while autumn has the advantage of warmer seas (welcome off northern coasts).

Desert regions are best avoided in midsummer; then temperatures are only tolerable very early in the morning or late in the evening and views are likely to be obscured by dust.

Although winter (December/January) temperatures can reach 23° C (73° F) in the popular holiday destinations of Sousse and Hammamet, a coolish 15° C (59° C) is more common. Desert regions still have abundant sunshine in winter months, but temperatures drop dramatically at night (be prepared). In deepest winter, snow falls in the Khroumir mountains around Ain Draham.

## WEIGHTS & MEASURES

Metric measures are used throughout Tunisia: distances are in kilometres, quantities in litres and weights in grammes or kilograms.

## ELECTRICITY

Most of the country's supply is rated 220 volts, but some places, notably a few old-fashioned hotels in Tunis, have a 110-volt supply. Sockets and plugs are the continental variety, with two round pins, so British

| MONTH | | J | F | M | A | M | J | J | A | S | O | N | D |
|---|---|---|---|---|---|---|---|---|---|---|---|---|---|
| Béja | Temp | 13.6 | 15.6 | 17.4 | 20.6 | 25.7 | 31.2 | 34.1 | 34.7 | 31.4 | 24.8 | 14.7 | 15.0 |
| | Rain | 123 | 74 | 61 | 55 | 33 | 11 | 5 | 9 | 27 | 81 | 63 | 103 |
| Bizerte | Temp | 14.6 | 15.4 | 17.1 | 19.4 | 23.3 | 27.4 | 30.5 | 30.7 | 28.6 | 24.3 | 20 | 15.6 |
| | Rain | 132 | 86 | 48 | 43 | 39 | 8 | <1 | 7 | 27 | 90 | 88 | 114 |
| Gabes | Temp | 15.9 | 17.8 | 19.7 | 21.6 | 24.2 | 27.6 | 30.5 | 31.2 | 29.6 | 25.7 | 21.9 | 172 |
| | Rain | 20 | 17 | 18 | 15 | 4 | 2 | <1 | 1 | 34 | 65 | 24 | 22 |
| Gafsa | Temp | 14.1 | 16.8 | 20.1 | 23.2 | 28.1 | 33.4 | 35.9 | 35.7 | 31.5 | 25.3 | 20.2 | 15.0 |
| | Rain | 18 | 14 | 17 | 17 | 12 | 7 | 5 | 5 | 25 | 28 | 13 | 16 |
| Hammamet | Temp | 15.3 | 16.6 | 18.3 | 20.8 | 24.3 | 28.7 | 31.5 | 31.4 | 29.3 | 25.3 | 20.9 | 17.0 |
| | Rain | 49 | 31 | 39 | 34 | 21 | 12 | 3 | 10 | 29 | 91 | 59 | 36 |
| Medenine | Temp | 16.7 | 19.6 | 22.1 | 24.9 | 28.8 | 33.3 | 35.6 | 35.9 | 32.7 | 28.2 | 22.6 | 18.1 |
| | Rain | 18 | 15 | 15 | 15 | 4 | 1 | 0 | 2 | 25 | 46 | 10 | 17 |
| Remada | Temp | 15.9 | 19.4 | 22.3 | 26.3 | 31.2 | 35.7 | 37.2 | 37.5 | 33.8 | 27.3 | 22.3 | 16.9 |
| | Rain | 19 | 10 | 10 | 14 | 2 | 3 | 1 | <1 | 7 | 10 | 8 | 3 |
| Sfax | Temp | 16.2 | 17.8 | 19.7 | 21.8 | 25.6 | 29.1 | 31.7 | 32 | 29.7 | 25.5 | 21.7 | 17.5 |
| | Rain | 19 | 16 | 20 | 13 | 11 | 3 | <1 | 5 | 32 | 66 | 23 | 17 |
| Sousse | Temp | 15.8 | 16.9 | 18.5 | 20 | 22.5 | 28 | 30 | 30.7 | 29.4 | 24.9 | 21.4 | 17.9 |
| | Rain | 31 | 17 | 22 | 32 | 14 | 4 | 1 | 17 | 18 | 48 | 36 | 42 |
| Tunis | Temp | 15 | 16.4 | 18.2 | 20.7 | 24.9 | 29.1 | 32.1 | 32.2 | 29.7 | 24.9 | 20.5 | 16.4 |
| | Rain | 79 | 48 | 41 | 41 | 29 | 12 | 2 | 14 | 26 | 85 | 56 | 47 |

**Key:**
*Temperature*: Average daily maximum (°C)
*Rain*      : Average monthly rainfall (mm)
*Source*    : Met Office Statistics

visitors will need a continental adaptor.

## BUSINESS HOURS

**Bank opening hours:** Winter, Monday–Thursday 8 a.m.–11.30 a.m. and 2 p.m.–5 p.m. Friday 8 a.m.–11 a.m. and 1.30 p.m.–4 p.m.
Summer, Monday–Friday 8 a.m.–11 a.m. During Ramadan (if it falls in winter) things are different again: 8 a.m.–11.30 a.m. and 1 p.m.–2.30 p.m.

**Post office opening hours:** Winter (approximately 16 September–15 June), Monday–Friday 8 a.m.–12 noon and 2 p.m.–6 p.m. Saturday 8 a.m.–12 noon. Summer, Monday–Saturday 8 a.m.–1 p.m. During Ramadan (if it falls in winter): Monday–Saturday 8 a.m.–3 p.m.

**Shops** are less restrictive. They, too, usually close for several hours at lunchtime – generally noon–4 p.m. (3 p.m. in winter) – but then open until at least 7 p.m. (6 p.m. in winter). During Ramadan traders always close in time for sunset, whatever time of the year it is, but once they have broken their fast they re-open and trade long into the night – not least because much money is spent on new clothes and children's toys during this time.

Although Fridays are normal working days and Sunday the day of rest for most shopkeepers (a pattern inherited from colonial days), in country areas Friday is still respected as the Muslim day of rest.

## HOLIDAYS

There are two types of holidays, religious and state. The religious holidays are based on the Hegira's lunar calendar and therefore change annually – they fall 11 days earlier each year (12 days in a leap year). State holidays (based on the Gregorian calendar) are the same every year.

**Muslim Holidays for 1991:**
Ramadan – from 19 March (N.B. this day is not a public holiday).
Aid es Seghir – (end of Ramadan) 17 and 18 April.
Aid el Kebhir – (feast of Abraham's sacrifice) – 22 and 23 June.
Ras el Am Hejri (Muslim New Year) – 12 July.
Mouloud – (the Prophet's birthday) 23 September.
State holidays:
New Year's Day – 1 January
Independence Day – 20 March
Youth Day – 21 March
Martyr's Day – 9 April
Labour Day – 1 May
Republic Day – 25 July
Women's Day 13 August

## FESTIVALS

Apart from national religious and state holidays and private family celebrations such as weddings, there are many regional festivals – celebrating harvests, traditional customs or the life of a local holy man – and some Arts festivals.

Below is a selection of the bigger events. For exact dates contact the Tunisian Tourist Office, as they vary from year to year.

**April/May**
Menzel Bouzelfa: Orange Festival (folklore and sideshows).
El Haouaria: Festival of the Sparrow Hawk (falconry displays and folklore).

**June**
Testour: Festival of Mahlouf (classical Tunisian music).
Houmt Souk: Festival of Ulysses (Djerban folk festival).
Dougga: Festival of Dougga (classical plays in Dougga's Roman ruins).

**July**
Kerkennah: Siren Festival (more allusions to Ulysses; celebration of traditional wedding customs).

**July/August**
Carthage: Festival of Carthage (music, theatre and dance).
Tabarka: Coral Festival (crafts, music, folklore).

**August**
Hammamet: Festival of Hammamet (theatre and music at the International Cultural Centre).
Sousse: Aossou Festival (music and folklore).

**September**
Grombalia: festival celebrating the wine harvest.
Kairouan: Festival of Cavalry (fantasias and displays of horsemanship).

**October**
Carthage: Film Festival of Carthage (festival of new Third World films, held every two years).

**December**
Douz: Oasis Festival.

**December/January**
Tozeur: Festival of the Sahara (fantasias, camel racing, folklore, dancing, etc).

## ISLAM

Much of Tunisia seems secular in character. Down-town Tunis and the city of Sfax do not appear so very different from economic and industrial towns in Europe. But to underestimate the role of religion in Tunisia is a mistake, as ex-president Bourguiba discovered. Bourguiba attempted to reduce the influence of Islam on daily life, almost blaming religious preoccupations for Tunisia's slow progress. His subsequent clash with the imams contributed to his downfall.

Islam is a religion that governs life. It began when a young merchant called Mohammed (570-632) living in Mecca started making regular visits to a cave to sit alone and think. He was a well-respected man from a good family and, as was usual then, unable to read or write. One day the archangel Gabriel visited him in the cave, began dictating the Koran, and instructed Mohammed to spread the word. This was the first revelation; over the next 23 years many others followed.

At first, Mohammed recited the verses to just his wife and his friends, but even so the growth of the new religion was explosive. Inevitably, the religion that proclaimed "There is no god but God" became a thorn in the side of the polytheistic rulers of Mecca, and Mohammed was forced to flee to Medina, an event that marks the beginning of the Hegira calendar (622). Within a few years he returned with his followers, conquering or converting his old adversaries.

The Prophet lived to the age of 63, by which time Islam had spread throughout the Arabian peninsula. Following his death, Abou Bakr, Mohammed's closest companion, became his successor (the first caliph), who was in turn followed by Omar ibn el Khattab, another close associate of Mohammed. But the Prophet, who had no direct heir (society being patrilineal), had never specified how successors to the role of spiritual leader should be chosen (or even whether there should be such a figure), and after Omar's death schisms began to develop in the new religion. Some felt that the caliph should be elected but others thought he should be descended from the Prophet and that Ali, the cousin of the Prophet, married to Mohammed's daughter Fatima, was the true heir. This latter group broke away from mainstream (**Sunni**) Muslims and formed the **Shia** movement, causing the biggest single split in Islam to date.

As in all religions, as time went on more sub-divisions developed. One, the **Kharidjite** sect, fiercely puritanical, found much of its support in North Africa, not least Tunisia where the Berbers felt estranged from the Eastern caliphs who were amassing more and more authority and wealth. Most Tunisians reverted to Sunni orthodoxy in the 11th century, but pockets of Kharidjites survive today, notably on Djerba.

**Sufism** is another deviation of Islam. Unlike mainstream Islam, which is very practical in outlook, it satisfies a need for mysticism. Sufi cults and brotherhoods, many practising strange, ecstasy-inducing rituals, are scattered all over the Muslim world.

Minor sub-divisions in the faith were caused by disagreement on how the Koran – not written down until 30 or so years after the prophet's death – should be interpreted. In Islam, God is the legislator: **Sharia**, the framework of laws laid down in the Koran, is the Law of God. But the Sharia did not meet every area of life in a rapidly developing world, and so various schools of Islamic law, each with its own interpretation and development of the Sharia, evolved. To complicate matters, the **Hadith**, the sermons of the Prophet (not held to be divine in origin), also had influence.

But there are five undisputed requirements of faith, which are firmly laid down by the Koran: to believe that there is no other god but God and Mohammed is his Prophet; to pray five times a day, beginning with dawn and ending with sunset; to undertake a pilgrimage (*hadj*) to Mecca at least once in a lifetime; to observe the Ramadan fast (no food, water, sex or tobacco during daylight hours for one month); and to give alms to the poor.

Islam is now the fastest-growing religion in the world. The Muslims' view on the other two written religions, Christianity and Judaism, is one of respect, seeing them as precursors to Islam (events in both the Old and New testaments are common to the Koran). But Jesus, though thought to be immaculately conceived, is not believed to be the son of God – just another prophet. Islam, Muslims believe, was necessary because the older religions had been distorted by the words of man. The Koran, in contrast, is the pure word of God.

# LANGUAGE

Classical Arabic is the official language (used by the media), but the spoken language tends to be an Arabic dialect. French is also used and it is taught as the second language in schools (during the protectorate all lessons, with the obvious exception of classical Arabic, were taught in French). Even in the humblest village someone will speak French.

Berber languages, alive and well in Morocco and Algeria, have practically died out in Tunisia. The following Arabic phrases may prove useful; they will certainly be appreciated:

| | |
|---|---|
| *Salamayokoum* | May peace be on you (used as a greeting) |
| *Salaama* | Goodbye |
| *Lebass* | How are you? (also serves as a reply to the same question, i.e. "Well, thank you"). |
| *Naam* | Yes |
| *Lu* | No |
| *Min fadlik* | please |
| *Shokran* | Thank you |
| *Bismillah* | In the name of God (said before embark ing on any activity, e.g. eating a meal) |
| *Hamdullah* | Thanks be to God |
| *Insh'allah* | If God wills (tacked on to the end of any statement of intent) |
| *Malesh* | Doesn't matter |
| *Shouf* | Look |
| *Kaddache?* | How much? |

## GLOSSARY

| | |
|---|---|
| *ain* | spring |
| *bab* | door |
| *bir* | well |
| *bordj* | fort |
| *chott* | dry salt lake |
| *dar* | palace, house |
| *djebel* | mountain |
| *erg* | sand dunes |
| *fondouk* | former lodging house for merchants |
| *ghar* | cave |
| *ghorfa* | barrel-shaped building, originally used for storing grain |
| *Hadith* | the sermons and sayings of the prophet |
| *Hadj* | pilgrimage to Mecca |
| *hammam* | Turkish bath |
| *imam* | prayer leader in mosque |
| *kef* | rock |
| *Kharidjite* | radical sect of Islam which developed among the Berbers in the 10th century |
| *Koran* | the word of God delivered through the Prophet Mohammed in 7th-century Mecca |
| *koubba* | tomb of holy man |
| *ksar (ksour)* | fortified granary, often one which has developed into a village (plural) |
| *Maghreb* | literally, west; but refers to the North African countries of Morocco, Mauretania, Algeria, Tunisia and Libya |
| *marabout* | holy man; sometimes refers to his burial site |
| *medressa (medersa)* | Islamic college, possibly attached to a mosque (plural) |
| *menzel* | community or dwelling place |
| *mirhab* | niche indicating direction of Mecca in a mosque |
| *minbar* | pulpit from which *imam* leads prayers in a mosque |
| *muezzin* | man who calls the faithful to prayer |
| *nador* | watchtower |
| *oued* | river |
| *ribat* | fortress/monastery, built in the 9th century along the North African coast |
| *sebkhet* | dry salt flat |
| *Shi'ite* | branch of Islam that recognises Ali as the successor to Mohammed |
| *Sufi* | belonging to mystical branch of Islam |
| *Sunni* | orthodox Muslim |
| *tourbet* | mausoleum |
| *zaouia* | centre of religious cult, often near the burial place of the cult's founder |

# COMMUNICATIONS

## THE MEDIA

**Newspapers:** The first newspapers in Tunisia were Italian: *Il Giornale di Tunisi*, in 1838, and *Il Corriere di Tunisi*, in 1855. Hot on their heels came the first Arab newspaper in 1860, and then, with the French protectorate, a number of "colonial" newspapers, including *Le Reviel Tunisien* and *Le progrès Tunisien*.

Today there are a host of publications, some in Arabic, others in French. The principal ones are *Es Sabah* (circulation 90,000), *La presse* (40,000), *L'Action* (50,000) and *Le Temps* (40,000). They are all pro the ruling RCD party, and hence pro-government, with *L'Action* being its mouthpiece.

However, in the spring of 1990 government control of the press was cautiously relaxed and the Islamic Fundamentalists, a group which the government had steadfastly refused to acknowledge, were allowed to launch their own paper.

Of the magazines available, one of the more controversial and respected is *Jeune Afrique*, published in France and distributed throughout Africa and the Middle East but edited by Bechir ben Yahmed, a Tunisian. At one point it was banned by Bourguiba.

In Tunis and the big resorts there is also a wide range of foreign publications, ranging from the *Wall Street Journal* to the UK tabloid *The Sun*.

**Television and Radio:** Television hit northern Tunisia in 1966 and the rest of the country by 1967. There are two **television** channels put out by *Radiodiffusion Télévision Tunisienne* (RTT), one broadcasts in Arabic, the other French. They are very pro-government. RTT produces over 45 percent of the total programmes and imports the rest from the West (41 percent) and from other Arab countries (just over 12 percent). In addition,

Tunisia is also able to receive Italian (RAI) stations.

There are numerous French language **radio** stations, and it is easy to pick up Italian, French and Algerian channels too. BBC World Service can be obtained on the following frequencies and wavelengths, though not on all of them at any one time in the day: MHZ: 17.70, 12.10, 7.320, 6.195. Metres: 16.94, 24.80, 40.98, 48.43

## POST & TELECOMMUNICATIONS

Airmail letters and postcards to Europe take about five days, and to the USA, Canada and Australia about two weeks. packages can take rather longer. *Poste Restante* is available at most post offices (PTTS); to take advantage of it, letters and packages should be clearly marked RP (meaning *Recette postale*). The main PTT in Tunis to which Tunis *Poste Restante* should be sent is Rue Charles de Gaulle. To collect it, the receiver must have identification.

Main PTTS also have **telex** and **telegram** facilities. In Tunis they are available at the *Centre d'Exploitation des Telecommunications*, 29 Rue Gamal Abdelnasser. **Fax** facilities are available in some stationery shops and hotels. For opening times of post offices, see *Business Hours*.

## TELEPHONE

It is possible to make direct international calls from some public call boxes in Tunisia (generally, main cities only) but it's more often necessary to phone through an operator in a PTT office. She or he will tell you how much you owe after you have finished. You can ask how much it costs per minute to your particular destination before you ring. It is supposed to be slightly cheaper after 8 p.m.

Reverse charge calls cannot be made to countries outside Europe other than Algeria. A small deposit is usually required in case reverse charges are not accepted.

To dial abroad, first dial 00, then the country code (44 for Britain; 49 for Germany; 33 for France; 1 for USA and Canada; 61 for Australia), then the area code (but omitting any initial zeroes), followed by the number.

To find a telephone, apart from going to a

PTT or seeking a telephone kiosk, look for signs saying "Taxi phone".

In Tunis, calls can be made from the *Centre d'Exploitation des Telecommunications*, 29 Rue Gamal Abdelnasser 24 hours a day.

Tunisian area codes are as follows:
Region of Tunis: 01
Region of Bizerte and Nabeul: 02
Region of Sousse, Mahdia and Monastir: 03
Region of Sfax: 04
Region of Gabes and Djerba: 05
Region of Gafsa: 06
Region of Kairouan: 07
Region of Le Kef and the North: 08
Telephone numbers in *Travel Tips* include the area code, which is bracketed.

# EMERGENCIES

## SECURITY & CRIME

According to a survey conducted for the British Consumer Association's magazine *Holiday Which?*, 2.1 percent of the holiday-makers that they questioned experienced theft in Tunisia, a statistic lower than in many other countries in the survey, including France, USA, Israel, Ireland and Holland.

Take obvious precautions to avoid crime: don't flaunt wealth, keep an eye on handbags in restaurants and cafés, always lock car doors, use the safe deposit box in your hotel.

**Lawyers:** Should you run into serious trouble and require a lawyer, your embassy will be able to supply a list of lawyers and specify which ones speak your language. An embassy will not, however, guarantee a lawyer's competence.

**Drug Offences:** Unlike Morocco, Tunisia does not have a big drug problem, and offers of cannabis or any other narcotic are rare. possession, use and trading in narcotic drugs is strictly illegal and and severely punished.

Conviction carries penalties of one to five years' imprisonment (there is no such thing as a suspended sentence) and 100 to 10,000D fines.

## LOSS OF BELONGINGS

Any documents or possessions lost or stolen should be reported to the police and a certificate of loss obtained for insurance purposes. Loss of passports must be reported to the local police as soon as possible and to your own consulate. Again, a certificate of loss must be issued by the police.

In Tunis, you can try the Lost property Office (*Bureau des Objets Trouvés*), Direction Generale de la Sureté Nationale, Caserne de Bouchoucha, Le Bardo.

## MEDICAL SERVICES

**Emergency treatment** is provided by the Aziza Othmana Hospital in Tunis (place du Gouvernement, La Kasbah; tel: 01-662 292) and in all regional hospitals. Treatment must be paid for; non-Tunisians are not entitled to free medical care. A certificate of treatment will be issued, so that costs can be reclaimed on insurance.

To find a **doctor,** consult the phone directory (where they are listed in alphabetical order under *Docteurs*. Your embassy will be able to supply a list of doctors who speak your language. Consultations are not expensive.

**Dentists:** are listed under *Chirurgiens-dentistes* in the phone book.

**Pharmacists:** are excellent, and can often solve minor problems. To find an all-night pharmacist in any major town consult a daily paper such as *La presse* or *Le Temps*. In Tunis there is a convenient late-night pharmacist at 43 Avenue 7 Novembre.

**Embassies:** Consuls cannot pay medical bills or bail you out if you have run out of or lost money, but will contact your family or friends on your behalf and ask them to help. If you still have a chequebook and cheque guarantee card, they may be able to cash a small cheque to tide you over. Only in cases of destitution can they make a repayable loan.

Should someone die, embassy staff will help family or friends deal with local bureaucracy.

Addresses of embassies are listed under Useful Addresses at the end of Travel Tips

# GETTING AROUND

## ORIENTATION

Signposts (in French and Arabic) are reasonably plentiful and orientation isn't a problem in well-frequented areas. In most towns, though not Tunis, hotels are also signposted.

## MAPS

It is difficult to buy a decent map of Tunisia in the country itself, so it is much better to take a good map with you. Michelin Algeria-Tunisia 972 is one of the best maps around, and Kummerly Frey's Tunisia is also good. That said, both are guilty of errors and omissions and neither are bang up to date as far as road conditions are concerned. As for city maps, the tourist offices are usually able to provide basic plans. Only their map of Houmt Souk on Djerba (for which they charge) is completely useless. In Tunis, it's worth buying a detailed map of the city from one of the many stationers.

**Guides:** Other than in Kairouan, local tourist offices do not supply official guides. In Tunis it is possible to hire one from a travel agent (costing about 30D per day), but a guide is not supposed to take tourists into the medina. The logic of this is to discourage guides from seeking to earn commission in the bazaars. As the medina is precisely where tourists most need a guide, this law is overcome by a temporary suspension of the business relationship, i.e. in the medina your guide is, should there be enquiries, your friend.

Most sites have their resident custodian, who will usually endeavour to show visitors around. They rarely speak languages other than Arabic and French and have little real knowledge, but they still expect a dinar for their trouble. There are exceptions to this damning generalisation, notably the custodian of Georges Sebastian's house in Hammamet.

If you do make use of a custodian's services, you should tip, but 500 millimes to 1D (depending on quality of service) is adequate. If you don't want to be accompanied around a site, politely make this clear beforehand. Occasionally, in the medinas of Tunis or Kairouan, you will be approached by a hustler of the type endemic in Morocco. Their main aim is to lure you into a carpet shop and earn a percentage on the amount you spend.

## AIRPORT-CITY LINKS

Trains and taxis operate from Monastir airport to Monastir and Sousse, and buses (no. 35) and taxis run from Tunis airport to the city centre. Taxi fares are supposed to be fixed for these routes, but check the price before driving off. If you want to know what the current price should be ask at the information desk or consult a rep from one of the holiday companies. Remember that journeys from and to airports are proportionately much more expensive than journeys around town.

If you have arranged to pick up a car from the airport and your flight is delayed, don't worry. The local agent will have been informed and will wait, even if you arrive in the early hours of the morning.

## CITY TRANSPORT

**Buses** are extremely cheap, of course, but they are usually crowded and, as in any city, can be confusing. In cities, destinations are written in French as well as in Arabic, which helps. In country areas this may not be the case, and the thing to do is to ask the driver; don't necessarily trust a passenger: sometimes you will be told anything just so that you will sit down and the bus can depart.

**Taxis:** In towns fares are metered, so there shouldn't be any confusion. Meters are set at 200 millimes when you start. Make sure you understand the meter: sometimes fares are clocked up in old French francs, which are equal to millimes, thus a fare of 500 francs = 0.5D. Large items of luggage cost 100 millimes each. Between 9 p.m. and 5 a.m.

there is a 50 percent surcharge. A taxi is not supposed to take more than four passengers.

**In Tunis:** As well as buses and taxis, there is the *Metro Léger de Tunis*, often called simply the Metro (but it does not go underground!) and the TGM, which operates every 20 minutes between Tunis and La Marsa via Carthage and Sidi Bou Said (trains run throughout the day, except 1 a.m.–3.40 a.m.) and leaves from the station at the foot of place 7 Novembre.

## DOMESTIC TRANSPORT

Because Tunisia is a small country, it is possible to use public transport to most towns without too many problems. That said, to save a lot of time waiting around at stations, it is essential to investigate timetables in advance. Often there will be only one or two buses or trains serving a particular destination in a day.

**By Train:** There are rail links between Tunis, Nabeul, Sfax and Gabes; between Tunis and Ghardimaou near the Algerian border; between Tunis, Bizerte and Tabarka; between Tunis and La Marsa (TGM); between Tunis and Kalaa Kasbah; and between Sousse and Mahdia. Any railway station will supply timetables on request. For long journeys, it is sensible to arrive at a bus or train station at least half an hour before departure in order to buy a ticket and secure a seat. Buses are extremely cheap – a journey of 200 km (12 miles) costs about 3D – with trains costing slightly more.

Services are operated by Société Nationale des Chemins de Fer Tunisiens (SNCFT). There are three classes of accommodation: Grand-comfort, first and second. Some trains contain air-conditioned carriages, for which a supplement is added to the cost of the ticket. Generally, trains are of a very high standard.

Children under 4 years travel free, those over 4 but under 10 pay 75 percent of the adult fare, and children over the age of 10 pay full adult fare.

**By Bus:** There is a wide network of bus routes operated by a variety of companies, and it is possible to reach even the smallest villages. Often the companies share the same bus stations, though sometimes there can be several stations in one town, each serving a different company. Tunis bus station at Bab Alleoua is well organised, with a central information unit.

**By louage (or shared taxi):** This is a very effective method of transport, generally fast (sometimes recklessly so) and costing only slightly more than buses or trains. Often the *louage* station is situated close to the bus station in a town. A driver calls out his destination, and as soon as his vehicle (usually a Peugeot 505) is full he departs. The fare, based on five passengers sharing a *louage*, is fixed, though for longer journeys, especially those into Algeria or Libya, it's often negotiable. If the car departs with only you and your friend in it, check the price. It may be that the driver is anxious to get home and so willing to leave without a full complement, or it may be he thinks you wish to "charter" the vehicle and will charge you accordingly.

## PRIVATE TRANSPORT

**Hiring a car:** Car hire in Tunisia isn't cheap. In high season (April to September) it costs a minimum of £200 a week for the smallest car, say a Citroën Visa or Fiat Uno, and it can be difficult finding a firm with cars left to rent. It is therefore advisable to book in advance from home (it's cheaper than in Tunisia itself) through one of the larger car hire firms. In the summer of 1990 Europcar was offering the cheapest deal.

Out of season, you are more likely to find a good deal, especially if you wish to hire a car for longer than a week. Then it can be worth shopping around local firms, but be prepared to bargain hard. In 1990 it was difficult to beat Budget's low-season price of £166 a week for a Fiat Uno booked in advance in London.

When you pick up your car, check its general state (particularly tyres, fan belt and brake hoses) and make sure it has a good spare wheel and jack – you are almost certain to need them. Also, examine the insurance and be clear about any exclusions. Don't assume the hire company has checked levels of oil and water – often they don't.

**Car rental firms:** Most firms (not just international companies) have offices in both Tunis and Monastir airports; if you arrive at a convenient hour, it can save time to shop around there and then. Djerba has plenty of car and bike hire places (try those along Avenue Abdelhamid Cadhi), though there are few bargains for short periods; if you're not intending to go beyond the island, bikes are more suitable.

## Tunis

Cartha-rent: 59 Avenue 7 Novembre (tel: 01-254 304/371/326), willing to negotiate.
Ben Jemaa: 53 Avenue de paris (tel: 01-240 060/240 023), little chance of a bargain.
Europcar: 17 Avenue 7 Novembre (tel: 01-340 348/340 303). Despite being an international firm, local agent may be willing to bargain.
Garage Lafayette: 84 Ave de la Liberte (tel: 01-280 284), expensive.
Carthago: 3 Avenue 7 Novembre (tel: 01-349 168), possible to get a good deal.
Mattei: 19 Rue Liberia (tel: 01-281 399), worth trying.

## Hammamet

Cartha-rent: Cité l'Oasis (tel: 02-80466).

## Nabeul

Mattei: Ave Habib Bourguiba (tel: 02-85967). This branch of this company provided the best deal we could find.
Express car: 146 Ave Habib Thameur (tel: 02-86873/87014).

## Sousse

Cartha-rent: place Farhat Hached (tel: 03-21020)
Mattei: Route de la Corniche (tel: 03-26632)

**Petrol:** Four-star petrol, *super*, costs about 0.490D per litre (a little less than in Britain), and petrol stations are plentiful. That said, don't risk breaking down for want of fuel: always make sure you have more than sufficient, especially when driving in remoter areas. The walk to the next village can be a very long way in hot conditions. If you take your own car to Tunisia, don't expect to find unleaded petrol.

**Breaking down:** There are plenty of mechanics even in small towns, and repairs are not expensive. Be sure to get receipts for any large repairs, the cost of which you will want to reclaim from the car rental firm. Punctures are common, so make sure you get a punctured tyre repaired as soon as possible; look out for *Clinique pneus* signs or simply a large tractor tyre and an arrow at the side of the road. Air pressure should be a little less than it would be in a cooler climate.

**Desert driving:** The most sensible time to visit desert regions independently is October–May. In summer the heat is intense (up to 122° F/50° C) and can be hazardous. But whatever the time of year you should inform the National Guard at Medenine about your itinerary and expected time of arrival/return. Unless you possess a 4-wheel drive vehicle and are in the company of a local guide, you should always stay on tarmac roads or well-defined tracks. Make sure you have sufficient oil and water in your car.

Even on short excursions you are advised to take plenty of water (5 litres per person per day) and food. In addition, it is a good idea to take suntan lotion, lip cream, throat pastilles, a large scarf to protect against wind and sandstorms, a hat, sunglasses, warm clothes for cold nights, and a small spade and sacking (to place under wheels) in case you get stuck. In the event of a sandstorm you should point your vehicle downwind to minimise the damage to your vehicle. **Most importantly**, if you get lost or break down, stay with your vehicle.

**Police:** Road checks are routine. Slow down when you see police (usually on motorcycles) and pull over if they gesture for you to stop. Usually they will simply examine your papers. If you have been speeding (**limit: 50 kph** in urban areas; **100 kph** on the open road) or committing any other motoring offence, you may be merely warned but you could face an on-the-spot fine.

**Parking:** In the centre of Tunis and in Houmt Souk in Djerba, you'll find parking meters (about 100 millimes for an hour), but elsewhere official (sometimes unofficial) attendants collect small fees and issue tickets. Apart from taking your money and directing your parking manoeuvres, they will also "guard" your car; occasionally attendants offer car-cleaning services for a small price.

Outside Tunis airport and around the centre of Tunis illegally-parked vehicles are clamped. Watch out for official-looking yellow Land-Rovers.

## INTERNAL FLIGHTS

As Tunisia is a small country with good public transport, internal flights are only likely to be necessary in an emergency. There are flights between Tunis and Djerba; Tunis and Tozeur; Tunis and Sfax; Tunis and Monastir; Monastir and Djerba; and Tozeur and Djerba. Prices are reasonable: Tunis to Djerba, for example, costs 22D; but there may be only one or two flights between towns in a week. If you are planning to take domestic flights in Tunisia, get a timetable in advance.

## ON FOOT & BY THUMB

Outside the hottest months, Tunisia is well suited to hikers. Distances are not generally too vast, and good but quiet roads pass through beautiful scenery. There are plenty of moderately high hills in the north and in the interior, but you don't need to be a mountaineer to survive. If you are also camping, in remoter areas it's usually possible to pitch a tent wherever you choose – so long as it isn't next to a military base – but always ask permission first.

Hitchhiking is fairly effective, especially if one of you is female.

# WHERE TO STAY

## HOTELS

Hotels fall in five categories. ☆☆☆☆ luxe, ☆☆☆☆, ☆☆☆, ☆☆, ☆ and non-classified. In addition, there is a growing number of *pensions familles* – family-run hotels which provide modest but comfortable accommodation at reasonable cost.

☆☆☆☆ luxe hotels are on a par with good European hotels in terms of comfort and service, though most are functional, modern establishments with little character. Prices are reasonable. A double room in a

☆☆☆☆ luxe hotel costs around 70D a night and in a ☆☆☆☆ hotel approximately 50D a night. ☆☆☆ hotels charge 25–30D; ☆☆ hotels 16–20D, ☆ hotels 12–15D and a non-classified hotel up to 10D a night. But these are rough estimates: prices vary according to the season and in popular areas, such as Sousse and Hammamet, they can be quite a bit higher during high summer – as much as 100D in a ☆☆☆☆ luxe hotel. When checking in, make sure you know whether a price is per person or per room; in more modest hotels the custom is to quote a price per person. A continental breakfast is usually included, even in non-classified hotels.

In establishments that are rated ☆☆ or above, you should expect reasonable comfort, including private facilities, decent plumbing and central heating out of season. A few two-star hotels run to a swimming-pool.

☆ hotels (generally clean but simple) and even some non-classified hotels normally have a few rooms with private facilities. If you don't like the room you are shown, ask if they have a better/larger/lighter one available.

Other than in Tunis, all hotels are signposted.

Prices quoted below are per night and based on double room occupancy. Single rates are likely to be about 25 percent less. In a few hotels (notably the *pensions familles*) weekly rates are available. The list is not exhaustive; the Tourist Office publishes a comprehensive list of hotels to suit all pockets – very useful for those touring independently.

## AIN DRAHAM

**Hôtel Hammam Bourguiba:** ☆☆☆
Hammam Bourguiba, tel: 08-47217
A hotel cum clinic offering thermal cures situated deep in the forests between Tabarka and Ain Draham and close to the Algerian border. Double with bath 26–30, treatments extra.

**Hôtel Rayani:** ☆☆
Tel: 08-47391
New hotel at the far end of the village. Totally lacking in character but with good views and comfortable rooms. Double with bath 26–30D.

**Hôtel Beau Séjour:** non-classified
Tel: 08-47005
Hunting parties' haunt covered with creepers and lined with stuffed boar. Cosy log fire in the dining-room and central heating in the rooms in winter. Friendly staff and reasonable food. Recommended. Double with shower 16D.

## BEJA

**Hôtel Vaga:** ✫ ✫
Tel: 08-50818
Functional but adequate. Dining-room; central heating in winter. Double with shower 16–20D.

## BIZERTE

**Hôtel Corniche:** ✫ ✫ ✫
Tel: 02-31844
Well-run, with a good restaurant. Most amenities, including a night-club and swimming-pool. Double with bath 21–26D.
**Hôtel Nador:** ✫ ✫
Tel: 02-31846
Resort-style hotel providing good value. Amenities include tennis, swimming-pool and night-club. Double with bath 18–25D.
**Hôtel Petit Mousse:**
Route de la Corniche, tel: 02-32185
Vacancies are rare at Petit Mousse, so book ahead. It's a small hotel overlooking the sea, with good food. Shame about the unhelpful staff. Double with bath 20D.

## DJERBA

Most of Djerba's hotels are on the east coast of the island, particularly along the best stretch of beach (between Plage Sidi Mehrez and Plage de la Seguia), several kilometres from Houmt Souk, the island's capital. They cater mainly for package tours, though off-season there are plenty of unoccupied rooms to be found. **Hôtel Abou Nawas** (tel: 05-57022), luxurious without being overtly flashy, is the best of the ✫ ✫ ✫ ✫ hotels, while the ✫ ✫ **Hôtel Tanit** (tel: 05-57016) at the easternmost point on the island, is said to be best value for money, with off-season rates of 18D for a double.

Houmt Souk's hotels are much more modest, but if you enjoy mooching about the local town in the evening rather than being marooned with other tourists in a large hotel, they can make better bases. Town centre hotels include:
**Hôtel Essada:** ✫
Avenue Mohammed Badra, Houmt Souk
Tel: 05-51422
Comfortable small hotel. Double 15–19D depending on season.
**Touring Club de Tunisie Marhala:** non-classified
Houmt Souk, tel: 05-50146
An attractive old *fondouk* (just behind Place Hedi Chaker in Houmt Souk) that has been converted into a simple hotel. Shared amenities, but clean, and very cheap. Double 8D.
**Arischa Hôtel:** non-classified
Tel: 05-50384
Another converted fondouk, whose central cistern has been converted into a very small swimming-pool. Double 10–12D.

## DOUZ

**Hôtel Saharien:** ✫ ✫ ✫
Tel: 05-95339
The most comfortable place to stay, and located in the middle of the palmerie on the road south of town. Swimming-pool. Double with bath 25D
**Hôtel Marhala:** non-classified
Tel: 05-95315
Best of several budget hotels (the others are in the town centre), situated in the palmerie south of town. Swimming-pool and dining-room. Double with shower 15D.

## EL HAOUARIA

**Hôtel l'Epervier:** ✫ ✫
Tel: 02-97017
As one of only two hotels in town, and the only classified one, it has pretensions, especially in its restaurant. Most of its business comes from its packed and noisy bar (it's possible and cheaper to eat in here). Rooms are adequate. Closed out of season. About 18–20D for a double room with bathroom.
**Hôtel dar Toubib:** non-classified
Tel: 02-97163
(Follow the signposts down track!)
The only other choice in town. Simple, brightly-painted rooms with rural views of the hills. Possible to have a room with shower and WC, though both could be a lot cleaner. Damp out of season. Double 10D.

## EL KEF

**Hôtel Sicca Veneria:** ☆ ☆
Tel: 08-21725/21561/21709
Situated in the centre of the old town in a mini high-rise that is already falling apart. Signs of lack of maintenance are everywhere. But clean, with plenty of hot water. Seems to make its money as a local drinking den: staff appear unused to bona fide residents. The drinking locals also eat here, so dinner is satisfactory, but you are advised to forgo breakfast. Compared with El Kef's other hotels, it is luxurious. About 20D for a double.

## GABES

**Hôtel Oasis:** ☆ ☆ ☆
Tel: 05-70381
Of the two hotels on the large unappealing beach, Hôtel Oasis is marginally better than **Hôtel Chems**. It has a swimming-pool and nightclub. Double with bath 25D.
**Hôtel Nejib:** ☆ ☆
Tel: 05-70381
Well-run and comfortable hotel in town centre at the intersection of Avenue Habib Bourguiba and Avenue Farhat Hached. Double with bath 22D.
**Hôtel Atlantic:** ☆
Good ☆ hotel with colonial character. Double with bath 18D.

## GAFSA

**Hôtel Mamoum:** ☆ ☆ ☆
Tel: 06-20931
Dining-room, pool and air-conditioning. Hotel strives to make Gafsa a more tolerable place. Double with bath or shower 30D.
**Hôtel Gafsa:** ☆ ☆
Tel: 06-22676
Best of the rest, and quite comfortable. Double with bath 25D.

## KELIBIA

In addition to **Hôtel Florida** and **Hôtel Ennasin,** there are two holiday club complexes: **Mammounia** (just along the beach from the hotels) and **Mansourah**, a collection of depressing bungalows on the headland past the fort, which may have rooms to spare off season.

**Hôtel Florida :** ☆
Tel: 02-96248
Neglected but adequate hotel with a sea terrace. Dining-room. Double with bath or shower 17–22D, depending on season.
**Hôtel Ennasin:** non-classified
Tel: 02-96245
Tolerable, with a dining-room. Double with shower 14–18D.

## HAMMAMET

**Hôtel Sindbad:** ☆ ☆ ☆ ☆ luxe
Avenue des Nations Unies, tel: 02-80122
Large and luxurious, with a relatively central position close to George Sebastian's former villa. Every amenity. Double 50–85D.
**Hôtel El Manar:** ☆ ☆ ☆ ☆ luxe
Tel: 02-81333
Ugly luxury hotel whose amenities include tennis courts, fitness centre and indoor and outdoor swimming-pools. It's a good 3 miles (5 km) from Hammamet on the Nabeul side of town. Double room with bath and separate WC 60D in winter, rising to 100D in high summer. It is much cheaper to stay here on a package deal.
**Hôtel Abou Nawas:** ☆ ☆ ☆ ☆
Typical member of the Abou Nawas chain, situated on the Nabeul side of town. All amenities. Double with bath 44–65D.
**Hôtel Yasmina:** ☆ ☆ ☆
Central position on the edge of the main bay (opposite side to the kasbah). More character than most, with attractive pool, shaded garden and even a tennis court. Double with bath, WC and balcony 36D, rising to 56D in summer.
**Hôtel Sahbi:** ☆ ☆
Avenue de la République, tel: 02-80343/807/288
Bright and pleasant. Comfortable rooms with doors opening on to a first floor terrace. Good bathrooms. Double with bath and WC excellent value at 15–20D.
**Hôtel Alya:** ☆
Rue Ali Belhouane, tel: 02-80218
Well-located and efficiently run. Double with bath 18–26D.
**Hôtel Olympia:** ☆
Avenue du Kuwait, tel: 02-80622
Not as well placed as Sahbi or Alya, but an adequate, spotlessly clean alternative. Bar. Double with shower and WC 16–20D.

## KAIROUAN

**Hôtel Continental:** ☆ ☆ ☆ ☆
Tel: 07-21135
Classy-looking hotel in extensive grounds, overlooking the Aghlabid Basins. Swimming-pool and decent restaurant. Double with bath and shower 40-45D.

**Tunisia Hotel:** ☆ ☆
Ave de La République, tel :07)-21855/21794
Welcoming hotel with spacious, comfortable rooms. Double with bath and shower 16D.

**Hotel Sabra :** non-classified
Rue Ali Belhaouane, tel : 07-20260
Clean, well-run hotel with an excellent location overlooking Bab ech Chouhada. No private bathrooms. Double 7D.

## MAHDIA

**Hotel el Mehdi:** ☆ ☆ ☆
Tel: 03-81300
Beachside package tour hotel with most amenities, including a nightclub, swimming-pool and hairdresser.
Double with bath or shower 24-30D.

**Hôtel Sables d'Or:** ☆
Tel: 03-81137
Low-key package-tour hotel which is good value at 13D for a double with bath.

**El Jazira:** non-classified
Tel : 03-80274
Simple well-run establishment on northern side of the medina.Good sea views, and hot showers. Very cheap:about 6D for a double.

**Le Grand Hotel:** non-classified
Avenue Habib Bourguiba, tel: 03-80039
In spite of its impressive entrance, *Le Grand* is a bit of a misnomer. In high summer it is busy enough but off season its caretaker/ receptionist, who operates from a bed in its lobby, seems astonished to see anyone. Clean, if gloomy. About 10D for a double.

## MATMATA

Several former troglodyte complexes have converted into quite large underground hotels. Nonetheless,due to the large number of tourists determined to sleep in a cave, it can be difficult finding a room; it's sensible to book or to arrive well before evening. There are no restaurants in Matmata so for once demi-pension is advisable. In the cheaper hotels dinner is invariably cous-cous.

**Hotel Matmata:** ☆ ☆
Tel: 05-30066
Troglodyte accommodation in the luxury bracket. Character is still kept authentically spartan but added comforts include a pool and air-conditioning. Double with shower 24-30D.

**Touring Club de Tunisie Marhala:**
Tel: 05-30015
Essential to book in advance, as tour companies use it as an overnight stop. Supposedly the best of the cheap troglodyte hotels. Part of the film *Star Wars* was filmed in its bar. Staff are notoriously surly, most unlike their colleagues in the other Touring Club de Tunisie hotels. Double about 10D

**Hôtel Sidi Driss:**
Tel; 05- 30005
Large impersonal warren, where many of those that cannot get into Marhala end up. Good showers.Double 10 D.

**Hôtel Les Berberes:** non-classified
Tel: 05-30024
Somewhat unfairly, this tends to be a last resort, mainly because it offers only cold showers (welcome during summer!). Pleasant owner. Double about 7D.

## MONASTIR

People without pre-booked accommodation arriving at Monastir Airport should head for Sousse, which apart from being a much more interesting town has a wider ranger of hotels. Many of Monastir's hotels flank the beach near the airport to the west of town, and are rather remote from the centre (though near the golf course).

**Hotel Regency:** ☆ ☆ ☆ luxe
Tel : 03-60033
Located next to the marina on Cap Monastir. Every amenity, and close to the centre—if Monastir can be said to have one. Double with bath expensive at 60-100D, depending on season.

**Esplanade Hotel:** ☆ ☆ ☆
Tel : 03-61147
Another centrally-located hotel,just along from the Great Mosque and close to the town beach. Swimming-pool..Double with bath 20-30D, depending on season.

**Hôtel Yasmin:**
Route de la Falaise, tel: 03-62511
Provides reasonable level of comfort and is

the only cheap hotel in town. Large bathrooms, with plenty of hot water. On the cliff road, not far from the airport, and a good 15-minute walk into town. Best to book. Double with bath 16–20D.

## NABEUL

Hotel development spans the coast between Hammamet and Nabeul, effectively linking the two towns. Of the two, Hammamet is the more attractive resort, with more to offer in terms of atmosphere.

**Kheops Hotel:** ☆ ☆ ☆ ☆
Tel: 02-86144.
Most luxurious of the big hotels, with vast outdoor and indoor pools, panoramic bar, tennis, jacuzzi and hairdresser. It's set well back from the beach, but has still managed to reserve a stake of sand for its guests. A short walk from the town centre. Double with bath, shower and WC 55–90D, depending on season. If you want to spend this kind of money, there are far better places to do so than Nabeul. High season is 1 July–15 September.

**Hôtel Les Pyramides:** ☆ ☆ ☆
Tel: 02-85444
The Pyramides complex (hotel and apartments) dominates the beach in front of the town. All the usual amenities, though nothing much to distinguish it from all the other package hotels. Double with bath 45–52D.

**Hôtel Jasmins:** ☆
Tel: 02-85343
Stylish pension set in olive orchards a couple of kilometres out of Nabeul on the Hammamet road, close to the Roman Neapolis. Relaxing, with decent dining-room and bar. Double with bath 20–25D depending on season. High season is 1 July–15 September. Mimosas is closed in winter.

**Pension Les Oliviers:**
Tel: 02-86865
Situated close to Hotel Jasmins and equally pleasant; just a five-minute walk from the beach. Double with bath 20–25D. Closed in winter.

**Pension Korbi Mustapha:**
Avenue Habib el Karma, tel: 02-22262
A new pension on the northern side of town en route for the camel market. Despite its unpromising exterior (and unfortunate position at the junction of two busy roads), inside it is bright, clean and cheerful. Double room

with shower and balcony 11–15D, depending on season.

## NEFTA

**Sahara Palace Hotel:**
Tel: 06-57046
Ugly and modern, but offering swimming-pool, night-club and even a hairdresser, all on the edge of the desert. Double with bath 70D.

**Hôtel Marhala Nefta:**
Tel: 06-57027
Another hotel in the Touring Club de Tunisie string which provides good value, simple accommodation. Double with shower about 7D.

## SBEITLA

**Sufetual Hotel:** ☆ ☆
Tel: 07-65244/330
This blot on the landscape is reckoned to be the best hotel in Sbeitla, but that does not mean a lot. Such luxuries as hot water and, out of season, central heating, are only available when tour groups descend. But it does overlook the site, and there is a swimming-pool. Poor value at 25–30D for a double with bath.

**Bakini Hotel:** ☆ ☆
Tel: 07-65074
Slightly less pricey than Sufetual, and better value, though less well placed. Swimming-pool. Double with bath 16D. Bungalows also available at 32D for two people.

## SFAX

**Sfax Centre:** ☆ ☆ ☆ ☆ luxe
Avenue Habib Bourguiba, tel: 04-25700
No-nonsense luxury hotel frequented by businessmen. Good position close to the medina. About 50D for a double with bath and WC.

**Novotel Syphax:** ☆ ☆ ☆ ☆
Jardin Public Sfax, tel: 04-43333
Large and low-lying in extensive gardens. Enjoys all amenities, though not a particularly inspiring hotel. Conveniently located for making a quick getaway via the airport but not for visiting the medina. Double with bath 50–60D.

**Hôtel Les Oliviers:** ☆ ☆ ☆
Avenue Habib Thameur, tel: 04-25188

An elegant old hotel with plenty of character. Preferable to the more expensive luxury hotels – pity that the somewhat snooty staff seem fully aware of this. Pleasant rooms, bar, terrace and pool; good dining-room. Sensible to book. 25–30D for a double with bath.

### Hôtel Alexander: ✮
Rue Alexander Dumas, tel: 04-21911
Adequate hotel with central location. Around 15D for a double with bath

## SOUSSE

During high season, from June onwards, the large hotels stretching for several kilometres north of the town are likely to be fully booked. Any spare rooms will be at least 40D a night, sometimes double that. Out of season (particularly before April), prices come down considerably; then, a double room in a **** hotel can be found for just 25D. Package-tour rates work out at a fraction of these.

Generally, the nearer hotels are to Port el Kantaoui the larger and flashier they are. Guests in these hotels have to rely on taxis to reach Sousse in the evenings.

Smaller and cheaper hotels such as the following are located in Sousse:

### Hôtel Justinia: ✮ ✮ ✮
Avenue Hedi Chaker,
Tel: 03-26866
Medium-sized hotel. Comfortable, if small, rooms with balconies. 22–35D for a double with shower and WC.

### Hôtel Hadrumette: ✮ ✮ ✮
Place Farhat Hached, tel: 03-26292
Doesn't enjoy the best view in town, but a well-run place with quite high standards. Less expensive than the big hotels. About 18D for a double with bath and WC.

### Hôtel Claridge: ✮
Avenue Habib Bourguiba
Simple hotel in the heart of town with popular downstairs café. Around 15D for a room with shower.

### Hôtel Medina:
Tel: 03-21722
Popular medina-based hotel with attractive central courtyard. Clean and lively. 15D for a double with shower.

## TABARKA

### Hôtel Mimosas: ✮ ✮ ✮
Tel: 08-44376
Nice position on a hill above the small town, with shady gardens, bar and decent restaurant. This is where the better-off head; if you want to stay here it's essential to book. 26–30D for a double with bath.

### Hôtel de France: ✮
Avenue Habib Bourguiba, tel: 08-44577
Old hotel with some character. No palace, but clean and comfortable enough. Bourguiba was interned here by the French. Rooms fill up quickly even out of season. price 16D for a double with bath.

### Hôtel Le Corail: non-classified
Avenue Habib Bourguiba
Basic but tolerable if everywhere else is full. Pleasant proprietor. 8–10D for a double.

## TAMERZA

### Hôtel Les Cascades: non-classified
Tel: 06-45365
Simple accommodation. Showers and meals available. 10D for a double.

## TATAOUINE

### Hôtel La Gazelle: ✮ ✮
Tel: 05-60009
This hotel is clean, with comfortable beds. Otherwise it is characterless. As Tataouine is a popular base for exploring the *ksour* and La Gazelle is the only half-way decent hotel, in the summer it is sensible to book or arrive early. Double room with bathroom around 16D.

## TEBOURSOUK

### Hôtel Thugga: ✮ ✮
Tel: 08-65713
Located in pleasant gardens, with rooms arranged around a courtyard. Each has a bathroom with WC. Heating out of season. Maintenance might be improved. Reasonable dining room. 20D double.

## TOZEUR

The great advantage of the first three hotels in the list is that they are on the edge of the palmerie and have shaded gardens and pools.

**Hôtel Continental:** ✩✩✩
Tel: 06-50411
A pleasant low-lying hotel with rooms arranged around the pool and garden. If you
decide to come here just for an evening
drink, arrive before 8 p.m. After that they do
not serve alcohol to non-residents. 34D for a
double with bath.

**Hôtel Oasis:** ✩✩✩
Tel: 06-50522
Attractive hotel that has recently been reno-
vated. 34D for a double with bath.

**Hotel El Jerid:** ✩
Tel: 06-50488
Not as classy as the Continental or Hotel
Oasis, but also on the edge of the palmerie,
with swimming- pool and air-conditioning.
26D for a double.

**Hôtel Splendid:** ✩
Tel: 06-50053 (sensible to book in the
summer).
A cheaper option, situated in the centre of
town. Worth getting here early to get a good
room – some are a lot more pleasant than
others, though all are clean. Rooms are
situated around a central courtyard occupied
by an enormous palm tree. Helpful staff.
Air-conditioning and, across the road, a pool
of sorts. About 15D for a double.

## TUNIS, SIDI BOU SAID & CARTHAGE

**Africa Meridien:** ✩✩✩✩ luxe
50 Avenue 7 Novembre, tel: 01-347 477
When it was built in the 1960s, the sky-
scraping Africa Meridien was considered an
architectural monster, but far worse has been
committed by architects since (Hôtel du Lac,
for instance). It has the best position in town
– on Avenue 7 Novembre, just down from
Café de France, giving it the edge on the
Hilton. All amenities and comforts, including a cinema, though apart from the night-
club on the top floor its facilities close very
early. Not much action after 11 p.m. at night.
Double room about 70D.

**Oriental Place Hotel:** ✩✩✩✩ luxe
29 Avenue Jean Jaures, tel: 01-348 846.
Flashy new hotel, with plenty of facilities
(including indoor pool). Very helpful service. Double room about 70D.

**Hôtel Le Belvedere:** ✩✩✩✩
10 Avenue Etats Unis d'Amerique, tel: 01-
784 119.
Small and comfortable; less ostentatious than
other luxury hotels.

**Hôtel Majestic:** ✩✩✩
36 Avenue de Paris, tel: 01-242 666/ 242
848.
Fine-looking building in the colonial style.
Popular with wedding parties. Comfortable
rooms. Double room with bath about 22D.

**Hôtel Capitole:** ✩
Avenue 7 Novembre, tel: 01-244 941.
Popular hotel, whose inflated prices reflect
its central position overlooking the main
avenue; serves surprisingly good food in an
inauspiciously empty dining-room. Double
room with bath about 20D.

**Hôtel Metropole:** ✩
3 Rue de Grece, tel: 01-241 377/240 028.
One of several old-fashioned but well-run
hotels just off Avenue 7 Novembre, in this
case alongside the theatre. Central heating
out of season; small lounge where residents
can order coffee or tea late at night when
everywhere else in Tunis has closed. Double
room with bath (plenty of hot water) 14D.

**Hôtel Transatlantique:** ✩
106 Rue de Yugoslavie, tel: 01)-240 680.
In similar style to Hôtel Metropole. Good
value at abut 14D for a double room with
bath.

Do as the beys did and escape the heat and
dust of Tunis for Sidi Bou Said or Carthage.

**Sidi Bou Said Hotel:** ✩✩✩✩
Tel: 01-740 411
Superb location, with well-appointed and
well-maintained rooms. Make sure of a room
with a view that is stunning (there are off-
shoots to the rear with rooms not of the same
standard). Reception helpful (welcoming
drink!), though quite a few hangers-on out
for tips. Definitely recommended, and good
value at 45D for a double.

**Dar Said Hotel:** ✩✩
Sidi Bou Said, tel: 01-270 792.
Hotel converted from a grand old house. It is
enclosed by a high wall on the left-hand side
just past Café des Nattes and signalled by an
Arabic-inscribed plaque on the wall. Comfortable, with excellent location. Double
room with bath 25D.

**Residence Carthage:** ✩✩
16 Rue Hannibal, Carthage, tel: 01-731 072.
Small no-frills establishment, but spotless
and very well run. Good restaurant. Double
with shower 18D.

You could stay in a Youth Hostel, where a bed (no bedclothes) costs a few hundred millimes though they are only recommended for the truly impoverished. Apart from primitive facilities, disadvantages include curfews, inconvenient locations and the fact that they are often occupied by group bookings. Tunisia's best Youth Hostel is said to be Ain Draham's. You don't have to be youthful to stay in a Youth Hostel, but you should have a YHA membership card.

**Ain Draham** (tel: 08-47087); **Béja** (tel: 08-50621); **Bizerte**, Route de la Corniche (tel: 02-50621); **Gabes**, Rue de l'Oasis (tel: 05-20271); **Gafsa** (tel: 06-20268); **Djerba** (tel: 05-50619); **Kairouan** (tel: 07-20309); **Kelibia** (telephone 02-96105); **Le Kef** (tel: 08-21679); **Matmata** (tel: 05-6070); **Medenine** (tel: 05-40338); **Menzel Temime** (tel: 02-98116); **Monastir** (tel: 03-61216); **Nabeul** (tel: 02-85547); **Rmel,** near Bizerte (tel: 02-33804); **Sfax**, 1 km out of town in pic-ville (tel: 04-43207; **Sidi Bouzid** (tel: 06-30088); Sousse, 2 km out of town at Plage Bougaafar (tel: 03-31269); **Teboursouk** (tel: 08-65095); **Tozeur** (tel: 06-50235); **Tunis**, at 23 rue Saida Ajoula in the Medina (500 metres from Place du Gouvernement; **Zaghouan** (tel: 01-75265).

# FOOD DIGEST

Tunisia shares many of the dishes found in other countries of the Maghreb, reflecting a common history of invaders. Some, such as *cous-cous* (a vegetable, meat or poultry stew served on a bed of steamed semolina grains), and *tajines* (a dryish ragout of meat, vegetables or fish cooked slowly in a clay pot on top of a stove) originated with the early Berbers. The Arabs introduced spices and *smen* (a cooked and aged butter), and the Andalusians incorporated olives, olive oil, nuts and fruits in their cooking. The Turks were responsible for the huge range of sticky, honey-oozing pastries and sweetmeats. Lastly, the French, as well as influencing restaurant cuisine throughout the country, introduced the concept of separate courses. As a rule, the only place to sample real Tunisian cooking is in a Tunisian home, and preferably a wealthy one. Only a handful of restaurants provide top-quality traditional cooking (M'rabet in Tunis is probably the most famous). Most good restaurants serve French food plus one or two Tunisian specialities of the day.

Anyone travelling around Tunisia will frequently rely on rotisseries (chicken, fried potatoes and salad for about 1D) or simple working-men's restaurants, partly because nothing else may be available but also because they are often very good. Menus in the latter seldom vary – *chorba* (a thick soup), *kebabs, kefta* (minced lamb meatballs), chicken, omelettes, *merguez* (spicy beef sausages common all over the Maghreb – and now in France – but which originated in Tunisia), sometimes beefsteak or fish, Tunisian salad (diced tomato, peppers and onion) and salad *mechouia* (a sensational aubergine dip). Invariably whatever is ordered will be accompanied by *harysa*, a fiery pepper condiment, which should be treated with caution, and French or flat Arabic bread. A Tunisian speciality which appears on almost every menu, high or low class, is *brik a l' oeuf*, a thin deep-fried envelope of *warkha* pastry containing egg, cumin, flat-leaf parsley and sometimes *kefta*, fish or potato. Sprinkled with lemon juice it is delicious.

During Ramadan, there is a daily fast from dawn until sundown which all Muslims (with some exceptions: see feature on Ramadan) are expected to observe. Most restaurants and cafés (for not even water should pass a Muslim's lips) are closed until the muezzin's call to evening prayer announces sunset. A few restaurants in tourist resorts such as Sousse and Hammamet or along busy road routes are likely to remain open, though some close for the whole month of Ramadan, taking it as an annual holiday. Other restaurants and bars do not serve alcohol during this time.

It is always possible to buy food from shops and markets during Ramadan, but it should be eaten with discretion. It is considered bad manners to eat openly in daylight even if offenders are non-Muslim. The same goes for smoking.

## WHERE TO EAT

As most meals, including lunch, are eaten in the home, the majority of restaurants are simple affairs used by men without women to cook for them. Other than in hotel dining-rooms or roadside restaurants catering for motorists, it is unusual to see Tunisian women dining.

The exceptions to this rule are in Tunis and its suburbs, where the middle classes have begun to dine out as a social activity and there are a number of suitably upmarket restaurants.

It is customary to leave a 10 percent tip, even in humble cafés. At most of the restaurants in the list below booking is not necessary, but where it might be appropriate telephone numbers are included.

### AIN DRAHAM

There are no fancy restaurants, but humble establishments punctuate the main street. Those wishing for something better, and wine, should head for the gloomy but atmospheric dining room of **Hôtel Beau Séjour** (soup, salad, entrée, fruit: 4D) or the well-situated but less interesting **Hôtel Rayani** beyond the village.

### BIZERTE

**Hôtel Corniche** is the best hotel in town and its restaurant is considered good, but **Le Petit Mousse**, a small hotel overlooking the sea a couple of kilometres along the corniche road, has a popular restaurant serving good food (plenty of seafood) at more reasonable prices. About 15D for two.

### DJERBA

As tourism is centred on Houmt-Souk, this is where the restaurants are. Most are situated around Place Hedi Chaker and they are all aimed at tourists wanting a change from the menu in their hotels. But standards are fairly high, with a wide choice of meats and seafood. For excellent fish try **Princesse**

**d'Haroun** at the Port de Houmt Souk. Less expensive restaurants (around 6–8D for two), with more limited menus, are found on Avenue Habib Bourguiba. Try **Les Sportifs** or **Restaurant Central:** both are cheap, clean and good – though neither serve alcohol.

### EL HAOUARIA

Apart from **Restaurant de la Jeunesse**, a cupboard-sized place (closes very early) serving simple meals, **Hôtel L'Epervier** is the only choice. The restaurant attempts to justify its high prices with pink napkins and fancy place settings; you'd do better to eat as the locals do, in L'Epervier's bar.

### EL KEF

There are virtually no restaurants in El Kef, but the chef of the **Hôtel Sicca Veneria** manages to rustle up a decent dinner. Don't, though, hold out hopes of a good breakfast or lunch; our inspector called Sicca Veneria's breakfast an embarassment.

### HAMMAMET

Among Hammamet's wealth of restaurants, **La Perle du Golfe** (tel: 82222/82110; closed Tuesdays), on Avenue de la République, and **La Pergola** (tel: 80993) in the *centre commercial* (the new development set back from the medina end of Avenue Habib Bouguiba) are the smartest – and most expensive, but worth a splurge. **Pommodoro**, an Italian/French restaurant is also highly-rated, and for a good pizza (rare in Tunisia, despite its proximity to Italy) visit the beach pizza bar of the Sheraton hotel. For rather cheaper food, try **Restaurant de La Poste** and **Le Berbère**, both overlooking the kasbah, or **Le Bistro**, on Avenue du Kuwait, which serves a surprisingly wide range of food at very cheap prices. For after dinner coffee and a smoke, you could adjourn to **Café Sidi M'Nasser**, a Moorish-style café in the centre commercial; it was clearly designed for the tourists, but local youths have made it their own.

### KAIROUAN

The agreeable patron of **Restaurant Fairouz**, signposted off Habib Bourguiba, the main drag in the medina, serves excellent and good value *brik*, salad *mechouia*, peppered steak, *tajines*, etc.

Kairouan also has numerous rotisseries, many beyond the tourist office outside the medina. For late night *casse-croûte* crammed with *merguez*, olives, fried potatoes and salad, visit the vendors on Avenue de la République.

## MAHDIA

Part of Mahdia's appeal is its unspoiled character. Consequently, other than in the hotels, there are few restaurants in the town. Near the market is the modest **El Medina**.

**Restaurant Moez**, close by the Skifa el Kahla, must rate among the worst places to eat in Tunisia.

## NABEUL

The obvious choice is **Les Oliviers** (follow the numerous signposts). It is pricey (at least 30D for two) but good, though its menu is almost exclusively French.

Alternatively, off the Hammamet road a kilometre or so outside town, are **Hôtel Jasmines** and **Pension Oliviers**, both of which serve reasonably-priced food in pleasant surroundings. To find them, turn left immediately after the large and flashy Restaurant Yugoslavie.

The dining-rooms in the big hotels on the front are not for epicures. They cater for package holiday-makers from various European countries and blandness rules.

Good basic fare (without alcohol) is best at **La bonne Heure** (Place Farhat Hached). Avoid **Restaurant Moderne:** the owner is surly and his food is poor.

## SFAX

For a relaxing ambience, try **Hotel Oliviers**, Avenue Habib Thameur: food is well-prepared and served in a dining-room with old-fashioned class. Alcohol is not served during Ramadan.

**Pizzeria Ristorante**, Rue Haffouz, offers reasonable pizzas for under 3D, and just inside Bab Diwan, on Rue Mongi Slim, there are a number of humble restaurants serving chicken, spaghetti, omelettes, *briks*, etc at around 5D for two.

## SOUSSE

Avenue Habib Bourguiba and Route de la Corniche are both very well-served by restaurants and pizza parlours. Out of season, most of them are empty but the best still manage to drum up trade. Try **L'Escargot** or **Le Pacha** on Route de la Corniche for quality French cuisine, **Le Bonheur** on Place Farhat Hached for good cooking at reasonable prices, and **Les Sportifs** on Avenue Habib Bourguiba for excellent value.

## TABARKA

**Hôtel Mimosa** is the best place to eat in town, but **Hôtel de France**, where Habib Bourguiba himself once dined, offers well-cooked simple fare (it's usually soup or salad followed by entrecôte steak, lamb cutlets or grilled fish). Its *table d'hote* menu includes several choices and is exceptionally good value at 4D (wine available).

Other than that there are numerous places serving simple seafood and grills. Try **Restaurant Triki** on Rue Farhat Hached.

## TATAOUINE

There are several simple restaurants in the town centre, all providing more atmosphere and no worse food than the town's best hotel, **La Gazelle d'Or**. Aim to arrive at a restaurant early: waiting staff are clearing away by 8.30 pm.

## TOZEUR

The large hotels along Avenue Abou el Kacem Chebbi all have restaurants open to non-residents, but you could eat a lot worse than what is available at **La République** or **Le Paradis**, both unpretentious restaurants off Avenue Habib Bourguiba. Food is fresh, well-prepared and cheap at around 3D for starter and main course.

## TUNIS

The capital contains Tunisia's best choice of restaurants, and in view of the limited choice elsewhere in the country it is as well to make the most of them (though bear in mind that even in Tunis you cannot expect to be served later than 9.30 p.m). Streets south of Avenue

7 Novembre are particularly well-endowed. For a good cheap lunch, there are several restaurants flanking the streets around the Great Mosque in the medina; but they get packed with businessmen, so get there early.

The following is a selection of the city's best restaurants (prices include a bottle of *vin ordinaire*):

**L'Astragale:** 17 Avenue Charles Nicolle, tel: 01-785 080. Highly respected French-run restaurant. Traditional and nouvelle cuisine. Little change from 60D for two.

**Restaurant M'rabet:** Souk el Trouk, tel: 01-263 681/261 729. Famous restaurant in the middle of the medina (close to the Great Mosque). French and Tunisian cuisine; traditional ambience, including exotic floor shows! 35–40D for two.

**L'Orient::** 7 Rue Ali Bach-Hamba, tel: 01-242 058. Plenty of atmosphere, first-rate food and good service. Menu changes daily and always incorporates one or two Tunisian specialities. Its position in a quiet side street off the northern side of Avenue 7 Novembre (opposite the offices of *La Presse*) shields it from most tourists. 20–25D for two.

**Chez Nous:** 5 Rue de Marseille, tel: 01-243 043. Popular restaurant recently refurbished, offering French cuisine at moderate prices. 15–20D for two.

**Le Colibri:** 218 Avenue 7 Novembre, tel: 01-731 317. New restaurant run by the son of the owner of *Chez Nous*. French cuisine. Again around 15D for two.

**Le Cosmos:** 7 Rue Ibn Khaldoun, tel: 01-241 610. Small busy restaurant, popular with Tunisians and tourists alike, serving mainly French food with occasional Tunisian specialities. Always a good choice of fish. 10–15D for two. Closed during Ramadan.

**Restaurant Le Baghdad:** 29 Avenue 7 Novembre, tel: 01-259 068. Flamboyant restaurant which attracts a lot of tourists. Offers well-cooked *tajines* and *cous-cous* as well as good fish and meat but serves it rather surlily. Around 15D for two.

**Restaurant Le Capitole:** 60 Avenue Habib Bourguiba, tel: 01-246 601. The dining-room of Le Capitole Hôtel is not the liveliest place in town, but its food is well-prepared and inexpensive. Views over Avenue 7 Novembre. 10D for two.

**Restaurant L'Etoile:** 3 Rue Ibn Khaldoun, tel: 01-240 514. If you cannot find a table at Cosmos, its staff will send you to L'Etoile just down the road. It is slightly pricier, with less ambience, but offers very similar food. 12–15D for two.

**Le Pub:** 1 Rue Kamel Attaturk, tel: 01-243 436. Serves large, quite good pizzas in a low-lit cavern. Not cheap at 15D for two.

## OUTSIDE TUNIS

**La Goulette** and **La Marsa** are known for fish restaurants, and indeed pavements are lined with idle waiters trying to coax tourists behind tables laid with flapping check table-cloths. But choose where you dine with care. Some restaurants profit from the reputation of the location and do not give good value, notably **La Victorie** in La Goulette. **La Corniche, Au Bon Vieux Temps** and **El Hafsi** in La Marsa have a sound reputation.

Sidi Bou Said has several restaurants of note: **Le Typique**, tables set on a small terrace shaded by cypresses, is a well-tried favourite, offering local specialities. Alternatively, try **La Bagatelle** near the Dar Said hotel, or **Pirates**, a pricier restaurant, located down near Sidi Bou's harbour, specialising in fish.

In Carthage, **Residence Carthage** (tel: 01-731 072), in Rue Hannibal near the Punic Sanctuaries, is stylish but expensive.

In Gammarth, choose between **Le Pecheur** (tel: 01-270 955), renowned for its excellent fish and oriental dancing (best to book), **Les Coquillages** and **Le Phenecien** in the Bay of Monkeys.

## DRINKING NOTES

As in most Mediterranean countries, cafés are social centres where men come to play dominoes or cards, smoke *checha*, the Turkish-style waterpipe, watch television or just sit and talk. Most serve only drinks, and generally just black **tea** (very sweet and stewed), **coffee** (either *kahwa bi halib*, with milk, or *kahwa kahla, black*) or soft drinks such as Coca-Cola and a lemonade called Boga. But some, particularly the more salubrious establishments and pâtisseries where women venture, celebrate the ritual with more style, offering mint tea or tea sprinkled with orange blossom or pine kernel; coffee laced with rose water, cinnamon or cardamom; a blend of coffee and chocolate (*café turc*); freshly squeezed juices; and milkshakes made with puréed fruit. If you want to eat pastries with your tea or coffee, you should visit a pâtisserie rather than a café, though café staff will not mind if you bring pastries with you.

**Alcohol** is normally only served in bars, hotels or upmarket restaurants, though a few colonial-style brasseries, notably Café de France in Avenue 7 Novembre in Tunis, still survive.

Tunisian **wines** are produced in the north of the country, particularly Cap Bon, either by state concerns or local co-operatives. In restaurants, a bottle of *vin ordinaire* such as Nahli sells for about 6D. Good robust reds include Coteaux de Carthage and Haut Mornag; and a popular rosé is Sidi Rais. Dry white wines are considered less good, with the notable exception of a dry Muscat from Kelibia on Cap Bon, though there are some excellent dessert wines of the Muscatel type (look for the *appellation* Vin Muscat de Tunisie). Other reputable red wines are Coteaux de Khanguet, Tyna, Tebourba, St Cyprien and Sidi Tabet.

Local **beer**, Celtia, is the light continental variety; it costs about 850 millimes a bottle. Stronger substances include **Boukha**, derived from figs and tasting rather like schnapps, and **laghmi**, a palm wine, and **thibarine**, also made from figs. Imported spirits and beers are much more expensive; a gin and tonic in a hotel is likely to cost 3–4D.

# THINGS TO DO

Distances are not great in Tunisia. With your own transport it is possible to travel almost anywhere in the country in a very long day. But for short comfortable excursions, which allow time to stop and sightsee, the following itineraries are recommended:

## FROM TUNIS

**Carthage and Sidi Bou Said**. Although many people are disappointed by what is left of Carthage, the remains are spread over a large area and require a day to view them properly. Cliff-top Sidi Bou is an excellent place to relax over a drink or dinner and recover from the exertion of visiting ruins.

The TGM railway (from the bottom of Avenue 7 Novembre in Tunis) stops at all the main Carthage sites and Sidi Bou Said; it is regular (every 20 minutes), cheap and convenient.

**Thuburbo Maius, Zaghouan, Takrouna, Hammamet.** This would be a day's drive, and you would probably arrive in Hammamet late afternoon or early evening, in time to visit the kasbah and have dinner. If you wanted to arrive earlier in the afternoon, in time for a swim, by-pass Zaghouan. If you don't have your own transport you could visit any one of these by public transport (buses or *louage* from Bab Alleoua at the southern end of Avenue de Carthage in Tunis).

**Utica, Ghar el Melh, Sidi Ali El Mekki/ Raf Raf.** This north-eastern corner of Tunisia is within an hour of Tunis. Car-drivers can combine pretty rural scenery, the Roman ruins of Utica, the sleepy village of Ghar el Melh and the really beautiful beaches of Sidi Ali El Mekki or Raf Raf. Bizerte and Lake Ichkeul could be included in a two-day itinerary.

**Dougga**. About two hours from Tunis. Perhaps Tunisia's most impressive Roman site yet one that sees few tourists.

**Dougga, Bulla Regia, Ain Draham**. An enjoyable two day trip would be to take in Dougga and Bulla Regia and then stay the night in Ain Draham in the Khroumir Mountains. Return via Tabarka.

**Cap Bon.** If you have your own transport and can explore, Cap Bon is ideal for a day's drive. You can visit quiet beaches, the fort at Kelibia, the Punic site of Kerkouane and the caves at El Haouaria all within a day. Scenery is very picturesque, full of idyllic picnic spots.

## FROM HAMMAMET

**Cap Bon**. (See *excursions from Tunis*.)

**Tunis** (including the Bardo), **Sidi Bou Said** and **Carthage**. It would be difficult to cover all three places in one day even with your own transport. You need at least two days: one for Carthage and Sidi Bou Said and another for Tunis and the Bardo. Tunis itself is definitely worth a trip; it has the most interesting medina in Tunisia.

**Thuburbo Maius, Zaghouan and Dougga**. A day of Roman ruins and delightful scenery (particularly in spring).

**Takrouna and Kairouan.** The old hill-top village of Takrouna, site of a famous World War II battle, may not be worth a special visit in itself but it makes an interesting stopping point on the way to Kairouan, former capital and religious centre of Tunisia with its Great Mosque, Zaouia of Sidi Sahib and ancient medina.

## FROM SOUSSE

The following places are each within an hour of Sousse: **Kairouan, El Djem, Takrouna** and **Mahdia** (capital of the Fatimid dynasty), and can all be reached by public transport. Further afield are **Tunis** (2 hours by road) and **Dougga** (see above). Excursions to the desert oases, such as **Tozeur, Nefta** and **Douz**, or to the deep south (**Matmata** and the **Ksour**) operate from Sousse (contact travel agents for organised trips) but a minimum of three full days are required. Some Sousse travel agents organise 4-wheel drive trips, lasting several days, to **El Oued** in the **Algerian Sahara.**

## FROM DJERBA

**Matmata and the Ksour.** By car it is possible to sample both the troglodyte village of Matmata and the *ksour* around Medenine and Tataouine in one exhausting day, but a two-day trip would be much more rewarding.

**The Chott el Djerid, Douz, Tozeur** and **Nefta**. At least two full days are needed to do justice to the chott and desert oases.

## FROM KERKENNAH

**Sfax**. The closest option, and quite an interesting town in spite of its industrial character. It has an impressive medina and a good museum of popular arts.

**El Djem.** The spectacular Roman amphitheatre set upon a plain of olive trees is just north of Sfax. Those with their own transport might drive on to Mahdia or Kairouan.

**Kairouan and Sousse.** Both these cities make a good day's trip from Kerkennah. Make sure you return in time to get the last ferry from Sfax.

**The Chott el Djerid, Douz, Tozeur** and **Nefta**. Even a whistle-stop tour of the chott and oases requires at least two full days from Kerkennah. To take in the Seldja Gorges as well, allow three days.

**The Ksour.** Allow a minimum two full days from Kerkennah.

## PLACES OF INTEREST

**Opening times** and admission charges of sites and museums (invariably, an extra 1D per person is charged for permission to take photographs):

## TUNIS

**Dar Ben Abdallah Museum of Popular Arts and Traditions:** Open: Monday–Saturday 9.30 a.m.–4.30 p.m. Closed: Sundays. Admission: 1D.

**The Bardo Museum:** Open: Tuesday–Sunday 9.30 a.m.–4.30 p.m. except public holidays. Closed: Monday. Admission 1D.

**The Zoo:** Open: every day, winter 7 a.m.–5.30 p.m., summer 7 a.m.–7 p.m.

## DJERBA

**La Griba:** Open: Sunday–Friday 8 a.m.–6 p.m. Donations more or less obligatory.

**Museum:** Open: Tuesday–Sunday 9.30 a.m.–4.30 p.m. Closed: Monday. Admission: 800 millimes.

## HAMAMMET

**The International Cultural Centre:** Open: 8.30 a.m–noon and 2 p.m.–5.30. Admission: 600 millimes.

## KAIROUAN

**Rekada Museum: Open:** Tuesday–Sunday 9 a.m.–4 p.m. Closed: Monday. Admission: 1D.

**The Great Mosque:** Open: Tuesday, Wednesday, Thursday and Saturday 9 a.m.–4 p.m., Friday 9 a.m.–noon. Closed: Monday. Admission: 1D.

**Tourist Information Office**, Bab ech Chouada: Open: Saturday–Thursday 7.30 a.m.–1.30 p.m. and 3 p.m.–5 p.m, Friday 7.30 a.m.–noon. N.B. Tickets for all monuments must be bought from here. Ticket: 1D.

## MONASTIR

**Museum and Ribat**: Open: Tuesday–Sunday 9 a.m.–noon and 2 p.m.–5.30 p.m. Closed: Monday. Admission: 1D.

## SOUSSE

**The Catacombs:** Open: Tuesday–Sunday 9.30 a.m.–noon and 2 p.m.–6 p.m. Closed: Monday. Admission: 800 millimes.

**The Great Mosque:** Open: Saturday–Thursday 8 a.m.–noon. Closed: Friday. Admission: 300 millimes.

**The Kasbah Museum:** Open: summer, Tuesday–Sunday 9 a.m.–noon and 3 p.m.–6.30 p.m; winter, Tuesday-Sunday 9 a.m.–noon and 2 p.m.–5.30 p.m. Closed: Monday.

Admission: 1D.

**The Ribat:** Open: Tuesday–Sunday 9.30 a.m.–noon and 2 p.m.–6 p.m. Closed: Monday. Admission: 800 millimes.

## SFAX

**Archaeological Museum** (in Town Hall): Open: 9 a.m.–noon and 3 p.m.–6 pm. Closed: Sunday. Admission 1D.

**Museum:** Open: Tuesday–Sunday 9 a.m.–4.30 p.m. Closed: Monday. Admission 1D.

## ARCHAEOLOGICAL SITES

**Bulla Regia:** Open: Tuesday–Sunday 8.30 a.m.–5.30 p.m. Closed: Monday. Admission: 1D.

**Carthage:** Open: Tuesday–Sunday 8.30 a.m.–5.30 p.m. Closed: Monday. Admission: 1.5D for each site, 1.5D for the museum, 2D to take photographs.

**Dougga:** Open: Tuesday–Sunday 8.30 a.m.–5.30 p.m. Closed: Monday. Admission: 1D.

**El Djem:** Open: daily 8.30 a.m.–5.30 p.m. Admission: 1.5D.

**Kerkouane:** Open: Tuesday–Sunday 8.30 a.m.–5.30 p.m. Closed: Monday. Admission: 1D.

**Makthar:** Open: Tuesday–Sunday 8.30 a.m.–5.30 p.m. Closed: Monday. Admission: 1D.

**Sbeitla:** Open: daily 8.30 a.m.–5.30 p.m. Admission: 1D.

**Thuburbo Maius:** Open: Tuesday–Sunday 8.30 a.m.–5.30 p.m. Closed: Monday. Admission: 1D.

**Utica:** Open: Tuesday–Sunday 8.30 a.m.–5.30 p.m. Closed: Monday. Admission: 800 millimes.

# NIGHTLIFE

## THEATRE

The French-built theatre at the intersection of Avenue 7 Novembre and Rue de Grèce might be compared with an old colonial dowager: heavily plastered to conceal the signs of age but determined not to admit defeat. It lies dormant in the height of summer but stirs in October and is active through to June, though never until at least 9 p.m. each night. Its range of events are varied, from classical Western and Arab concerts to Arab comedies to performances by foreign theatre companies (French and Italian especially), but audiences are rarely so large that tickets (from 4D upwards) need to be booked. If you can catch something interesting, a visit is recommended.

## CINEMA

There are over 80 cinemas in Tunisia. Many appear to show only kung fu/horror/adventure films, compared to which a James Bond or Clint Eastwood film can seem heavyweight. However, in Tunis there are usually a few good French films and one or two worthy Tunisian ones (these normally have French subtitles). To find out what's on, consult the main national newspapers. One of the best venues for films is the cinema in the Africa Meridien Hotel on Avenue 7 Novembre.

The **Carthage film festival**, held every two years, is building a reputation for Arab and Third World films. (For information on the Tunisian film industry, see *Further Knowledge*.)

## CONCERTS

For information about concerts – *mahlouf* (classical Tunisian), occasionally Algerian *rai* (a distinctive Maghrebian rock) or performances by popular Arab singers – scan the main newspapers (*La Presse* or *Le Temps*). For classical Western music, also look out for posters in embassies and cultural centres (for example, in the window of the library of the British Embassy, Place de la Victoire). Note: like theatre, concerts usually begin around 10 p.m.

## NIGHTCLUBS

Outside Tunis, the very large luxury hotels provide the best nightlife. Predictably Sousse, Port el Kantaoui and Hammamet offer the widest choice. An evening invariably entails cabaret (often a belly-dancer), a band or well-known Arab singer and a supporting discotheque. The slightly less grand hotels, ☆☆☆☆ and ☆☆☆ establishments, will only run to a discotheque with occasional tourist-orientated performances by local musicians and dancers. In small towns the only life in the evenings is likely to be in a hotel bar or, failing that, a café.

For nightlife in **Tunis**, try **Crazy Horse** (45 Avenue 7 Novembre), **Le Jockey Club** (Hotel International), **Tunis Club** (Avenue de Paris), **Monseigneur** (11 Rue de Hollande) or the nightclub in the Africa Meridien. Most of what action there is in Tunis takes place in the streets off Avenue 7 Novembre. The medina is absolutely dead in the evening, though during Ramadan Place Halfaouine, just outside its northern gate, is said to be one of the most lively places in the city. **Sidi Bou Said** is always animated during the evening – Café des Nattes and the bar of Hotel Sidi Bou Said attract students – but particularly so during Ramadan. For more sophisticated entertainment, say dinner and cabaret, in Sidi Bou Said, try **La Barraka**.

# SHOPPING

Like those of other Arab countries, Tunisia's crafts include brassware, leatherwork (jackets, handbags and open-back slippers known as *babouche*), pottery, gold and silverware, carpets and embroidery. Unfortunately most of the examples that fill the souks in the resorts are not of a very high quality – some of it is actually imported from the far east – and made purely to serve the tourist trade. Only a few upmarket shops in Tunis, Hammamet, Sousse and Houmt Souk on Djerba offer anything better.

That said, **L'Office National de l'Artisanat Tunisien** (ONAT), a government-run body which aims to promote traditional crafts, controls the quality of carpets and each one must have an official stamp stating whether it is *Deuxième choix, Première Choix* or, best of the lot, *Qualité Supérieure*. All the carpets are hand-made, but some are woven (*mergoum*) and others, the more expensive ones, are knotted. The more knots they have to the square metre the better the carpet. To get an idea of upper price limits for each category, go to an ONAT official shop, even if you do not buy there.

Sometimes *mergoum* rugs are sold as antique; this may or may not be the case. The ONAT shops in Gabes and Kairouan (where mergoums are traditionally made) have some genuine antique examples which should help you judge the bona fide item.

A few regions are renowned for particular crafts and these are likely to present the best buys. Tabarka, in the northwest, is known for coral, Ain Draham for wooden crafts (including very handsome salad bowls costing far less than in Europe), Hammamet for embroidered *silk gilets*, Djerba for silver filigree and Kairouan for carpets.

Other than in ONAT shops, where prices are fixed, the cost of an article is arrived at by haggling. When Tunisians shop, they start by suggesting a price to a shopkeeper, who then tries to force it up. Tourists, afraid of starting too high, generally prefer to let the shopkeeper begin the process, and then offer a sum that is a fraction (perhaps a quarter) of the one he initially wants. Bargaining can be tiresome; it can be fun. For a large item, such as a carpet, it will involve lengthy deliberation over several cups of very sweet tea.

In some shops, either the more exclusive ones or those in the big resorts, expensive purchases can be made with a major credit card – American Express or Diners Card are most welcome, but Visa and Mastercard are gaining acceptance. ONAT shops are supposed to give a 10 percent discount to anyone paying with hard currency cash (but check this first).

To save customers from transporting large items such as carpets, shops will ship goods home on your behalf; often no charge is made for this service (in fact, it is included in the price of the carpet) and in the end (often after a couple of months) it usually turns out to be reliable. If in doubt, however, use a credit card rather than cash – then you may have some comeback if things go wrong. ONAT shops are absolutely reliable.

## EXPORT PROCEDURES

You are allowed to export goods up to a value of £900 without paying duty. Keep all receipts for purchases; customs may wish to examine them.

Tunisian dinars may not be exported. Needless to say, neither fauna nor objects of antiquity may be exported without government permission.

## MARKETS

Market day can turn a town or village into a much more exciting place than it normally is. Markets are found in these towns on the following days:

**Friday:** Midoun, Thala, Zarzis, Nabeul, Testour Ksar Essaf, Sfax, Mateur, Tabarka, Zaghouan, Mahdia.
**Saturday:** Ben Guerdane, El Alia, El Fahs, Thibar, Monastir.
**Sunday:** El Djem, Enfidha, Hammam Lif, Ksar Hellal, Sousse, Fernana.
**Monday:** Ain Draham, Kairouan, Mahares, Mareth, Chebba, Houmt Souk, Makthar, Tataouine.

**Tuesday**: Béja, Haffouz, Kasserine, Menzal Temime, Ghardimaou, Ksar Hellal.
**Wednesday**: Djendouba, Nefta, Sbeitla, Moknine.
**Thursday**: Douz, Teboursouk, Gafsa, Menzel Bouzelfa, Bou Salem, Siliana.

# SPORTS

## GOLF

The government has invested a considerable amount of money in golf facilities in recent years and the Tunisian Open Golf Tournament (held in April) is now a major tournament.

There are four courses: Monastir, the most beautiful and challenging; Hammamet, the newest; El Kantaoui (most easily accessible); and Tunis, the original 1924 course. Shortly (sometime in 1991) an 18-hole course surrounded by pine and oak forest will open in Tabarka (contact Tourist Office for progress report) and in 1992 a second course is due to open near Monastir, along the Dkhila Corniche. Other courses are being planned, including a second course at Hammamet and two courses on Djerba.

All fees must be paid in dinars. Equipment can be hired (a full set of golf clubs, approximately 10D a day; half set, 5D a day; trolley, 3D a day). A caddy can be hired for approximately 6D a day. It is usually necessary to make reservations.

**El Kantaoui Golf Course**: Port El Kantaoui, tel: 03-31755. 27 holes, 9,576 metres. Fees: 25D per 18 holes.
**Monastir Golf Course**: Route de Ouardanine, tel: 03-61120. 18 holes, 6,140 metres. Fees: 27D per 18 holes.
**Hammamet Golf course**: Bir Bou Rekba, tel: 02-82722. 18 holes, 6,115 metres. Fees: 23D per 18 holes.
**Tabarka Golf Course**: Montazah Tabarka, tel: 08-44321. 18 holes 6,400 metres.

**Tunis** (Soukra): Route de la Soukra, tel: 01-765919. To be extended to 18 holes.

## TENNIS

The Tourist Office publishes a booklet listing hotels with tennis courts, stating the number of courts at each.
The hotels with the most extensive facilities are as follows:

**Djerba**
Club Méditerranée Djerba la Douce: 20 courts. Tel: 05-57129.
Dar Djerba: ☆ ☆ ☆ and ☆ ☆ complex (8 courts). Tel: 05-57191.
**Hammamet**
El Fell: ☆ ☆ ☆ (5 courts). Tel: 02-80744.
Salammbo: village-style complex (7 courts). Tel: 02-80197.
**Korba**
Club Méditerranée: 5 courts. Tel: 02-88411.
**Nabeul**
Al Diana Club: ☆ ☆ ☆ (10 courts). Tel: 02-85400.
Les Pyramides: ☆ ☆ ☆ (5 courts). Tel: 02-85775.
**Port el Kantaoui**
Les Maisons de la Mer: apartment complex (11 courts). Tel: 03-41799.
El Hambra: apartment complex (11 courts). Tel: 03-40300.
Open Club: ☆ ☆ ☆ (11 courts). Tel: 03-48063.
Hasdrubal: ☆ ☆ ☆ (6 courts). Tel: 03-41944.
**Mahdia**
Club Cap Mahdia: ☆ ☆ ☆ (7 courts). Tel: 03-81300.
**Monastir**
Regency: ☆ ☆ ☆ ☆ luxe (8 courts). Tel: 03-60033.
Club Méditerranée: 12 courts. Tel: 03-31887.
Club Robinson: ☆ ☆ ☆ ☆ (10 courts). Tel: 03-27515
Sahara Beach: ☆ ☆ ☆ (10 courts). Tel: 03-61088
**Sousse**
Tour Khalef: ☆ ☆ ☆ Tel: 03-41844.
**Tunis**
Cap Carthage: ☆ ☆ ☆ (30 courts). Tel: 01-740 600.
Dar Naouar: village-style complex. Tel: 01-741 000.

## HUNTING

In mid-winter, the hills around Korbous on Cap Bon and the Khroumir mountains around Ain Draham and Tabarka are crawling with hunting parties. Their sport is boar, jackal, fox, mongoose and genet; thrush and even the poor starling. Seasons (they vary year to year, so check exact dates with the Tourist Office) are as follows: end-October to end-January – boar, jackal, fox, mongoose and genet; end-November to mid-March (on Friday, Saturday and Sunday only) – thrush and starling.

Hunting can be arranged *in situ* but the Tourist Office strongly recommends that you do it through a travel agent, either at home (in Britain, try Panorama or the Tunisian Travel Bureau) or in Tunisia. They can take care of necessary arrangements, including organising a licence, permission to import firearms, and book accommodation in hotels, which can be scarce during winter. To do it all independently, you will need to apply to *La Direction des Forêts* (30 Rue Alain Savary, Tunis) for a licence, and the Home Office (*Ministère de l'Intérieur*) for an application to import firearms. They must receive your requests at least 10 days before your arrival in Tunisia.

Foreign hunters are allowed to import 50 bullets for boar and 500 bullets for thrush and starling. They are not allowed to bring gun-dogs into Tunisia.

## RIDING

Stables, often affiliated to hotels, have proliferated on Djerba and the east coast. Their horses and ponies are generally excellent, and prices are reasonable (about 6/7D an hour). Supervision is often inadequate, so don't allow headstrong children free reign.

## GLIDING

The Federal Gliding Centre at Djebel Rassal (25 km/15 miles from Tunis) can provide gliders to experienced visitors. Tel: (Djebel Rassas) 01-906 712.

## SWIMMING

All luxury hotels have swimming-pools, and even if you are not staying in one it is often possible to use a hotel pool for a small charge. In the very hot south sometimes even modest hotels have pools. In Tunis, there are three municipal pools: *La Piscine d'El Gorjani*, Boulevard du 9 Avril; *La Piscine Municipale du Belvedere*, Place Pasteur; and *La Piscine d'El Menzah*, Cité Olympique Bourguiba (heated in winter).

## WATERSPORTS

The resort beaches are packed with watersports paraphernalia. Windsurfing paragliding and cavorting around on a jet scooter are the most popular activities, with some water-skiing and sailing too. Sousse, Port el Kantaoui, Monastir, Hammamet/Nabeul and Djerba have most to offer. A few minutes of paragliding, 10 minutes of waterskiing and an hour of wind-surfing each cost around 10D. For watersports in Tunis, contact *Club Nautique de Sidi Bou Said* (tel: 01-270 689).

## FISHING

Species include mullet, bream, sea perch, whiting, sardines, eel, octopus, and crayfish. The Tourist Office provides a booklet outlining the best seasons and locations for fishing. A licence is not required for regular angling and fishing gear may be taken into the country.

In many areas it is possible to take trips with local fishermen – either to watch or participate. Make enquiries at the ports or Tourist Office.

## UNDERWATER FISHING

This is much more tightly controlled. Fishermen must file a request, accompanied by a medical certificate stating fitness to undertake undersea diving and comprehensive insurance cover, to the Director of Fisheries or his regional representative. The Tourist Office and the *Centre Nautique de Tunisie* (22 Rue de Medine, Tunis, tel: 01-282 209) can advise on the procedure and issue a booklet containing conservation regulations. A specialist tour company such as the London-based Tunisian Travel Bureau will make the necessary arrangements on your behalf.

## DIVING

There are three diving centres: the International Diving Centre at Port el Kantaoui (tel: 03-30500), the Underwater Diving School SHTT in Monastir (tel: 03-61156) and the Tabarka Yachting Club (tel: 08-44478). They offer tuition and hire equipment; it may be necessary to take out temporary membership.

## BIRD-WATCHING

Lake Ichkeul in northern Tunisia is one of the most important waterfowl sites in the world. Many kinds of birds winter (October–February) here, including pochard, widgeon, greylag geese, black-tailed godwits, sandpipers and redshanks. Other birds breed in the lake's reedbeds, notably blackwinged stilts and herons, and birds of prey – kestrels, peregrines and marsh harriers – hover round about.

Other good bird-spotting areas are Cap Bon (especially in spring when the sparrowhawks and peregrine falcons are nesting) and, just off its coast, the island bird sanctuary of Zembra, famous for gulls and terns. During April and May buzzards, kites, eagles and hobbies set off to Europe from Cap Bon. Along the salt lagoons on its eastern coast flamingos, spoonbills and avocets congregate.

Even Tunis has some impressive bird life. Lac de Tunis looks dismal most of the year but in winter its southern quarters are visited by flamingos.

A few tour companies offer specialised bird-watching holidays (try the Tunisian Travel Bureau or Panorama); their expertise will help determine the place and time to go.

## SPECIAL INFORMATION

## DOING BUSINESS

Business customs are a blend of Arab and European. French business methods were inherited after independence but Arab traditions of hospitality and personal contacts are important and should not be underestimated. Correspondence should be in French (never English) but personal visits are infinitely more effective, especially at the beginning of a business relationship, and can usually be arranged at short notice. Business visitors are advised to avoid the Ramadan period.

Anyone intending to do business in Tunisia should contact the ministry in charge of trade in their own country. In Britain this is the Department of Trade and Industry, 1–19 Victoria Street, London SW1H 0ET (tel: 071-215 4947/8). The DTI can supply a trade pack containing hints (on current political situation, employing an agent, making contacts, setting up a company there, etc), the latest economic report and forecast and details of laws relating to business in Tunisia. They also publish a booklet entitled *Hints to Exporters* costing £5.

Other useful contacts include the Tunisian Trade Centre, 29 Princes Gate, London SW7 1QS (tel: 071-225 1710) and, in Tunisia, *Agence de Promotion de l'Industrie* (API), 63 Rue de Syrie, Tunis (tel: 01-287 600).

## CHILDREN

Other than in the extreme heat of high summer, Tunisia is a suitable destination for children. Abundant sand, safe bathing along most of the east coast and the promise of camel rides keep them fairly happy. They are welcomed everywhere, from the largest hotels to the humble *pension famille* (often full of Tunisian children), and many restaurants in the tourist resorts cater for their narrow tastes. Food in local establishments may not be to their liking – Tunisian children are reared on hot, spicy dishes – but it's nearly always possible to order plain omelettes or chicken with chips. If all else fails, even the smallest village will have a grocer selling cheeses, yogurt, bread, milk, etc, and these stay open until 9 or 10 at night.

Many hotels offer baby-sitting services. To find out which, enquire at the Tunisian Tourist Office before you go.

Children under the age of four travel free and those under 10 for half price on buses and trains.

## GAY

Homosexual practices are against the law. Tunisia is not the gay mecca that Morocco has been in the past (and still is to some extent), though offers of male homosexual relations are not unusual around Hammamet and Sousse, where some young men see European homosexuals as an easy way of making money. Unlike in Morocco, there are no specifically gay bars.

## DISABLED

Facilities for the disabled (slopes rather than steps, special toilets, etc) in hotels and restaurants are rare, but some low-lying hotels have rooms on the ground floor and will place ramps against any small steps. The attitude of the Tunisian people towards disability couldn't be more helpful, as the wheelchair bound traveller and writer Quentin Crewe, points out in his book *In Search of the Sahara* about his expedition across the Sahara.

A helpful British organisation called Holiday Care Service can give specific information on the suitability of hotels and resorts, specifying number and heights of steps, widths of doors, and access to beaches. It identifies four categories of hotels: category 1, offering good access for guests who use a wheelchair all the time; category 2, offering reasonable access but which will require negotiation of occasional single steps or ramps with a maximum gradient of 1:8; category 3, offering basic access for wheelchairs, but which may require guests to walk short distances, including not more than one step up or down at any one place; and category 4, providing access only for guests

who can walk short distances, including not more than 3 steps up or down at any one place. It claims there are no category 1 or 2 hotels in Tunisia but there are several in the 3 and 4 categories. For more information contact: Holiday Care Service, 2 Old Bank Chambers, Station Road, Horley, Surrey RH6 9HW, tel: 0293-774 535. Holiday Care Service is a registered charity.

Tour companies which make a special effort to advise disabled people on the suitability of their holidays include Cadogan Travel, Thomson and Lancaster (see *Useful Addresses*).

The Tunisian organisation L'Association Générale des Insuffisants Moteurs de Tunis, AGIM Centre d'Orthopedie, Kassa Said, Manouba, Tunisia, may be able to answer queries.

## STUDENTS

Some sites and museums (for example, Carthage) offer free entry to those with an international student identity card (a useful saving for those on a budget, as admission charges are comparatively expensive). There are no concessionary fares on trains or buses. Although Inter-Rail is expanding its network yearly, it does not yet extend to Tunisia.

## FURTHER READING

*The Handbook of Off-road Driving*, by Julian Cremona and Keith Hart. (Ashford.)

How to choose, equip and maintain four-wheel drive vehicles. Suitable for beginners and experts keen to get the most out of their vehicle.

*In Search of the Sahara*, by Quentin Crewe. (Michael Joseph.)

Relates the adventures of Crewe and his hand-picked team of travel companions as they undertake a two-year crossing of the

Sahara, starting from Tunis.

*Fountains in the Sand*, by Norman Douglas. (Oxford University Press.)

Xenophobic, it has to be admitted, but still an entertaining and finely written book describing the author's adventures in the Djerid regions of Tunisia at the turn of the century. The following extract, ruminating on the drawbacks of purchasing a bedouin bride, imparts some of the flavour of Douglas's book: "These little wildlings are troublesome to carry about. They are less nimble and amiable than the boys, and often require more beating than a European has time to give them. You can always sell them again, of course; and sometimes (into the towns) at a good profit."

*Tangier to Tunis*, by Alexandre Dumas. (Peter Owen.)

Dumas visited Tunis in 1846 at the invitation of the French government which had just acquired Tunisia as a colony. Unfortunately his book displays much of the bland politeness typical of writers on all-expenses-paid trips who hope another trip might be in the offing. Dumas even had a French warship placed at his disposal.

*Salammbo*, by Gustave Flaubert. (Penguin Classics.)

Novel set in 3rd-century Carthage and purporting to be about the so-called Truceless War. Lots of action, plenty of sex, but not considered one of Flaubert's best efforts.

*Roman North Africa*, by E. Lennox Manton. (Seaby.)

An entertaining, highly-readable and illustrated history of the Romans in North Africa, with plenty of material on Tunisia.

*On the Shores of the Mediterranean*, by Eric Newby. (Picador.)

Only two chapters on Tunisia in this book, one relating to Newby's impressions of Carthage and another on a north-south excursion from Bizerte to Douz, but worth reading. Newby's prose flawlessly interweaves information, history, impressions, anecdotes and, above all, humour – as dry as the desert he describes.

## FILMS

Egyptian films have dominated Arab cinema since the 1930s, but the 1970s and 1980s brought a big increase in films from other Arab countries, particularly those made in North Africa. The Carthage Film Festival – which was inaugurated by Tahar Cheriaa, one of the fathers of Arab cinema – is an important venue for Arab and Third World films, but international recognition of Tunisian cinema didn't happen until *Soleil des Hyènes* – a cautionary tale about the ravages tourism makes on a small fishing village, directed by Ridha Behi – was presented at the 1977 Cannes film festival.

Other notable Tunisian films include *Sejnane* (Abtellatif ben Amar, 1974), *Aziza* (Abtellatif ben Amar 1979), *Shadow of Earth* (Taieb Louhichi, 1982) and *Les Baliseurs du Désert* (Nacer Khemir 1984).

The documentary *Camera Arabe* (Ferid Boughedir 1987) tackles the touchy subject of censorship in Arab cinema.

# USEFUL ADDRESSES

## TOURIST INFORMATION OFFICES

**Tunisia**: There are National Tourist Offices (ONTT) in all large towns and they are usually complemented by a municipal Syndicat D'Initiatif. Both can give maps, leaflets and advice, though Syndicats D'Initiatifs have more information on local matters.

## NATIONAL TOURIST OFFICES

**Bizerte**: 1 Rue de Constantinople. Tel: 02-32703.
**Monastir**: Rue de l'Independence, Quartier Chraga. Tel: 03-61960.
**Nabeul**: Avenue Taieb Mehiri. Tel: 02-86737.
**Sousse**: 1 Avenue Habib Bourguiba. Tel: 03-61960.
**Tozeur**: Avenue Abou Kacem Chebbi. Tel: 06-50503.
**Tunis**: 1 Avenue Mohammed V. Tel: 01-341 077.

## SYNDICATS D'INITIATIFS

**Ain Draham**: Centre Ville. Tel: 08-47115.
**Djerba**: Jardin Boumeswer, Avenue Habib Bourguiba. Tel: 05-50915.
**Douz**: Rue Farhat Hached. Tel: 05-90930.
**Gabes**: Place de la Liberation. Tel: 05-70254.
**Gafsa**: Place des Piscines. Tel: 06-21664.
**Hammamet**: Avenue Habib Bourguiba. Tel: 02-80423.
**Kairouan**: Bab Chouhada. Tel: 07-20452.
**Nefta**: Avenue Habib Bourguiba. Tel: 06-57184.
**Port el Kantaoui**: Tel: 03-41799.
**Sfax**: Place de l'Independence. Tel: 04-24606.
**Sousse**: Place Farhat Hached. Tel: 03-20431.
**Tabarka**: 32 Avenue Habib Bourguiba. Tel: 08-44491.
**Tozeur**: Place Ibn Chaabat. Tel: 06-50034

## CONSULATES

**Algeria**: 18 Rue du Niger, Tunis. Tel: 01-283 166.
**Austria**: 17 Avenue de France, Tunis. Tel: 01-282 209.
**Belgium**: 47 Rue du 1er Juin. Tel: 01-282 650.
**Canada**: Rue du Senegal. Tel: 01-286 577.
**Denmark**: 5 rue Mauritanie. Tel: 01-286 804.
**Egypt**: 16 Rue Essayouti, El Menzah. Tel: 01-230 004.
**France**: Place de l'Independance. Tel: 01-245 700.
**Great Britain**: 5 Place de la Victoire. Tel: 01-245 100.
**Italy**: 37 Rue Gamal Adelnasser. Tel: 01-247 488.
**Libya**: 48 Rue du 1er Juin. Tel: 01-283 166.
**Morocco**: 39 Rue du 1er Juin. Tel: 01-288 063.
**Norway**: 7 Avenue 7 Novembre. Tel: 01-245 933.
**Portugal**: 2 Rue Chakib Arsalane. Tel: 01-286 711.
**Sweden**: 87 Avenue Taieb Mehiri. Tel: 01-283 433.
**Switzerland**: 12 Rue Chenkiti, Mutuelleville. Tel: 01-28191.
**USA**: 144 Avenue de la Liberté. Tel: 01-282 566.

## TOUR OPERATORS

**Cadogan Travel**: Cadogan House, 9–10 Portland Street, Southampton SO9 1ZP. Tel: 0703-332 661.
**Club Mediterranée**: 106–110 Brompton Road, London SW3 1JJ. Tel: 071-581 161.
**Cosmos Air**: Tourama House, 17 Homesdale Road, Bromley, Kent BR2 9LX. Tel: 061-480 5799.
**Enterprise Holidays**: Groundstar House, London Road, Crawley, Sussex RH10 2TB. Tel: 0293-517 866.
**Falcon Holidays**: 33 Notting Hill Gate, London W11 3JQ. Tel: 071-221 6298.
**Horizon Holidays**: Broadway, Edgbaston, Five Ways, Birmingham B15 1BB. Tel: 021-643 2727.
**Panorama's Tunisia Experience**: 29 Queen's Road, Brighton BN1 3YN. Tel: 0273-206 531.
**Portland Holidays**: 218 Great Portland Street, London W1. Tel: 071-388 5111.
**Saga Holidays**: The Saga Building, Middleburgh Square, Folkestone, Kent CT20 1AZ. Tel: Freephone 0800-300 500.
**Sovereign Holidays**: Groundstar House, London Road, Crawley Sussex RH10 2TB. Tel: 0293-517 866.
**Swan Hellenic**: 77 New Oxford Street, London WC1A 1PP. Tel: 071-831 1616.
**Thomson Holidays**: Parway House, 202–204 Finchley Road, London NW3 6XB. Tel: 081-493 9191.

**Tunisian Travel Bureau**: 304 Old Brompton Road, London SW5. Tel: 071-373 4411.

Most of these offer only sun, sand and sea package holidays to the big resorts – Hammamet, Nabeul, Monastir, Sousse and Port el Kantaoui – 5-day additional excursions to the South are as adventurous as their programmes get.

The exceptions are Tunisian Travel Bureau and Panorama, who can arrange bespoke holidays to almost anywhere in the country. Panorama specialises in golf holidays.

The only company concentrating on Roman Tunisia is Swan Hellenic. It runs a 13-day Arts Treasure Tour which includes Tunis, Carthage, Bulla Regia, Dougga, Thuburbo Maius, Makthar, Kairouan, Sbeitla, Thelepte, Nefta, Tozeur, Sfax, El Djem and Mahdia. Each tour group is accompanied by an informed lecturer.

# ART/PHOTO CREDITS

*Photography by*

| | |
|---|---|
| *62* | **Associated Press** |
| *Cover, 3, 9, 14/15, 16/17, 18/19, 20/* | **David Beatty** |
| *21, 22, 25, 26/27, 29, 30, 34, 35, 36,* | |
| *37, 38, 41, 45, 48/49, 50, 52, 55, 65,* | |
| *66/67, 68/69, 70, 72, 73, 74, 75, 78/79,* | |
| *80/81, 82, 84, 88, 89, 92/93, 94, 95,* | |
| *96, 97, 99, 105, 108/109, 110/111,* | |
| *112/113, 114/115, 120/121, 122, 123,* | |
| *124, 125, 126, 129, 130, 131, 132,* | |
| *133, 134, 135, 136, 137, 138, 139,* | |
| *140/141, 145, 146, 148L, 148R, 149,* | |
| *150, 151, 152/153, 154, 155, 156, 157,* | |
| *158, 159, 160, 161, 162, 163, 164,* | |
| *165, 166/167, 168, 169, 171, 172, 173,* | |
| *174, 175, 176, 177, 178, 179, 180/181,* | |
| *182, 183, 184, 185, 186, 187, 188,* | |
| *190, 191, 192, 193, 194, 195, 196,* | |
| *197, 198, 199, 200, 201, 202, 203,* | |
| *204, 205, 206, 207L, 207R, 208/209,* | |
| *210/211, 212, 214, 215, 216, 217, 218/* | |
| *219, 220/221, 222, 223, 224/225, 226/* | |
| *227, 228, 229, 230, 231, 232, 233,* | |
| *234, 235, 236/237, 238, 239, 241, 242,* | |
| *243, 244, 245, 246, 247, 248/249, 250/* | |
| *251, 252, 253, 254/255, 256, 257, 258,* | |
| *259, 260, 261, 262, 263, 264/265, 267,* | |
| *268/269, 274, 275, 277, 280, 282/283,* | |
| *284/285, 286, 287, 289, 290, 291, 292,* | |
| *293, 294, 295, 297, 298, 299* | |
| *83, 85* | **Bodo Bondzio** |
| *100/101, 102, 103, 104, 106, 281* | **Julian Cremona** |
| *56/57, 60, 61, 63* | **Hulton Picture Company** |
| *42, 43, 44, 51, 53, 54, 58, 59, 64, 128,* | **Alain Le Garsmeur** |
| *276* | |
| *28, 32, 39, 47* | **Mary Evans Picture Library** |
| *107* | **Neill Menneer** |
| *266* | **Christine Morley** |
| *71, 76/77* | **Donald G. Murray** |
| *40, 98, 270/271, 278, 300* | **Kim Naylor** |
| *33, 86/87, 90/91, 127, 142, 143, 147,* | **Hans Schork** |
| *244, 272/273, 296* | |
| | |
| *Maps* | **Berndtson & Berndtson** |
| *Illustrations* | **Klaus Geisler** |
| *Visual Consultant* | **V. Barl** |

# INDEX

A
B
C
D
E
F
G
H
I
J
a
b
c
d
e
f
g
h
i
j
k
l